Keys to the City

Keys to the City

HOW ECONOMICS, INSTITUTIONS, SOCIAL INTERACTIONS, AND POLITICS SHAPE DEVELOPMENT

Michael Storper

PRINCETON UNIVERSITY PRESS

Princeton and Oxford

press.princeton.edu

Cover Art: Lucian Freud,1922–2011. *Man and Town*, 1940–41.
  Private Collection, courtesy of Harry Moore-Gwyn/Moore-
  Gwyn Fine Art Ltd. UK. Courtesy of ©The Lucian Freud
  Archive/Bridgeman Art Library.

First paperback printing, 2020
Paperback ISBN 978-0-691-20295-2

The Library of Congress has cataloged the cloth edition as follows:
Storper, Michael.
  Keys to the city : how economics, institutions, social interactions,
  and politics shape development / Michael Storper.
  pages   cm
  Includes bibliographical references and index.
  ISBN 978-0-691-14311-8 (hardcover)
1. Cities and towns—Growth—Economic aspects.   2. Regional planning—
Social aspects.   3. City planning—Social aspects.   I. Title.
  HT371.S76 2013
  307.76—dc23
  2013003220

British Library Cataloging-in-Publication Data is available

This book has been composed in Sabon

Contents

Dedicated to
les jeunes de Crouy-sur-Ourcq
and
Franck Monfort (1965–2011):
L'écho de ton rire: nous nous en souviendrons pour toujours.

Acknowledgments

This book builds on research that I have carried out alone and in collaboration, in my three "home" universities. In the Department of Geography at the London School of Economics, there is an unusually large group of geographers and economists who share the language of geography and economics. I would particularly like to acknowledge my coauthors on other works, including my current colleagues Riccardo Crescenzi and Andrés Rodríguez-Pose along with my former colleagues Gilles Duranton and Tony Venables. I also have the pleasure of regular stimulating conversations with other colleagues who work on economic geography: Simona Iammarino, Ian Gordon, Henry Overman, and Christian Hilber. Working with Tom Farole, a former PhD student at the London School of Economics, and Fabrizio Barca on a team with Rodríguez-Pose on regional policy issues was important to my thinking as well.

My thinking in this period has also been influenced by working with my PhD students at the University of California at Los Angeles, notably on a project supported by the John Randolph Haynes and Dora Haynes Foundation that explored the foundations of urban growth. I am grateful to Tom Kemeny, Naji Makarem, and Taner Osman for their intensive participation in this project, and our interactions in struggling with how growth is sorted into different places. I have benefited also from coauthorship with Tom Kemeny, Mike Manville, and Allen J. Scott.

Last but not least, since 2003, I have been privileged to be a member of the faculty at Sciences Po in Paris, where I am a member of the Center for the Sociology of Organizations. The partnership of economic geography and economic sociology proposed in this book comes from that experience. My colleagues at Sciences Po have helped me think about how social forces make certain kinds of institutions possible in certain places. I thank Erhard Friedberg, with whom I codirected our master of public affairs program, for many stimulating discussions about how organizations and institutions "really work"; Patrick LeGalès for our many exchanges on urban political economy; and Christine Musselin, the director of the Center for the Sociology of Organizations, for the ongoing welcome I have had there. In the master of public affairs program, we have had a lively concentration in "territorial development policies," and the colleagues who have taught in that area have given me much to draw on in this book. In Paris, I would also like to thank Jean-Claude Prager and Pierre Veltz for many years of stimulating discussions about regional development, and Riel Miller for working with me on the question of technologies of telepresence.

My editor at Princeton University Press, Eric Schwartz, provided me supportive and well-conceived advice on rewriting, and Susan Christopherson of Cornell University and Jacques-François Thisse of the Université Catholique de Louvain each gave me many suggestions about how to improve the arguments.

The book draws on much research that has been published, but I have significantly modified or rearranged it, and complemented it with new material. The specific contributions are acknowledged in notes to each chapter, yet none of my coauthors should be held responsible for what I have done with the results of our research in creating this book. Presentations at a number of conferences and universities sharpened the arguments. Ideas from a wide circle of friends and colleagues in the disciplines of geography, economics, and sociology at many universities around the world have been important to my intellectual development.

Keys to the City

INTRODUCTION
Cities and Regions in the Twenty-First Century: Why Do They Develop and Change?

Divergence and Turbulence

If the current residents of many countries were transported back just a few decades, they would not recognize many aspects of their cities and regions. This is paradoxical, since cities are durable structures made of concrete and steel, and in many ways, slow to change. The iconic dimensions of cities—Manhattan's skyscrapers, Los Angeles' long boulevards and freeways, and the historical core of Paris—stay with us. But many other dimensions of cities, from the granularity of their neighborhoods to the size and organization of entire metropolitan regions, and the map of winning and losing regions, change radically in small amounts of time.

In 1950, the average American would barely be glimpsing what would come to be the current "American way of life" in the suburbs and would not be paying much attention to what we now call the Sun Belt. In 1960, few were worried about the decline of dozens of major metropolitan areas in the Manufacturing Belt, and the average resident of Detroit gave nary a thought to the idea that their metropolitan region would be considered the poster child of failure several decades hence. Nor would many have imagined that Houston and Las Vegas would be considered big success stories soon thereafter.

As late as 1980, the average American was not thinking about the resurgence of certain cities in the Frost Belt, such as New York, Chicago, or Boston, as would occur in the 1990s, or the gentrification of their forlorn center-city neighborhoods. In the 1980s, few scholars thought about the rise of "world cities," such as Hong Kong or Shanghai, or how London or Paris would or would not be in their ranks. Nor would the Parisian in 1950 be able to imagine the massive suburbanization of that region and thorough gentrification of central Paris, erasing most of its characteristic raucous rough *parigot* edges. The resident of Rio de Janeiro in 1940 would have laughed scornfully if presented with the prospect of São Paulo becoming Brazil's as well as South America's biggest, richest metropolitan area. The deck of economic development is constantly being reshuffled, and the cards are being dealt out over different places in an uneven and changing pattern.

Urbanization has been on a sharp upswing since the trade revolution that began with the age of exploration in the late 1400s. It intensified with the advent of the Industrial Revolution in the eighteenth century. This period has also witnessed the "Great Divergence" at the global scale, whereby the West after 1750 left the rest of the planet behind in wealth and income. As part of this divergence, in the eighteenth and nineteenth centuries the world's big cities became its richest places, but some cities became a lot richer than others. In the merchant period, cities like Venice, or Xi'an at the other end of the Silk Road, found themselves losing out to Manchester in terms of wealth. The industrial period generated a patchwork of higher- and lower-income regions. The Industrial Belt of northern Europe first had the highest incomes, followed by the core regions of North America. In the Old Northeast of the United States, cities such as Buffalo and Cleveland were points of high wealth in 1900, especially when compared to Atlanta or Houston. The rise of California and the "first" New Economy in the early twentieth century added wealthy and growing city-regions on the Pacific coast to the ranks of the ten-richest large urban regions.

By the late 1960s, across Europe and North America, many of the formerly richest urban regions were losing employment and struggling to maintain their income levels. The change in the United States was particularly dramatic, as a host of Sun Belt cities not only grew bigger than old manufacturing cities but also grew richer (Kim 2002). Some of the old manufacturing cities even had absolute declines in employment. Though the US case is particularly marked, the same thing happened to European manufacturing cities such as Lille, Manchester, or Torino. This turbulence for the United States can be seen in table 1.1.

The late 1980s and 1990s brought further change in the West. Certain cities that had been written off as declining manufacturing centers, including New York and London, began to attract people again, and most dramatically, moved back up the urban income hierarchy as their economies were recomposed around high-paying New Economy industries and jobs. Indeed around the world, a set of major urban regions started to resemble one another and became essential switching points of the emerging global economy. Hong Kong, Tokyo, Singapore, São Paulo, Sydney, Toronto, Zurich, and many other cities grew bigger and richer, while many formerly rich, mostly middle-size industrial cities lagged them more and more. With the increase in global trade and integration, major

TABLE 1.1
U.S. Consolidated Statistical Areas with 1970 Population Greater Than 2 Million, Ranked According to Per Capita Personal Income Levels

Area Name	Income Rank		Pop Growth 1970–2009
	1970	2009	
San Jose-San Francisco-Oakland, CA	1st	1st	55.3%
New York-Newark-Bridgeport, NY-NJ-CT-PA	2nd	3rd	13.0
Chicago-Naperville-Michigan City, IL-IN-WI	3rd	12th	21.1
Los Angeles-Long Beach-Riverside, CA	4th	25th	78.2
Washington-Baltimore-Northern Virginia, DC-MD-VA-WV	5th	2nd	57.2
Detroit-Warren-Flint, MI	6th	52nd	1.7
Minneapolis-St. Paul-St. Cloud, MN-WI	7th	11th	60.0
Seattle-Tacoma-Olympia, WA	8th	6th	96.6
Cleveland-Akron-Elyria, OH	9th	36th	−6.6
Philadelphia-Camden-Vineland, PA-NJ-DE-MD	10th	10th	13.6

NOTE: Bureau of Economic Affairs REIS data.

industrial cities in developing countries, especially China, kept attracting people yet also moving up the world income hierarchy of cities; Guangzhou, Belo Horizonte, Bangalore, Johannesburg, and Kuala Lumpur are just a few of these places. Reflecting this reality, Richard Dobbs and his colleagues (2011) show that the six hundred largest cities in the world house about a third of the global output, and two thousand urban centers produce the majority.

In addition to this broad picture of urbanization, metropolitan areas are continuing to spread out physically. The great suburban wave in the West is slowing, but suburbanization is gaining in emerging economies, perhaps with a slight nod to environmental concerns that push for greater density and more collective transport—although it is unlikely to be abandoned. Many metropolitan areas in the twenty-first century will expand not only through greater employment density in their core but also by replicating the polycentric metropolitan region model that is already found in Los Angeles, London, Paris, São Paulo, Mexico, and San Francisco.

Thus, within this shared global process of development, the pattern of development will remain territorially unequal. There are two senses of such inequality. The first is that urbanization is itself a form of extreme unevenness: it packs people, firms, information, and wealth into small territories. About 40 percent of US employment is located on 1.5 percent of the country's land, and about 60 percent is situated on 12.5 percent of the land. In most countries, this has led in recent years to an increase in income divergence between major metropolitan areas and the remaining parts of the national territory. Some of this is offset through income transfer to those areas, but the basic dynamic—of a split between the middle- and large-size metro areas and the rest—will likely characterize development in the opening decades of the twenty-first century. The second type of unevenness of development is that individual metropolitan regions, over the medium run of thirty to forty years, undergo considerable turbulence in their fates, rising and falling in the income ranks, and gaining or losing population at different rates.

City-regions are the principal scale at which people experience lived reality. The geographical churn, turbulence, and unevenness of development, combined with the sheer scale of urbanization, will make city-region development more important than ever—to economics, politics, our global mood, and our welfare. And managing it will pose one of the most critical challenges to humanity. The winning side of the process will excite us and motivate talent, but the losing side will create displacement and anger, both within and between countries.

Growth and Change: The Challenge to Theory and Evidence

Social science has paid abundant attention to describing urban growth and change—or more broadly, to the regional and geographical dimensions of growth and change. Notwithstanding the progress that has been made, we are still far away from identifying the causes of such change. Change and its causes are what matter most to human welfare. The big game to be hunted is insights into the drivers of changes in the geography of economic development and population. The problem is that we still mostly account for patterns in a post hoc manner, or attribute causes to them by oversimplifying, thus bracketing out most of the interesting interactions ("if this, then that" kinds of approaches).

Explaining the growth and change of regions and cities is one of the great challenges for social science (Perloff 1963). Cities or regions, like any other geographical scale of the economic system, have complex economic development processes that are shaped by an almost-infinite range of forces. The thorny question is, What should social science aim to do in the face of such complexity? It would be unrealistic to ask any field of theory and research—especially in an area of such complex human-technical interaction as the spatial economy—to meet all these challenges fully. But a focus on change and causality, by which I mean studying cities and regions as forward-moving development processes—should determine what is most relevant in defining the ambitions of the field. Concretely, then, the field should be able to respond to such questions as: Why do city-regions grow? Why do some decline? What differentiates city-regions that are able to sustain growth from those that are not? What are the forces that cause per capita income to converge or diverge, and under what conditions do they operate? Why are some city-regions so much more productive than others? What is the relationship of a region's material-physical structure to its economic performance? What are the principal regularities in urban and regional growth, and what are the events and processes that are not temporally or geographically regular but instead affect pathways of development in irreversible ways?

Urban and regional development is a noisy and complex phenomenon. Its most significant causes cannot be understood through the tools of any single discipline or theory, even the "economic" ones. This book's main purpose is to consider the explanations we use for city and regional growth and development, and organize the major questions along with the toolbox we have for attempting to answer them. It draws principally from economics, economic geography, and economic sociology. Four contexts of the development of city-regions compose the toolbox for explanation that this book constructs: economic, institutional, social interaction, and political or normative. In each context, I focus on identifying microfoundations: how individuals, households, firms, and groups interact to make cities and change them.

Economics and Geography

I begin with the task for economics and then move on to the other disciplines. The geography of uneven economic development is the central concern of development economics, economic geography, and regional science and urban economics. This book engages with all these fields. The main difference that characterizes studying the mechanisms of development at the urban-regional scale from the national scale has to do with the degree of openness of the economies in question. International flows of goods, people, capital, and information are important to national development, and arguably ever more so in a period of intense globalization such as the present one. But there are still many significant limits to openness. Nation-states have sovereign state structures with powerful tools to shape development. These include property rights, fiscal and monetary policy, the ability to intervene in the economy's supply of factors through education, border controls as well as research and development (R & D) and tax policy. In addition, countries have informal institutions such as common languages, traditions, and social and economic networks. This allows countries to limit their degrees and types of openness in a wide variety of ways.

City-regions within a country do not have that kind of sovereignty or separation. There are fewer barriers to trade as well as the mobility of firms, capital, and people inside national economies than in the global system as a whole. City-regions also have limited fiscal capacities compared to nation-states and no independent monetary policy. City and regional governments do not set fundamental laws about such things as property rights, tax policy, and other basic institutional issues. In some countries, there are local education systems, but they usually depend on national norms and, often, national budgets. R & D may be more intense in some regions than others, but its basic structure and magnitudes are strongly shaped by national policy. In a few countries such as Spain, Belgium, or Switzerland, the social and economic networks are sharply segmented by language and history. In most countries, though, the national language and culture have strong unifying influences on city-regions.

In standard economic models of regional development, this high degree of openness is captured by assuming the unlimited mobility of labor (people) and capital (firms), and low trade costs for goods and services (output) between regions. In these approaches, we thus assume high openness and low costs of interaction with other regions, allowing research to turn to what we might call patterns of "sorting" of firms and people. This means that urban and regional economics tends to reduce the question of regional development to the interregional economics of the sorting of capital and labor. In part I of this book, I argue that standard urban and regional economics attributes too much importance to sorting, and that it gets the principal sources of sorting wrong. Whereas standard urban and regional economics sees sorting as driven principally by costs of living, housing markets, and local business climates, I see it as driven principally by changes in technology and trade costs.

International development studies, by contrast, identifies concerns that should be at the heart of analyzing city-region development. Since countries have significant barriers to trade and factor mobility, development is structured not just by what is sorted to them but also by what they do internally with the resources they have and create (Helpman 2011). Regional development—like national development—is strongly influenced by interaction processes within the economy—notably in innovation, know-how, human networks, labor markets, and local social interactions and political processes related to development. These internal developmental dynamics of the productive economy in turn contribute to sorting, in a two-way interaction between the local and other scales of the economy.

The location of the leading-edge tradable activities of the economy—in shorthand, the "innovation sector"—is not just a sorting response to factor costs and factor prices. In many ways it is the other way around. Regional business ecosystems or clusters generate or attract their own factor supplies, and create their institutional and interaction environments. These conditions cannot be readily imitated, nor can their costs or prices be bid down through interregional competition and sorting of firms and people.

Geographers, sociologists, and many students of urban politics typically concentrate on these internal dynamics of regions. Unfortunately, these scholars inhabit separate worlds of academic and policy debate from those explored principally by economists. The disciplines of geography, sociology, and urban politics think about how business networks affect entrepreneurship and specialization; how politics affect local labor markets and wages; how social networks influence political attention and problem solving; how ideas, traditions, and cultures impact the environment for firms; and how land use is shaped by many such local forces. All these contribute to the internal developmental dynamics of city-regions, and they differ strongly from city to city.

The Book

For the noisy and complex problem identified above, there will be no single "big-bang" model, but rather four analytic contexts, covering several disciplines: again, economic, institutional, innovation or interaction, and political or societal.

The economic context explored in chapters 2 through 5 concerns the geography of production, or where firms and jobs go, and the geography of individual household and worker locational choices. In chapter 2, I ask whether it is movements of people seeking quality of life or jobs/firms seeking production locations that set off major sequences of change in urban and regional development. The response is that city-regions develop mostly as workshops of firms, not playgrounds of individuals. In chapter 3, I discuss why industries concentrate in general, and what kind of spatial-economic pattern of population and production they trace out. In chapter 4, I look at why some cities and regions have prices and wages that are so much higher than others, and how this fits into the overall economic process of wealth creation.

In chapter 5, I consider the role of individuals and their preferences for where to live; for firms, I examine their preferences for where to locate; and for both, I look at their preferences for public goods. Any broad economic process such as city-region development is the result of innumerable individual choices. A critical issue in all studies of urban development is the extent to which the pattern of urbanization responds to such preferences. I will argue that the relationship between preferences and urban outcomes is fraught with tensions. This means that we can only rarely use the characteristics of existing cities and urban systems to deduce "what people want," or what they would "prefer to prefer."

For economists, this book attempts to occupy a middle ground of respect for the technical workings of theory, although using mostly words and stories to communicate, with some numbers and models (Leamer 2012). The goal is not to build models but instead to find a framework for the economics of cities and regions that captures the main forces of their development.

The principal economic models take us a long way, but cannot fully explain the selectivity of development among city-regions. Any major wave of fundamental changes in the drivers of urban economic development will consolidate around certain "winner" regions and generate a set of less successful places. There are many possible reasons for such selectivity: "first-mover accidents" (i.e., luck), institutions, the geography of innovation, and the deliberate actions or policies of states. Did New York become a great financial center by just being there first, or did Silicon Valley locate near San Francisco because one of its founders needed to be near his aging mother? Did something deep about the institutions and social structures of these places attract these industries to these locations? Was it their capacity to innovate, and what is that? Or did the actions of states and governments favor these places?

It is widely thought that "good institutions" have something to do with the economic development of nations—and increasingly, this notion is applied to city-regions. For the most part, development economics considers institutions in the capital I sense of Institutions (states, constitutions, rules, laws, and formal policies). But there is also a small i sense of institutions, as the organization of the key "groups" or "communities" in the economy—from elite networks to civic associations and neighborhood groups. I am interested in knowing how they interact, often in unintentional ways, to shape labor markets, schooling, attitudes, and even formal policies.

Metropolitan regions within countries have similar formal Institutions, but they differ greatly in the communities they have, and how these communities bridge together to form the overarching society of the region. The social structure of Dallas has important differences compared to that of New York, and the social structure of Toulouse looks quite different from that of Bordeaux. Paris and London differ not only in their formal institutions, since they are in two different countries, but also in this small *i* institutional sense. These differences have a strong influence on how metropolitan regions perform over time in the way they capture, develop, or repel economic activities. In part II, I concentrate on the economic sociology of city-regions and especially on informal institutionalized action at the regional scale.

Economics and sociology are then heavily mobilized, in combination, in part III of the book, where I consider the local interaction context and its role in a globalizing world economic system by examining its role in the geography of innovation. Innovative sectors tend to be highly concentrated—agglomerated—in a relatively small number of cities, where their firms, talent pools, and knowledge are located. Why, for example, does information technology locate in San Jose, finance in London and Hong Kong, entertainment in Los Angeles, and pharmaceuticals in Basel? The location of these industries in certain cities (and countries, by extension) is key to where the high-skilled jobs are and the hierarchy of incomes.

Innovation is a special concern of the economic context of development, because the geography of innovation transforms not just the major centers of innovation but also the whole economy and all of its regions. Innovation centers get many local benefits from being innovative: high-wage jobs, high incomes, and high fiscal capacity. Innovations that emerge from the principal metropolitan centers have effects that wash across the economy when they are applied to processes and products in other industries, and because the innovative industries themselves ultimately mature and can be relocated elsewhere. Understanding the space and time pathway of innovation and growth is the holy grail of development economics and geographical economics. And it is the most elusive and complex question in the study of economic development.

The space-time pathway of the economic rents from innovation is explored in part I, the economic context section. In this part, I get into the human interactions underlying innovation and cities. Each way of being innovative has its own specific supply architecture—the way that ideas, entrepreneurs, partner firms, and consumer tastes and habits are brought together. This is why different countries and cities still have their particular "genius." The genius of cities, in the form of the behavioral context in which different elements of know-how come together, is analyzed in chapter 10. Moreover, much proximate interaction takes a specific form, which I analyze in chapter 11: face-to-face contact. Why is face-to-face contact so central to innovation and local genius? Why do certain cities and regions have many overlapping worlds of face-to-face contact, giving them a "buzz?"

City-regions also develop in part as a result of politics. They are shaped by national policies in different ways, and in turn, they enter into national political and social life in a variety of ways that are often not apparent to the naked eye. They are also the subject of heavily normative judgments by their residents, experts, and policymakers. In the final section of the book, I look at cities and city-systems within the overall political-economic process.

Four broad mechanisms of politics are examined: the ability to create new city and regional authorities and governments, expressing the difference between more centralized and more decentralized societies; the rate of migration of firms and people from region to region; the role of land and land development in the economy; and the degree of differences in labor regulation and wages among regions. These four mechanisms influence important economic and geographical outcomes: the dynamics of reorganizing factors of production (labor, firms, and knowledge) across regions, which is one of the main components of innovation; the pattern of togetherness or separation of social groups; and the use of geographical "exit" (mobility) versus the use of "voice and loyalty" to affect political and economic processes. The existence of all these differences means that even in a more and more globalized world, cities and regions will have different roles in the political and normative debates in different national states and societies.

The world of metropolitan development that I analyze in this book will, as noted, create a huge amount of opportunity, innovation, and creation, yet it will be turbulent and uneven, and necessarily conflict filled. There will be a cleavage not only between the basic winner territories of the world economy—middle- and large-sized metropolitan regions—but also increasingly between them and the vast territories that they do not include. The viability of countries has long depended on their ability to hold the winners and losers of society together—in both people and place terms (winner and loser categories of the population, and winner and loser regions). In some cases, the failure to do so has led to the breakup of countries; in others it has led to policies that backslide on integration, trade, and even cultural openness. The question of what to do about uneven development and churn will be more relevant than ever in the twenty-first century, within and between countries. Given the reality of uneven development and turbulence, what—if anything—should public policy do? In chapter 13, I explore efficiency and equity in relation to territorial development. Determining the right mixture of efficiency and equity is the question of *justice* in relationship to development. Getting the cities and regions we "want" involves engaging with the mix of efficiency and equity consequences we want to be embodied in the number, size, form, and interrelationships of our cities.

PART I

The Economic Context of City and Regional Development

Workshops of the World Economy

PEOPLE, JOBS, AND PLACES

People or Jobs: Chicken or Egg?

The development of cities and evolution of urban systems occurs through the movement of people and jobs (firms) between places.[1] Consider the major changes in the geographical distribution of people and jobs that have taken place in just a few decades. The biggest and richest cities in the US urban system today include many places that were not there just a short while ago, and many of the formerly biggest and richest have slipped well down the ranks of size and wealth (see table 1.1 again). Houston and Dallas are big and rich; Seattle has become relatively richer; San Francisco is both bigger and has retained its status as the highest-income metropolitan area in the country. Cities that were once considered to have fallen on hard times in the United States—such as Boston or New York—are now dynamic and rich again.

In Europe, London is rich and vital, after decades of losing jobs and income; Zurich, Copenhagen, and Munich have maintained high per capita income with modest population growth, while Marseille, Lille, and Manchester have done poorly. In developing countries, the story is fundamentally different, because there is a primary urbanization effect at work that favors a few big cities in most industrializing countries, such as Shanghai, Beijing, and Guangzhou.

In this chapter I focus on a classical question, formulated crisply by Richard Muth (1971): Is the migration of individuals the chicken or egg of regional development? Urban systems change as the result of an endless series of mutual adjustments of people and jobs to one another across neighborhoods and regions; some people or firms move, this attracts more people, which in turn makes the region attractive to more firms, and so on. Change is two-way and circular over time. But this is only a way of wriggling out of providing an answer to the question of what sets off major change in the pattern of urban and regional development. For a hundred years up to the 1940s, the core of the US urban-regional system was the Northeast and Midwest, with an outpost in California. Then some kind of floodgate opened, though, and rapid change happened in just a few decades, at the end of which was a fundamentally redefined urban system.

In the recent US version of this debate, a great deal of urban economics and regional science claims that migration is the chicken, and that migration is fundamentally driven by consumer choices for cheap housing in the Sun Belt and various kinds of quality-of-life features of places, such as climate or landscape. A still more recent version of this argument is that "creative" people lead the way to development, as they migrate in search of talent and tolerance (Florida 2005); another version is that skilled people lead the way by seeking to be with other skilled people (Glaeser and Maré 2001). The contrary view that I will defend in this chapter is that individuals and households do indeed make such choices, but that they are the egg, with the chicken being the location of jobs and opportunity to earn income.

The New Neoclassical Urban Economics

To consider this question, I need to introduce the dominant perspective in the field of urban and regional economics: new neoclassical urban economics (NNUE). The NNUE focuses on the locational choices of individuals, firms, and households. Empirically, the NNUE is strongly influenced by Philip Graves (1976, 1980, 1983) and Jennifer Roback (1982), North American regional scientists who theorized that preferences for amenities are central to the choices of individuals and households. For them, the principal amenities are climate and "quality of life," which both households and individuals seek to maximize utility, and do so through mobility. The NNUE assumes some set of constraints (such as budgets for households, skills for workers, or supplier structures for firms), and then determines the equilibrium spatial distribution of population (people decisions) and output (firm decisions), which together define the size of cities, cities' income and output levels, and specialization patterns between city-regions.

Edward Glaeser (2008), and Glaeser and his colleague Joshua Gottlieb (2009) take things further, offering a comprehensive "general spatial equilibrium" (GSE) framework, in which the locational decisions of firms, migration decisions by individual workers, and developers' choices to construct housing are jointly determined. Consumers seek to maximize utility, which is a function of their wages, housing expenditures, and amenities; firms seek to maximize profits, and they have the possibility of full factor substitution across locations. Builders supply housing in response to demand and regulation, providing more space and a low price for land, where the latter is determined mostly by the level of land use regulation, and in some cases, natural ("first-nature geography") differences between regions.

The GSE claims that housing prices, wages, and city sizes are simultaneously determined by the interaction between workers, firms, and developers, and that they in turn simultaneously determine city sizes, income levels, and rates of population and income growth. After some shock disturbs any of the key variables, workers and firms change locations, and builders adjust housing stocks until they collectively bring the system back into general equilibrium. If workers in city x enjoy higher utility levels—a function of either differences in amenities, productivity levels, or housing costs—workers in city y will migrate to x and ultimately eat into those premiums. In equilibrium, the presence of high nominal (money) wages should be bid down by some combination of high housing prices and disamenities, while cities with low nominal wages must offer some compensating advantage—cheap housing and/or some bundle of desirable amenities, such as a pleasant climate that requires no access payment. Crucially, in this framework, population growth is alleged to be the most relevant yardstick for economic performance, as individuals vote with their feet, and real income—as the index of utility—is equalized among locations.[2]

Employing this reasoning, many North American regional scientists claim that a shock to urban amenities—the widespread commercialization of air-conditioning in the postwar period—set off a major, long-term transformation of the US urban system (Borts and Stein 1964; Graves 1983; Rappaport 2007; Partridge 2010). Air-conditioning, combined with the construction of the interstate highway system, permitted many individuals to act on their built-in preferences for living in a pleasant climate, or being near mountains and the seashore. Large groups of workers therefore moved from cold, dense locations in the Northeast to warmer, less dense southern ones. According to Mark Partridge (2010), building on Graves (1976, 1983), people in this era migrated for housing and climate, jobs then found those people, and housing construction shifted to places that had less restrictive building rules, usually in the warm, less developed places, with per capita nominal income levels below the national median.

In addition, they argue that certain areas that they consider to have less desirable climates and natural features, such as New York and other old large metropolitan areas, resurged in the 1990s because their quality of life, or "amenity value," increased. These cities offer the amenity of interaction among highly skilled workers; the demand for such workers increased sometime in the 1990s. These cities are also said to offer the amenity of superior consumption opportunities, and the exogenous event of declining crime rates made it possible for this preference to be accessed at a lower cost than previously.

These researchers are, of course, not alone in observing that many Americans enjoy sunshine and suburbs, New York is now much safer than it was during the 1970s, and highly skilled workers are more productive when clustered together. What is distinctive about the explanation put forth by these urban economists is the way it ties these processes together. This perspective contends that because workers can relocate so easily, and because money and amenities are substitutes for one another, the utility of similar workers—where their utility is composed not only of nominal (or gross) wages but also spending on housing and the availability of local amenities—will tend toward equalization across urban areas. In this general spatial equilibrium, an individual worker cannot be made better off by moving from one city to another. New Yorkers may earn higher nominal wages because of the concentration of skill-demanding industries there, but the reason why the residents of Phoenix do not migrate to New York en masse is that New Yorkers are not better off once we account for their icy winters and the relatively high cost of their apartments.

According to this view, the Sun Belt grew because many workers chose sunshine and housing in exchange for lower nominal wages, while certain highly productive workers opted for higher wages accompanied by higher housing costs as well as a mix of good and bad amenities, such as cultural activities, traffic, crime, and so on. And although air-conditioning and lax land regulation might temporarily make certain locations more attractive, the utility levels of workers in the Sun Belt, Rust Belt, and those on the two coasts ought to tend toward equalization, because when those people move to the Sun Belt, they ultimately "pay" for the sunshine and cheap housing in the form of lower money wages.

This vision has become increasingly dominant in discussions about the causes and consequences of the transformation of urban systems, and not just in the United States. At first glance, table 2.1 seems consistent with this general story. The list of cities that most rapidly increased their per capita income between 1980 and 2000 include some resurgent northeastern metropolitan areas and their suburbs, wealthy parts of Silicon Valley, and a group of Sun Belt newcomers. The ten cities with the highest rates of population growth are all in the Sun Belt, except for San Bernardino–Riverside area, a satellite of the Los Angeles region.[3] Declining industrial hubs dominate the list of cities at the bottom of the population ranking. A group of fairly small urban areas in interior California and Texas share the dubious distinction of having the lowest rates of income growth.

TABLE 2.1
Population and Income Growth, U.S. Metropolitan Areas, 1980–2000

	Population Growth Rate	Nominal Income Growth Rate
Top 10	Las Vegas, NV	San Jose, CA
	Fort Myers-Cape Coral, FL	Norwalk, CT
	Austin, TX	Stamford, CT
	Ocala, FL	Bridgeport, CT
	Riverside-San Bernardino, CA	Boston, MA
	Orlando, FL	Raleigh-Durham, NC
	Phoenix	Austin, TX
	McAllen-Edinburg TX	Charlotte-Gastonia, NC
	West Palm Beach, FL	Fort Walton Beach, FL
	Atlanta, GA	San Francisco-Oakland, CA
Bottom 5	Decatur, IL	Odessa, TX
	Johnstown, PA	Bakersfield, CA
	Duluth-Superior, MN/WI	Fresno, CA
	Pittsburgh-Beaver Valley, PA	Visalia-Tulare-Porterville, CA
	Youngstown-Warren, OH-PA	Riverside-San Bernardino, CA

NOTES: Population growth rates based on authors' calculations from U.S. Census data (N=331); Income growth rates based on authors' calculations from Bureau of Economic Affairs data on nominal metropolitan per capita gross domestic product (N=387). Nominal refers to gross income, as opposed to income net of expenditures (real income). Unless otherwise stated, income data has not been adjusted to reflect inflation.

Figure 2.1, from Kemeny and Storper (2012), shows scatterplots of the relationship between population and nominal and real median household income in 1980 and 2000 for a consistent set of 244 metropolitan areas. In the left column, we observe the expected upward-sloping relationship between nominal income and population: "raw" wages are higher in large cities. In contrast to Edward Glaeser and David Maré's (2001) finding with 37 cities in 1990, however, this figure depicts that in 1980 as in 2000, the median household in large cities earns considerably more, even after accounting for housing costs, than the median household in smaller cities. The slope of each line diminishes when moving from nominal to real income levels, but the relationship remains significant and strongly positive. Additionally, the intercity distribution of incomes shows no tendency toward some distant moment of equalization. The coefficient of variation for real median household income actually increases from 0.137 to 0.145 over the study period.

In order to be consistent with spatial equilibrium, we should expect any externality from unpriced or "free" amenities to be negatively related to real wages (Glaeser, Kolko, and Saiz 2001). Cities with pleasant climates, vibrant nightlife, or other amenities should also be those cities with comparatively lower real income. With this relationship in mind, some urban economists have seized on average January temperatures as a major driver of the later twentieth-century growth of Sun Belt population and income (Borts and Stein 1964; Graves 1983; Partridge 2010), while others argue that an expansion of the housing supply in southern cities is the more compelling cause (Glaeser and Tobio 2008). If either amenities or a construction boom are exogenous determinants of the rise of the Sun Belt, then workers have revealed their willingness to trade wages for warmer winters or cheap, spacious accommodation. In table 2.2, January temperatures are significantly and negatively associated with real wages in 1980, just as general spatial equilibrium models predict.

But is average January temperature a broad enough indicator of the amenities likely to affect locational decisions? Ultimately this question would best be answered with data on the motivations and preferences of migrants. Lacking data that peer inside the heads of human actors, we still have some indications that winter temperature is insufficient as a gauge of overall amenities. One could begin with the commonsense observation that Houston's summers are about as uncomfortable as Detroit's winters. Other hints come from several sources. Publications such as the *Places Rated Almanac* (Boyer 1985) and *Cities Ranked and Rated* (Sperling and Sander 2004), though far from perfect, combine survey and secondary data on amenities with the goal of providing information to assist with migration decisions. Each suggests that even examining climate factors alone, individuals consider a wider range of qualities of place. Table 2.2 also presents the relationship between real income in 1980 and the *Places Rated Almanac*'s "Climate and Terrain" variable, which combines information on temperature extremes, the number of days where heating and cooling would be needed, and other considerations. Although negative, the correlation is both weak and insignificant, suggesting that the relationship between climate, population, and income does not survive a wider consideration of climate characteristics. Just to bring this down to an image, coastal Southern California (from Santa Barbara to San Diego)

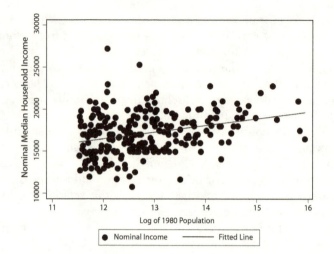

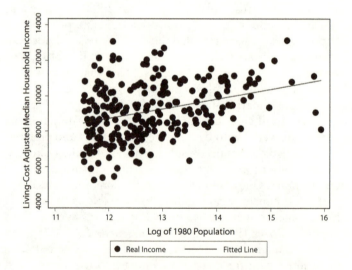

Figure 2.1   Median income and population levels for metropolitan areas, 1980 and 2000.

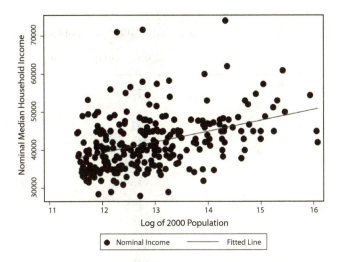

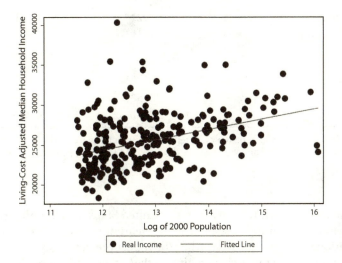

TABLE 2.2
Correlations between Amenities and Real Income and Population

Amenities	Real Income, 1980	Population, 1980
Mean January Temperature	−.41** (.00)	.004 (.95)
Climate & Terrain	−.002 (.98)	.23** (.00)
Transportation	.16** (.01)	.44** (.00)
Health Care & Environment	.34** (.00)	.84** (.00)
Crime	−.03 (.63)	−.42** (.00)
Recreation	.02** (.01)	.35** (.00)
Arts	.23** (.00)	.89** (.00)
Education	.15** (.02)	.38** (.00)

NOTES: Standard errors in parentheses. Asterisks denote significance levels:
**Significant at 1%. Amenity variables are described in the data appendix.

has the most temperate climate in the United States along with high real income net of housing costs, but its population growth rates are just at the national median, far from what the model predicts.

As noted, some researchers maintain that other kinds of quality-of-life factors shape urban performance, including leisure attractions (Carlino and Saiz 2008), coastal access, and a host of consumer amenities (Rappaport 2007; Glaeser, Kolko, and Saiz 2001; Clark et al. 2002; Florida 2002). This claim is consistent with the broader theoretical discussions in Roback (1982) and elsewhere. The remainder of table 2.2 presents the relationship between real income in 1980 and other amenities as measured in the *Places Rated Almanac* with indicators of the arts, recreation, health care and environment, crime, education, and transportation. Surprisingly, all the other amenity indexes are positively associated with real income, except for crime. All but crime are also positively correlated with metropolitan population in 1980, which accords with general quality-of-life patterns in Albouy (2008): large cities offer better amenities, no matter how unpleasant their winters. Of all the quality-of-life measures I consider here, only mean January temperature displays the expected relationship to real income.[4]

In order to fully understand the relationship between amenities and urban growth, we would need more detailed data on the prices of amenities, the supply of unpriced amenities, and the detailed preferences of individuals everywhere. It is important to note that despite thirty years of publication on the topic, supporters of the amenity-driven growth hypothesis have not generated these detailed data. Are amenities more abundant, but more expensive in, say, New York as compared to Houston? As of this writing in fall 2011, the Metropolitan Opera of New York and Houston Grand Opera are presenting Gioacchino Rossini's *The Barber of Seville*. The Met's prices range from $25 to $430, and Houston's prices range from $38 to $400, as indicated by their respective Web sites. A budget-constrained individual can pay one-third less to attend this opera in New York than for the cheapest seat in Houston. It is a fair guess that New York has a greater total supply of entertainment amenities than Houston, though we lack the data to calculate convincing estimates on a per capita basis, or determine whether there are varying effects of access and crowding. But the existing literature offers no proof that amenities are more expensive in high-income cities or that such cities have lower supplies of free amenities, except for warmth, than in rapidly growing cities. General spatial equilibrium theory demands that "high amenities should be associated with lower real incomes since high real incomes are needed to offset low amenities in unattractive places" (Glaeser 2008, 59). When we unpack the evidence and examine it closely, the role of amenities in explaining population movements—which are the yardstick of the Glaeser-Roback-Graves tradition—is far from convincing.

One could then ask whether such real wage and income differences are caused by different quality of labor and skills between cities. But the real wage gaps reported above remain after we account for differences in the composition of cities' workforces. Kemeny and Storper (2012) finds that 12 percent of the variance in real household wages is a function of metropolitan-level differences in characteristics (not differences in household member characteristics, in other words) in 1980 and 2000. To put it another way, households composed of people with similar individual characteristics do better in larger metropolitan areas where, as we have already seen, they also have access to better amenities.

One of the main claims of the NNUE is that the best gauge of what drives the urban system is population change because this view claims that real utility is equalized. Since that doesn't hold up to scrutiny, however, do people maximize their utility by migrating toward places with a combination of high real incomes and higher amenities? If migration—driven by personal preferences—really is the chicken of regional and urban development, people should be flowing to the places that combine these two things.

Because we cannot neatly combine amenity values and real income into a single index, we arrange cities into four quadrants: those with above-average amenities and real income, those with below-average amenities and real income, those that have high income and low amenities, and those cities with low income and high amenities. To facilitate this grouping strategy, we standardize and then calculate a single mean amenity score for each metropolitan area, combining indexes for climate, health, crime, transport, education, arts, and recreation.[5] This requires that we weight each kind of amenity equally—no doubt an imperfect assumption, although the different amenity measures are strongly positively correlated, except for crime. Figure 2.2 presents the relationship between the standardized amenity measure and real income in 1980. In it, we also distinguish between Sun Belt and non–Sun Belt cities.[6] Top performers in the high-utility quadrant in 1980 include Washington, DC, Chicago, San Francisco, and Boston, among the heartlands of the innovation-based economy. Few of these high-utility cities are in the Sun Belt; Atlanta and Dallas are among the exceptions. Most Sun Belt cities lie in the low-utility quadrant, and to a lesser extent in the low real income and high-amenity quadrant. Non–Sun Belt cities are more evenly dispersed throughout the four quadrants. A number of high-utility cities in 1980 are on their way down, including Detroit, Cleveland, and Philadelphia. Unsurprisingly, these old manufacturing centers do not remain in this quadrant if we recalculate based on year 2000 values.

To determine whether population growth rates differ significantly between quadrants, table 2.3 shows the relationship of population growth on a set of dummy variables indicating quadrant membership, with the high-amenity, high-wage quadrant as the reference group. None of the quadrants have population growth rates that are significantly different from the group with both high real income and high amenities.[7] This runs counter to the prediction that the highest population growth rates ought to be found in locations with higher-than-average levels of real income and amenities. If there has been some shock that has led to higher utility in certain cities, whether cheaper housing, higher nominal wages, or more pleasant amenities, workers should seize on this opportunity to increase their utility levels by moving from lower- to higher-utility cities. The evidence for this proposition, central to the NNUE, is not apparent.

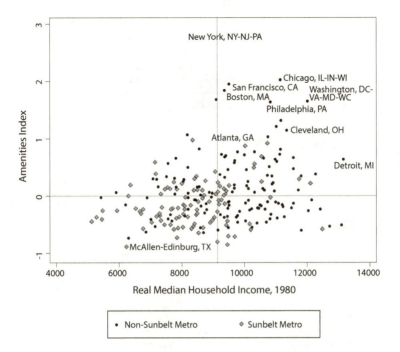

Figure 2.2 Amenities and real income in US metropolitan areas.

A More Plausible Story of Sun Belt Development and Urban System Change in General

What set off all these complex changes in the US urban system (and for that matter, in many other countries)? Both general spatial equilibrium theory and its more modest cousin, amenities theory, hold that such sequences of change can be set off when individuals and households are given access to environments that were previously inaccessible to them—thus the importance of air-conditioning and better highways to unleashing massive population flows between regions. The initial cause is that people move; jobs follow. Translated into an image, these theories suggest that enormous numbers of people woke up in the late 1950s and early 1960s, and decided it was now time to move to the Sun Belt. The question is not whether infinite incremental and circular relations between population/labor supply and firms/labor demand reshape the spatial economic system. It is about what could set off a new sequence of developmental events that ultimately led to the metropolitan system we have today.

TABLE 2.3.
Utility as a Determinant of Metropolitan Population Growth
Rates, 1980–2000

Dependent Variable: Population Growth Rates	
Low Amenities, Low Real Income	0.150
	(0.205)
Low Amenities, High Real Income	0.139
	(0.205)
High Amenities, Low Real Income	−0.017
	(0.249)
Constant	0.127
	(0.204)
Observations	239
R^2	0.008
p-value	0.613

NOTE: Reference group is high income, high amenity quadrant.
Standard errors in parentheses.

Let's consider the specific US version of revolutionary change in the urban system. If we cannot find evidence that there is spatial utility equalization today or a recent tendency toward it many decades after the development of the Sun Belt began, then how likely is it that wages and amenity conditions in the South were good enough in, say, 1947 to attract large numbers of northern workers away from their jobs? In 1947, the US Congress passed the Taft-Hartley amendments to the National Labor Relations Act. Nearly all the southern states responded by becoming right-to-work states, where unionization would be (and still is) much more difficult than in the Northeast or Midwest, thereby creating a distinct labor relations system in the South. Just two years later, Congress commissioned a report titled *Why Industry Moves South* (McLaughlin 1949) to try to understand why eighty-eight plants had relocated to the nascent Sun Belt. Both the legislative change and this report predate the widespread adoption of air-conditioning, or the construction of the interstate highway system.

This historical context points to an alternative set of drivers of recent US urban change. Instead of being led by workers seeking warm

sunny winters and sprawling suburbia, the plausible story of the bur-
geoning Sun Belt and declining Frost Belt starts with firms moving from
the Northeast to the South and West in sectors like mill processing (tex-
tiles, etc.). These were firms in sectors at the mature end of the product
cycle—industries whose innovative days were mostly behind them. Many
such firms, once locked into high-wage and highly unionized northern
cities, found their production processes increasingly easy to routinize and
mechanize. Routinization reduced the skill level required in the labor
force, which allowed those firms more locational freedom. Firms seized
on this freedom, relocating to cities in the Sun Belt that offered cheap
land and less skilled, less expensive workers along with little regulation.
These and other firms were and are not spatially indifferent but rather
have semifixed locational requirements at each stage in their life cycle,
and their locational choices are driven by the uneven geographical distribution of factors as well as transport costs. Once a certain number
of northern firms learned that the South was a suitable location, others
copied their decisions to move.

A great deal of research indicates that unemployment strongly conditions mobility decisions for US workers (for a review, see Greenwood
1997). Therefore, once the initial plants located in the Sun Belt, subsequent waves of migration to the Sun Belt were driven first by the slowing
down of job creation in many northern industrial cities and later by the
growing structural unemployment there, as the mature phase of the product cycle hit a wide range of capital-intensive traditional manufacturing
industries. It just so happens that the places where wages have been low
also have warmer winters than the places employment has been leaving
for the last half century or more in the United States—a coincidence, but
not an initial cause.

In US Sun Belt cities, there were institutional changes in the 1940s
(right-to-work laws; local economic development policies in the South;
and a decline in farming opportunities for abundant labor in some southern states). These interacted with industries that were maturing technologically and less dependent on labor skills than before. Then there
were important innovations: improvements in infrastructure, notably the
construction of the interstate highway system, radically reducing transport costs to market. And there were massive federal expenditures for
regional development in certain politically influential southern metropolitan regions.

We can thus establish that it was the changing geography of production that developed the Sun Belt. Exactly which of the forces named
above—institutions, industries, infrastructure, and federal investments—
was most important in setting off the sequence cannot be established
with certainty.[8] Individuals entered into the development of the Sun Belt

first as southern rural populations were drawn into manufacturing jobs that were relocating from the North and then as former northern workers were drawn to the South as job opportunities dried up in the industrial cities of the North.

What Kind of Assumptions Should We Use?

Let's now think about more recent changes in the US urban system. The emergence of major regional innovation powerhouses—the winning cities and regions in the New Economy—surely cannot be explained by the spontaneous migration decisions of workers and households, their supposedly superior amenities, or any other kind of lifestyle change. The geography of production drives the geography of urban development today, just as it has in the past.

Take the example of the ten-county San Francisco metropolitan area and five-county Los Angeles region. Both are in the general class of high-wage, high-income metropolitan areas, where housing prices have increased at a higher rate than population in the last few decades. Whereas their per capita incomes converged between 1945 and 1970, they have diverged since, leading to a one-third difference today.[9] The NNUE attributes such differences to a different position in the builders' equilibrium, assuming that San Francisco had less housing expansion than did Los Angeles, thereby limiting population growth and driving wages up. Most empirical indexes suggest that the overall quality-of-life amenities are slightly "higher" in San Francisco than in Los Angeles, so according to the model workers should actually be prepared to take lower nominal incomes in San Francisco, ceteris paribus.[10] The builders' equilibrium would need to be a powerful force for income divergence. But since 1970, the two regions have both had population growth near the national average, and proportional growth in the number and size of housing units.[11] Long-term average housing prices are, however, higher in the San Francisco metro area than in Los Angeles, in spite of the facts that the two regions are closely ranked in terms of regulatory strictness and their rates of housing expansion in the past thirty years are nearly identical. Moreover, money (nominal) wages in the Bay Area are higher in almost every category—that is, even when controlled for education, ethnicity, gender, and industry—suggesting that no trade-off for amenities is in evidence. It is conceivable that housing expansion is severely limited by existing regulatory regimes such that this becomes a determinant of overall regional growth. But most cases of highly limited housing expansion are on the neighborhood or central-city scale, not the regional one. It's unlikely that a significant change in the rate of population or income could be caused by changes in housing supply; housing construction is the egg, not the chicken, of regional growth.

Consider an even more extreme extrapolation of the model's role for housing supply. Again, take the case of San Francisco and Los Angeles since 1980. During this period, San Francisco grew to be the center of the world's information and communication technology economy, and Los Angeles lost much of its previous high-tech base in aerospace. How can this be explained? According to the model, this should be the result of these two cities being at different points on the builders' equilibrium, with San Francisco restricting housing construction, limiting population growth, and hence selecting for a more skilled migration stream, in turn attracting information technology industries; Los Angeles would have a more elastic, cheap housing supply, attracting lower-skilled people and in turn attracting industries that follow such people, as in low-wage light manufacturing. San Francisco did indeed get a more skilled migration stream, but it seems quite a stretch to place the weight of labor force, skills, and specialization on the price of housing. It is more likely that in regions with high housing costs, poor people will crowd into small and dense housing to a greater extent than they would in regions with cheaper housing. Housing cannot be the fundamental motor of an elaborate set of substitutions of people, jobs, and industries.

If it's not these lifestyle amenities and cost-of-living considerations, then what could explain the growth of the high-wage sector principally in places such as New York, San Francisco, and London? The GSE model holds that this could be due to preferences for the highly skilled to interact with other highly skilled people (Glaeser 2007). In this version of the people-jobs story, such preferences cause these individuals to cluster together, and in turn the industries—jobs—will follow. The reason that the financial industry grew so much in New York or London after 1980, according to this account, is that worker preferences for those two cities attracted the financial firms. Even if we grant that workers in such cities augment their productivity through various kinds of interactions within the large regional labor pool, it does poorly on the chicken-and-egg question, since such large-scale interaction could have only occurred once a large pool of people in the relevant industry were already in place. In the case of new industries such as microelectronics in Silicon Valley in the 1970s, the pool of talent did not even exist prior to the emergence of the industry. The emerging information technology industry and its labor force coevolved through the initial invention of skills in tandem with the initial growth of the new industry. Such a pool, once established, then may have many recursive effects on productivity and specialization, but it has to start with some other force that is omitted from the model. Thus, to model the interaction of the three constituent markets (builders, firms, and households) as simultaneous and without direction or starting points is to empty the account of any meaningful causality. City and regional development is the consequence of temporal sequences as well as hierarchies of causes.

The eschewing of history or sequence in this modeling strategy is done via the "spatial indifference assumption" in the firms' and individuals' choices. According to this assumption, firms go anywhere where they can maximize productivity, in an infinite combination of trade-offs of such things as worker skills and wages. But this can only be made tractable by assuming that the production system can be divided out at will into different places, and that each piece of it can have its factor proportions made to measure according to the factors available in each location (the firm as "putty"). In this world, a firm scans all the possible locations available to it and chooses the place it can trade-off, for example, some more labor for less capital and transport costs. As we will see in the following two chapters, though, in the critical leading-edge sectors of the economy—those that drive economic development—there is little spatial indifference. In a slightly more realistic, alternative view of this hypothesis, different firms or industries, with their different mixtures of capital, labor, and transport, can sort themselves to places in such a way that all supply and demand in the local-factor markets for capital, labor, and transport all balance out. But this would require a really happy coincidence in a world with an infinite number of firms, industries, and need structures.

In place of this way of thinking, in the chapters to follow I will use different assumptions. Spatial unevenness in wages, prices, and incomes comes about because there are different local equilibriums, even in a highly connected economy. There is no general economy-wide spatial equilibrium but rather a set of what economists call "multiple equilibriums" that reflect the location of leading-edge activities in certain places and sorting of other types of activities to other places. In turn, they unleash different local development processes, manifested in interregional differences in wages, incomes, and housing prices. These development processes can have durable effects on the skill and wealth accumulation of individuals, the fiscal and investment capacities of localities, and the social multipliers of their human networks.

Conclusion

Future major transformations of urban and regional patterns will come from shifts in the location of firms and industries, with people, amenities, and local consumer markets largely following. Even though London, New

York, and Paris have central-city neighborhoods that are consumption playgrounds for the rich of the world, they are above all major productive hubs in the global economy. The vast majority of their people come to these cities in order to work. The world urban system—from its richest to poorest cities—is not a set of playgrounds or amenity parks but instead a vast system of interlinked workshops.

The Motor of Urban Economies

The Geography of Employment

Many of the world's most notable city-regions are identified with their iconic industries: New York, Hong Kong, and London with finance; Los Angeles with entertainment; San Francisco with information technology; Houston with oil equipment; Milan with fashion; and Nashville with country music. In the nineteenth century, many manufacturing industries that are today quite spread out were typically concentrated in clusters in certain cities (Scranton 1983; Krugman 2011). This is still true now of some smaller and less well-known cities. Packaging machinery is produced in a cluster in Bologna; Stuttgart is involved in mechanical engineering, but all in all, manufacturing has spread out. In the developed countries, cities now specialize in services: high technology, health care, medical instruments, software, logistics, and finance (Fujita and Thisse 2009; Krugman 2011).

Specialization can sometimes be hard to see with the naked eye. One reason for this is that some cities are identified with many different industries rather than a single iconic cluster. In the developing world, the biggest cities such as Mexico City, São Paulo, Guangzhou, or Shanghai bring together many different sectors, and are thus often described as being "diversified" rather than specialized. This is because the national urban systems of those countries offer fewer alternative locations for industry clusters, so many activities crowd into the limited number of available locations. In developed countries, city-regions tend to have narrower economic bases given that economic activities can choose among many different city-regions offering the basic conditions of production (infrastructure and market access). But even there, some cities have diversified economies. For instance, the Los Angeles region has large clusters in entertainment, aerospace, mortgage lending, logistics, and light manufacturing. Part of this diversity is an optical illusion, however, in the sense that the size of each of these clusters in a huge region like Los Angeles will be bigger than the size of a cluster that accounts for a much bigger share of a smaller region's economy.

There are many regions and cities with successful economies that are not home to strong, easily identifiable clusters. Instead, they group together many functionally similar types of work, but not necessarily in a single or related industry. For example, there are many cities in the US South with manufacturing jobs, where what is similar among them is the type of work that is done—assembly, say—rather than the type of product. This is also now true of some developing world cities—those that are "functionally specialized"—as manufacturing and services shift there. Guangzhou specializes in assembly functions; Bangalore specializes in online customer service.

These two types of cases summarize a great deal of what we know about the geography of jobs in the tradable industries: they either concentrate or cluster together as industries (or "areas" of activity), or the industry in question spreads its different functions or phases out, choosing locations that are right for each type of work it does. In the third case, activities can be "greenfielded," meaning that they are not located in a cluster of anything but instead are isolated from most other tradable sectors. The economies of city-regions are then filled out with nontradable sectors such as home construction, haircutting, and supermarkets that respond to local demand. They increasingly rely on tradable (imported) inputs, so the distinction between tradable and nontradable activities is a rough one, and the borderline is constantly changing.

The motor of a city-region's economy is the tradable sector; it provides the jobs that come in and anchor labor as well as incomes to a place, on the basis of which the home market is built. However big the locally serving sector might appear at any given moment in time, it will always shrink if the tradable jobs go away, as cities such as Detroit know all too well. Tradable sectors are where the principal productivity gains of the economy are realized. This is because the main reason that certain industries are not tradable is that they must be located close to their markets, and this in turn usually means activities where the labor input is hard to squeeze out (haircutting, health care, and restaurants), and where the income to spend on these activities comes from the income that the region earns in producing tradable goods and services along with selling them to other places. Even the nontradable end-of-pipe activities in the economy—such as Walmart stores—get most of their productivity increases by incorporating tradable technologies (information technology for logistics) and tradable goods that they sell (their worldwide supplier chain). There are limited exceptions to this logic—city-regions with high proportions of retirees, for example, who live via income they bring with them, or in some countries, regions where the local population lives largely through government-sponsored income redistribution and services. But if one thinks closely about these instances, in effect the economy is the result of trade—in this case, in the income base that is imported by people who worked in other regions, and then came to retire or have fun. In this sense, the Florida or Costa del Sol "home markets" are the markets created by income coming from somewhere else and then being spent locally.

The location of jobs has two principal dimensions. One is the basic geographical structure of each sector in the economy. To put it simply, industries either concentrate or spread out, and in sectors involving complex production chains, they can manifest varying combinations of these two patterns. For now, I will focus on the recent efforts made by geographical economists to explain the concentration and spread of jobs along with how they affect patterns of city and regional development. The main recent contributor to this is known as the new economic geography (NEG), the second major branch of spatial economics that needs to be considered in this book. NEG has made major advances in explaining spatial concentration and the spreading out of industries, and some steps toward the ways concentrations of jobs, people, and firms arise.

Why Do Industries Concentrate? The Basics According to NEG

NEG stems from founding papers by Paul Krugman (1991a), the expansion of his work into a field of interrelated models (Fujita, Krugman, and Venables 1999), and roots in trade theory and applications to international development (Krugman and Venables 1995). These researchers wanted to know why countries with such similar underlying characteristics (comparative advantages) trade so much with one another. The answer provided is that places with similar underlying characteristics—the type and price of labor and capital, knowledge, transport access, and so on—can efficiently specialize in different things as well as trade with one another if industries or firms have economies of scale, such that by concentrating production in a small number of places, it is cheaper to produce goods there than to spread production out. If the cost savings of such concentration are greater than the extra transport or trade costs incurred to get products to markets that are rendered more distant by such concentration of production, then specialization and concentration will generate trade (Krugman 1991b; Fujita and Thisse 2002).

From this initial insight, a number of additional ones were added to the basic model of NEG. The scale economies can, for example, exist within firms or production units, or they may be "external." In the latter case, the relevant scale is that of a set of interlinked firms or industries that form an entire production chain. Each firm operates at a higher scale than would be possible than if it were isolated, because dense trade within the production chain enables more efficient sharing of work tasks, leaving less downtime for each firm. Moreover, if this process of sharing out tasks within production chain involves trade costs that are relatively high—meaning the intermediate or business-to-business trade—then the firms will tend to concentrate together spatially, leading to the formation of an agglomeration or cluster. This is especially true if the business-to-business trade costs are higher than those from getting outputs to their final market.

Another essential reason for trade among similarly developed economies is the differentiation or variety of products: when a market is fragmented into many different varieties, this can lower the scale of producing each variety; but if the many varieties are concentrated in large firms or clusters, and each transported to larger markets, then the system can combine efficiency and variety. The key to such gains is the increased size of market areas. Instead of many regions all producing many varieties at a low scale or dropping production of the varieties that have inadequate scale under markets that are divided from one another by high trade costs, regions specialize and trade in different varieties. In this way, for example, France can produce Peugeots and sell them to its European neighbors, combining all the demand to produce many Peugeot models, each at a high efficient scale, while Germany can sell many types of Volkswagens in the same way. For trade to make this possible, however, the costs of trade have to be low enough so as not to wipe out the gains from combining production into larger, but farther away, production units. Thus, NEG shows us how the ongoing transport and telecommunications revolution feeds back to economic development through geographical specialization.

Another feature of NEG, which is critical for thinking about city-region development, is that the concentration of production—whether as big firms or many externally linked firms in a cluster—does not depend on the uneven distribution of natural resources, climate, or proximity to coasts and rivers. For much of history, trade relied on being close to natural features such as waterways; these first-nature features therefore determined the pattern of urbanization. But it is now possible to create good transport links virtually anywhere we like. Natural factors are thus no longer the major reason that cities locate where they do or why they attain a certain size.

So then why have cities at all, if we can create transport access abundantly and in many places? One answer is the first lesson of all urban economics: it still makes sense to concentrate transport hubs, even if they don't have to be on coasts and rivers, and it still makes sense to concentrate a lot of local infrastructure to serve firms and households. These "urbanization economies" remain as important as ever, yet their location depends less on nature than it once did.

NEG adds a second major element to our understanding of why cities exist. Large numbers of firms in the same industry or closely linked industries sometimes locate together, even though transport services are now so cheap and abundant. Of course, in other industries, they don't locate close together anymore; this is reflected in the extensive worldwide procurement (outsourcing) of inputs by firms. But for the industries that cluster, NEG says that as long as some intermediate trade costs are significantly positive, it will make sense to concentrate suppliers close to where their buyers are located. Cities can arise from a natural and circular process of workers following jobs to big firms and clusters, the reverse effect of firms then following the workers in order to take advantage of the big consumer markets that are concentrated in those places, and so on. So we are back to the chicken-and-egg of jobs and people, and the response of NEG is that it is both chicken and egg, as long as something happens—even an accident (some people go to some place, firms follow, and things get bigger, or reverse that, some firm first gets big and draws in workers, and then more firms come). NEG is agnostic about what sets off the causal sequence, but it has a powerful microfounded model of what happens once the system is tipped in one direction or another (Martin and Ottaviano 1999). This way of thinking is known as the "endogenous core-periphery model," because the concentration of firms, jobs, and people doesn't depend on nature. Workers seek jobs and the income they provide, but also seek variety of consumption opportunities and lower prices. A sequence of self-reinforcing concentration—urbanization— comes from these behaviors.

These are significant achievements, though most of the underlying insights have been around quite a long time. An earlier generation of development economists, typified by Albert Hirschman (1958), Gunnar Myrdal (1957), Celso Furtado (1959), and Raúl Prebisch (1950), and drawing on other seminal thinkers such as François Perroux (1950), argued that economic development was circular and cumulative, and hence uneven among regions. The greater scale of markets in the wealthy countries propelled this circularity, attracting more production in order to serve local demand, and the income generated by such employment then enlarged the market even more. This is what NEG theorizes as the role of the home market of wealthy or large city-regions in generating core-periphery patterns (Melitz and Ottaviano 2008). These observations are consistent with the descriptions by scholars of cities of agglomeration as the basis of urban economies (Pred 1977; Hall 1998). But these earlier thinkers did not place their insights in a framework with a consistent view of trade costs and open-economy relationships, and they lacked micro-foundations. Moreover, NEG not only allows us to see how economic development could be circular and cumulative but also how declining trade costs could break or at least alter the core-periphery dynamic by allowing activities to move away from cities or core regions. In this sense, NEG is a fundamental leap forward, in that it opens up avenues for much more precise understanding of how trade costs, variety, and scale interact in a dynamic way.

The main challenge for NEG is how to get from what it teaches us about industries and jobs to then apply that to whole cities and regions. This is the classical issue of "aggregation" in social science: cities and regions combine many different industries and sectors. Can we build up from industries to places or at least broad patterns of development using the NEG toolbox?

NEG AND DEVELOPMENT: THE ORIGINS
OF SPATIAL CONCENTRATION

In order to consider the issue raised above, we need to dig into the details of NEG. The reader less interested in technical detail than the bigger picture may want to skip this section. The key NEG model is known as Dixit-Stiglitz-Krugman (DSK). It incorporates the three important, realistic features of the contemporary economy that I noted above—that is, labor mobility, product variety, and firm-level economies of scale. The main challenge for the DSK model is that it is analytically insolvable. Specific patterns of interplay between scale, variety, and trade can be created by simulations of them, which in turn means that the specifications of these forces have to be invented by the author (Fujita and Thisse 2009).[1] This raises the specter of having a speculative view of the world, which while useful in identifying basic causes of spatial behavior, cannot be used to see how they shape real-world development patterns.

Another criticism of NEG is how it considers the costs of trade over space. It does so through the use of "iceberg" trade cost assumptions, where a portion of the value of a good "melts away" in transit, usually as a function of distance. For many goods and services, however, the reality of trade costs could be quite different from this—not a linear function of distance, for example, and hence lumpy ("all or nothing"). Another technical critique is that there are overlapping gray zones of competition between places in the real world rather than clean, distinct market areas. And finally, consistent with the first critique, the model can only be worked out when the analyst makes assumptions about the substitutability of different products, because this determines how many clusters one gets and how far away from each other they can be. All of this means that there is a strong risk that modeling results will make predictions about the pattern of jobs in systems of cities and regions that are far from reality, or that the model will simply be massaged until it gets close to reality, with a risk that it is therefore not establishing anything insightful about hierarchies or sequences of causes.

The DSK model also has overly restrictive views of the behaviors that initiate spatial concentration. Both the DSK and classical "Loschian" central-place models represent the spatial economy as hierarchical market areas for goods that are differentiated by variety and scale. The DSK adds labor mobility as the dynamic force, and the size of the home market and hence core regions are then endogenously determined. The behavior that motivates this determination is the workers' pursuit of consumer utility. The causal story has agricultural workers search for utility by following product variety and lower prices (as a consequence of firm-level scale economies). This then leads to spatial concentration as firms crowd in to follow them, unleashing more scale economies, followed by a "snowball" process of mutual reinforcement. In this light, the DSK is formally committed to being agnostic about Muth's (1971) chicken-and-egg question of people and jobs. As with the NNUE approaches examined in the previous chapter, once the snowball of jobs and people begins to roll, then the rest of the dynamic is modeled as two-way causality, in the form of a spatial dance of jobs and people. This dance is itself determined by complex elasticities of trade costs and scale economies, giving rise to a number of possible stable patterns and unstable states, where instability can be augmented by lower trade costs (Baldwin and Forslid 1997).

In this type of reasoning, the location of jobs, industries, and consumers becomes, like its neoclassical counterpart, a story of endless marginal knife-edge trade-offs. This might appear paradoxical to the technical follower of this discussion, since economies of scale—which are the key motive force in theory—are lumpy. They don't change marginally or incrementally but rather jump from level to level discontinuously. In modeling, this is dealt with by assuming that in the aggregate, there are enough varieties of products and scales that the economy *as a whole* functions "as if" the scale economies that affect competition in particular industries or segments of markets are not really lumpy in a way so as to generate any important monopoly effects, not even locally. Industrial economists are at endless pains to show that such effects are minor in the economy; but spatial economists in NEG want to have it both ways: monopolistic competition in industries, but no serious lumpiness and monopoly effects in real geographical space. The evidence I presented in the previous chapter suggests that development, reflected in real wages, is really lumpy. This is a technical issue that nobody can resolve at the present state of research, but it has crucial implications—the central concern in chapter 4.

NEG also has potentially much to say about the local, cumulative dimension of economic development through the relationship between the traded and locally serving sectors. In labor and regional economics, this is known as the question of the employment "multiplier." As noted above, the NEG core-periphery model is a dance of firms that have scale economies with workers seeking jobs, but also those workers as consumers dancing with purveyors of cheaper and more diverse products in big central-place market cities, with this latter known formally as the "home market effect." The core-periphery model holds that product varieties tend to cluster together; with large home markets, more varieties are supported, because of bigger individual production units for homogeneous goods. The problem with this result is that it goes against another NEG result, which is that different varieties of product can be shipped over long distances (cross hauled) into each other's distant markets. Home market effects are no longer present in much routine, large-scale manufacturing.[2] Such manufactures, both intermediate and final, have sufficiently low trade costs today (in the developed countries) at almost any level of product variety, so they are not going to crowd into the same places—except in developing countries, where primary urbanization services are still scarce.

The realistic contemporary case of home market effects is not in tradable services and manufactures but rather in end-of-the-pipe retailing, and especially personal and consumer services. New York specializes in financial services because its intermediate producers concentrate together to serve a large concentration of banks and brokerage houses, but the latter are not concentrated in New York City because of its large population; they are the tradable end of financial services and have distant markets. For retail banking, however, New York is just like anywhere else. For these reasons, empirical research on home market effects has not turned up convincing results (Behrens et al. 2004; Redding 2010; cf. Ciccone and Hall 1996; Head and Mayer 2004). As an extension of this point, NEG cannot tell us why New York is so big.

This is not to say that the geography of home markets is unimportant. But NEG has probably missed the boat on the role of the home market. It devotes too much attention to scale/variety interactions in manufacturing and distribution, and not enough to the diversified service sector that provides the nontradable activity sector to city economies in developed countries today. Personal services, construction, and other labor-intensive activities have demand structures that are highly elastic in relation to the income generated in the tradable part of the contemporary urban economy. The issue for demand here is not bringing the unit costs down through the scale of the local market but instead providing goods and services that have a cost disease (labor intensive by nature) in proportion to the income available in the regional economy. This is the way home markets largely operate today. So we need to go back to the drawing board to update the models of the multiplier effect; NEG home market models do not do the trick.

WHAT GOES ON INSIDE CLUSTERS: SHARING, MATCHING, AND LEARNING

In contrast to the problems encountered by NEG in explaining the origins of spatial concentration, the size of cities, and the multiplier effect, NEG has made unambiguous progress in getting inside the spatial organization of particular industries, notably in theorizing about and measuring trade costs, agglomeration, and trade patterns (Anderson and van Wincoop 2004; Head and Mayer 2004; Rosenthal and Strange 2001). Gilles Duranton and Diego Puga (2004) felicitously capture the major sources of spatial concentration in their monikers of "sharing, matching, and learning."

We know the most about *sharing*, and especially the influence of trade costs on the degree of colocation within the input-output system. Sharing (local trade in intermediates) seems to be the weakest source of agglomeration in developed economies (Puga 2010).[3] In developing economies, by contrast, local input-output sharing remains important because these territories have immature infrastructure systems, so that trade costs remain high enough to concentrate suppliers together.

In "top-of-the-food-chain" activities—Wall Street, Silicon Valley, and Hollywood—local input sharing is probably quite elevated because long-distance sharing is costly and substantively complex. These activities have high levels of product variety, specialization, and market uncertainty, which raise intermediate trade costs. Since these industries generally do not have high weight-to-value ratios, however, one can still ask what level of trade costs would be sufficiently high to merit colocation. Two such sources come to mind. First, uncertainty makes knowledge difficult to stabilize and codify; the fixed costs of doing so are too high. Second, these sectors have complex divisions of labor because product variety and uncertainty inhibit vertical integration (Baumgartner 1988). Such complex divisions of labor are then coordinated using a wide variety of tools, ranging from lots of negotiation and contracts, involving shared knowledge, and many informal conventions and "cues." The more informal these systems are, the more they tend to be localized within geographically concentrated networks of actors (Granovetter 1995).

In this case, then, we must ask, What is being shared? NEG theorists have come full circle, in a way, to what geographers and economic sociologists have claimed for a long time about the nature of spatial clusters. It's the human relationships and "untraded interdependencies" in them, supported through lots of face-to-face contact, that are the high-cost glue holding them to places and one another (Storper 1995; Storper and Venables 2004). This point exists also in trade theories that argue that incomplete contracts (a result of complex relationships) can limit long-distance trade (Antràs 2003), and relationship skills are nonroutine and highly remunerated (Levy and Murnane 2005).

The second feature of spatially concentrated industries identified by Duranton and Puga (2004) is the *matching* of people to jobs. Industries with high levels of uncertainty about their future products and processes cannot smooth their output levels. They therefore need to avoid labor hoarding during downturns and rapidly access highly specialized labor during upturns. Their workers need to be able to move fluidly from job to job in these unstable markets, rematching their highly specialized skills to employers. Large pools of employers and workers are the solution to this matching-without-hoarding problem (Jayet 1983).[4]

The question of whether a large pool of specialized people attracts a large group of fragmented but interrelated firms, or whether the firms cluster and then generate their own labor pool, raises the chicken-and-egg, jobs/people issue again. In thinking about the sources of an urban structure and possible major change in it, we need to think about origins. Many states in the United States have attempted to lure Hollywood away from Los Angeles, and they have done so for shooting films. What they have not lured away is the home locations of the firms and people who supply the specialized services to entertainment. That is because the people who are involved in the high-turnover part of the business stay in Los Angeles in order to get access through their intricate networks and relationships to new jobs. These people aren't going to migrate spontaneously to Orlando or any of the many other cities that are trying to build a film industry.

How did specialized labor pools get where they did in the first place? In the case of Hollywood, the preexisting entertainment industry in New York—based on Broadway and vaudeville—was subject to a radical organizational break when a number of its impresarios went to Los Angeles to work in the new technology of film in the early twentieth century (Scott 2005). The firms initially brought the key people with them. From there, the pool built itself up in situ in Hollywood as workers flowed in when the studios grew and multiplied. To take another case, the current financial services industry in New York grew in the 1970s and 1980s by using some of the talent that was in the city from its long history as a banking and corporate headquarters center; but the people were there because they had jobs, and they had jobs because the firms were there.

Turning to the last angle of Duranton and Puga's triangle, there is increasing evidence that clusters are sites of technological *learning* and localized knowledge spillovers (Jaffe and Trajtenberg 2002; Feldman 1994, 2003). This long-standing theme—known from Alfred Marshall's (1919) celebrated phrase "the secrets of industry . . . are in the air"—has been imported to urban economics. There is convincing evidence that even in a world with global flows of technology and ideas, specialized local economies concentrate communities of innovators, and this is a key reason for the persistence of certain clusters. But what causes such spatial concentration of these people? Agent-based models in urban economics hold that workers congregate together in order to interact, and this explains the high wages of certain places. Yet on closer examination, this is just working backward from the aggregate observation that skilled people do indeed cluster together. It does not answer the chicken-and-egg question of whether jobs move to people or people move to jobs that I tackled in chapter 2.

All in all, NEG teaches us about how spatial clusters function and why they are so efficient. Uncertainty about technology and markets—typical in the innovative, leading-edge parts of the economy—intensifies the need for the localization of sharing, matching, and learning. Still, we are far from being able to model or predict the sequence by which specific clusters form, the initial events that set them in motion, and hence the precise "where" of clusters. Yet the where of clusters is the reason for the specific pattern of winner and loser regions, turbulence within city-systems, and concerete pattern of uneven economic development. Thus, one of the thorniest issues in the field of urban and regional development is the origin of specialization—a question that I will return to in chapter 6.

Jobs Spread Out: New Centers and Peripheries

The other side of the spatial behavior of industries is that they spread out. There are two different types of deconcentration. In the first, industries respond to a combination of routinization (lowering skill content), lower trade costs, and increasing economies of scale by deagglomerating to peripheral regions. In the second, new agglomerations arise in formerly peripheral regions, hosting mature activities that are deagglomerating at a world scale, but doing so via reagglomeration in less developed regions. This has been the case for mature manufacturing industries leaving developed countries, generating in the process major new industrial cities in emerging economies, just as it was the case earlier with the development of many cities in the US Sun Belt.

The most recent episode of massive spreading out is the globalization of manufacturing, which has been made possible by the decline of trade costs for manufactured goods that occurred in the second half of the twentieth century (Glaeser and Kohlhase 2003). As a consequence, production systems have been increasingly unbundling themselves into different territories (Baldwin 2006). In the 1940s, mill-based industries moved south in the United States; by the 1950s, the mechanical engineering core industries of the Northeast and Midwest began to go south and west; and by the 1990s, all went offshore. Even Silicon Valley and Wall Street are now mostly the brains—the conception, design, and innovation centers—of far-flung production systems for their final outputs.

Product cycle models propose stylized descriptions of this sequence (Norton and Rees 1979). In them, technological maturity reverses the forces that lead to agglomeration, enabling increases in the scale and scope of production units, and lowering the volume and unit costs of intermediate trade; this, in turn, allows for deagglomeration. Product cycle models are simplified, stylized descriptions of this dynamic. Scale and scope do not always move in one direction, from small to large volumes. Technologies and market structures also change in different ways, sometimes involving more product variety and sometimes less. The pace of basic technological changes and innovations in trade costs (logistics or management) are not the same from one industry to another. So there is no single pathway or life cycle for production as well as the spatial organization of production. In this sense, observing intermediate trade costs directly, as instructed by NEG, is an improved way into understanding the changing geographies of sectors. But trade costs are not the cause. Technological change in products and production technologies is what defines scale and scope opportunities, and in turn, that drives the basic dynamic of being able to fragment a production chain into different steps. Trade costs then determine how far the steps in a production chain can be located from one another.

The "where" of deagglomeration is sectorally specific (the type of product along with its associated specific trade costs and market locations). Firms seek cheaper land because they are no longer constrained by agglomeration economies to colocate in an innovative milieu, and because the rise in the scale of production as technologies become routinized makes production more land intensive, while the lowering of intermediate and final trade costs (because of increasing scale and standardization) allows a wider choice of locations involving cheaper land.[5] This enables firms to seek cheaper, less skilled labor, as in the successive waves of relocation from the Frost Belt to the Sun Belt in the United States since the 1930s. Initially, then, jobs move to people in such deagglomeration-driven development.

In some cases, the deagglomeration of production can induce local population change in receiving areas, either through rural-urban intraregional migration or through interregional long-distance migration. If enough jobs and people arrive, the snowball of local development gets rolling. What began as a deconcentration of jobs from industrial agglomerations can lead to the beginning of new job concentrations in less developed places. This certainly seems to be the case concerning metropolitan areas in the US Sun Belt, though the composition of those economies is still quite different from places like New York. Once again, though, if we think about change as a sequence of events, the initial cause of the sequence is the movement of jobs, itself defined by the internal trade cost as well as scale and scope dynamics of the industry. The directions of causality are ultimately two-way, but do not appear to be in the same proportions.

As noted above, another major contemporary example of the spreading out of industries takes the form of this "concentration via deconcentration" as in the development of major manufacturing cities in China and other East Asian countries. These manufacturing agglomerations are not based on specialization in an industrial sector but rather in accumulating firms in many industries and performing similar types of tasks for each, such as assembly. The initial seed of creation of these major manufacturing agglomerations is the evolution of such industrial sectors in such a way that they can be located far away from their final markets, and increasingly far away from the sources of many of their primary (raw) materials and manufactured intermediate inputs. So at the world scale, they are in the deagglomeration phase of their product cycle. But at the local scale, because primary urbanization services are only efficiently available in a limited number of urban centers in developing East Asia, these industries agglomerate there.

To the naked eye, this looks much like some of the manufacturing agglomerations that characterized cities in the Northeast and Midwest of the United States in the nineteenth century. On closer examination, however, those industries locating in Guangzhou and Shenzen are in the mature phase of their product cycle and are export oriented, unlike their nineteenth-century British and US counterparts, which were highly innovative and far from technological maturity. So while it has become commonplace to call contemporary Guangzhou the "Manchester of the twenty-first century," this analogy is basically wrong. Manchester in the nineteenth century was more like Silicon Valley today, whereas Phoenix, Arizona, or Birmingham, Alabama, play roles closer to that of Guangzhou.

In any case, the combination of deagglomeration through urbanization in the developing world and the agglomeration of innovative activities globally propels the powerful new wave of urbanization today.

Innovation-Based Agglomerations

Where will regional sharing, matching, and learning occur, following a major innovation? New technologies open up "windows of locational opportunity," where the sharing, matching, and learning processes of existing places may no longer provide them decisive productivity advantages over new places (Scott and Storper 1987). This occurred in the nascent semiconductor industry in the 1950s. It broke free of its roots in the communications industry firms that were located in the Northeast of the United States and ultimately locked in its center of gravity in Silicon Valley.

When first-mover agglomerations are generated, sometimes they can go through the window of locational opportunity that was referred to above and create major new industrial-urban centers outside the existing major cities of the urban system. The development of California in the twentieth century, where two major core metropolitan areas (Los Angeles and San Francisco) were added to the US urban system, but well outside its core regions, is a case of agglomerated first-mover industries having been created in what were then greenfield locations or provincial cities. But major new innovation centers can also be created in older metropolitan areas, as has been the case for Boston, Paris, and London in the wave of urban-economic resurgence that has been observed in selective older cities in the West since 1990. Local learning can thus "reseed" the process of agglomeration over and over because it re-creates activities with higher intermediate trade costs (new or continuously improved products often involve substantively complex knowledge or fluctuating markets). The snowball of this effect is not initiated, as in NEG, by drawing in consumers, but instead from the "nursery effect," as dynamic new firms are formed or existing firms engage in local learning, and hence are able to move up the economic quality ladder. Duranton and Puga (2001) improve on the product cycle by linking the creation of new products to "nursery cities," where local learning is centered, while Duranton (2007) shows that there are different time lags for the diffusion of innovations from such cities to other places. A subtler version of the link between innovation and product variety builds on the quality ladder concept of Gene Grossman and Elhanan Helpman (1991). This latter concept allows the inclusion of a price ladder, which is useful for modeling.

Some NEG models derive the formation of such centers by experimenting with models of trade costs, some of which can predict big new centers ("black holes") (Thisse 2010). By incorporating labor mobility, they have also developed intriguing suggestions about dynamic possibilities, such as tipping points and instabilities in patterns of spatial-economic development. These models are heuristically stimulating in the way that they present different ranges of trade costs and locational outcomes, but they do not concern themselves with the initial sources of demand for local sharing, matching, and learning,

Another contribution to this theme of the link between innovation, learning, and resilience comes from Richard Baldwin and Philippe Martin (2004), through the device of the spatial distribution of the innovation sector. Yet consistent with what I said in the previous paragraph, the real dynamic problem is not the allocation of an existing innovation sector but rather its ongoing dynamic of self-creation and regeneration, itself involving both local interactions and long-distance factor mobility and absorption. Baldwin and Martin then operationalize endogenous growth by transforming it into an investment (capital accumulation) function, thereby returning to the initial inspiration of Myrdal (1957). But merely investing is not enough to secure dynamic advantage, if the investments are not linked to innovation and staying on top of the product quality ladder, as many older industrial regions know only too well.

As we have seen, work on agglomeration has progressed considerably in NEG, urban economics, and regional science. The time-space dynamics of agglomeration and deagglomeration are the basis for the expansion and rearrangement of urban systems. It still lacks a precise "where" of winning and losing regions, but it gives us a sense of system dynamics.

Urban Systems

Major change in urban systems is the result of incremental thirty- to forty-year changes, and thus is not readily apparent to the naked eye or sharply on the minds of the average citizen. Consider three major change processes. Rapidly developing emerging economies are building their city-systems. The most dramatic case of this is China in recent decades, where population, activity, and income have crowded into the coastal regions; as the economy grows, it is "moving west," much as the US economy did in the late nineteenth century. A second case is the transition to the US Sun Belt, which began in earnest in the 1940s, but continues today, in a country that is used to high levels of people and firm mobility as well as a tolerance for letting cities compete with one another. A third case is in Europe, which is affected by the twin processes of slow population change and continental integration, in an old urban system characterized by the presence of a high proportion of middle-size cities, and where there is a strong political emphasis on maintaining the viability of all cities and regions. A holy grail of research on city-systems has been to try to determine whether there is a right—most efficient—mix of the number of cities and their sizes, and whether urban systems are moving toward this first-best equilibrium for territorial development. There is a small industry of scholarship and a big industry in consultancies on building urban systems in developing countries, or generating the right kind of change in developed ones.

Moving from the dynamics of agglomeration and dispersion of industries to the broad evolution of the urban system has proven to be one of the most difficult tasks for geographical economics and regional sciences (Henderson 1974; Thisse 2010). Ultimately, theorists want to be able to understand the rate at which urban units are added to a system, how old ones expand or decline, and how this affects the turbulence of population and jobs in the system—a laudable goal shared by this book. Masahisa Fujita, Paul Krugman, and Tomoya Mori (Fujita and Krugman 1995; Fujita, Krugman, and Mori 1999) made early attempts to deal with the formation of new urban centers, but were limited by considering old-fashioned monocentric cities rather than contemporary polycentric metropolitan areas. As noted above, Fujita and Jacques-François Thisse (2002) then added the spatial distribution of the innovation sector, as a way to deal with new products and agglomerations. Duranton and Puga (2001) formalized the product life cycles that I alluded to above, and Duranton (2007) added a time dimension, based on the relationship of innovation to diffusion. In all these cases, the ambition is to understand the connections between the technological evolution of industries, their spatiotemporal dynamic, and the dynamic of the urban and regional systems of people and jobs.

The "ground-up" part of NEG—which looks at firms and industries, technology, and sharing, matching, and learning—is not yet able to "add together" all the dynamics of scale, scope, and clustering, or the spread of all *industries*, and by doing so, get to a comprehensive picture of the distribution of types and quantities of employment in different *cities*. Building on the roots of NEG in international trade theory, there have been some interesting beginnings of work toward this goal (Rossi-Hansberg, Sarte, and Owens 2009). These attempts ask how declining trade costs influence the scale and scope of firms and industries, and hence their broad locational patterns. But there is no result that brings these general insights down to the level of the urban units of each country.

In contrast to the bottom-up approaches reviewed above that start with industries, other NEG theorists go downward from markets and prices to cities as "organizations" in the economic system (Gabaix and Ioannides 2004; Rossi-Hansberg and Wright 2007). Thus, cities and regions are modeled as the intermediate level of organization of the economy, situated in between markets (at a higher level of scope) and industries as well as individuals at lower levels of aggregation. Agents choose cities because of the benefits of agglomeration, yet the number and size of cities react to industry-level productivity shocks in a way that wipes out their economies or diseconomies of scale at the local level. In this view, when product and factor prices get too high in Boston and San Francisco, Phoenix and Las Vegas enter the system to tame them by attracting firms and people away from them.

These models claim to have resolved the puzzle suggested earlier: firms and industries generate the benefits of agglomerations in such a way that individual agents also distribute themselves in space so that there is a regular spatial distribution of jobs and output, and both are consistent with overall efficiency and perfect competition in the economy as a whole.

These approaches draw NEG toward a neoclassical synthesis that includes cities and regions as just one more scale in the system—from agents to firms to industries to cities to the economy—and the urban scale has no real lumpiness that counts in economic terms (i.e., it does not generate monopolistic competition effects). It would be miraculous if all levels of organization of the economy—cities, industries, firms, and agents—lined up in this way, like Russian dolls. If they do, then the only really important task in maintaining an optimally efficient economy is to keep lowering trade costs, and make sure that enough land and housing are available. Just as in the NNUE, the rest will take care of itself by generating an optimal urban and regional system in spite of the lumpiness of firms, their interconnections, and the lumpiness of home markets. As can be seen, these are intriguing claims in the abstract, but basically there are no bottom-up detailed empirics to back them up. They are pure modeling deductions and depend on strong assumptions about the world that are not themselves backed up by much data.

In the end, we have no single convincing model of what shapes the overall spatial distribution of people, their jobs, and income levels in a way that incorporates turbulence along with change in the fates of places within that system over time. Urban systems may have certain average regularities (a tendency for there to be a certain number of big, medium, and small cities, and certain sizes of cities). But we still don't understand much about how robust such regularities are, or how they are created and maintained via the turbulence in the fates of individual cities that allows New York to remain rich and big even as Detroit gets smaller and poorer. In part IV of this book, I will argue that the limits of economic and geographical models in this regard are not due to errors in modeling. Instead, some of the structural determinants included in NEG models are not identical everywhere; they are shaped by social and political forces lying outside these models' scope of interest.

Efficiency and Spatial Distributions of Jobs and Income

The relationship of efficiency and equity is an important concern for spatial economics. Above, I outlined the NEG approach to an efficient landscape of production, where efficiency effects largely come from trade-offs between scale, trade costs, and factor costs, and a major empirical flavor of the analysis is that agglomerations of producers have significant positive effects on efficiency. Cities are key, in other words, to greater wealth creation, but they involve equity or distributional effects: higher average incomes in some places than others, and possibly higher inequality within them. Consider three examples of this in the form of questions: What would be an efficient way to urbanize China? What would be an equitable way? Is the Sun Belt transition in the United States efficient, equitable, or both, or neither? Can the emphasis in Europe on keeping enough activity spread around its highly decentralized urban system reconcile more equitable local economic development with aggregate economic efficiency?

NEG reasoning can basically be plugged into any standard elementary model of the gains from trade and specialization: agglomeration should have an efficiency effect in the form of higher potential aggregate output; it probably then generates losses to potential competing producers in other locations; and its efficiency gains are then distributed as some gains to consumers, who are in turn unevenly distributed across cities and regions. The net of all these would be the aggregate gain to the economy from agglomeration (Charlot, Gaigné, et al. 2006; Baldwin et al. 2003).

This is a good first step, but it is incomplete. Any change in the spatial configuration of production most likely also involves aggregate employment effects along with social costs of employment changes in both agglomeration centers and other places that are receiving or losing employment. Social costs include income gained or lost to individuals over their career cycle as well as the possible externalities thereof and pecuniary costs to be picked up by the public sector. These latter types of costs are not part of the mainstream debate about the efficiency or distributional effects of changes in spatial organization. Some social costs can also be purely because of where the jobs go. For example, if jobs move from a region with high minimum wages, workplace safety regulations, and benefit laws to one with less of those conditions, then social costs will change. Agglomeration or deagglomeration may also be associated with crucial changes that affect the skills and wage mix of the workforce, both through locational and technological change. It will then have income distribution effects that are not exclusively local (Yellen 1977). Most important, there is a long list of ways that there could be wedges between private and social costs, between aggregate gains and the distribution of gains and losses. This is exactly a geographical-economic way of framing the debate about the current effects of globalization.

For urban and regional economics—like its cousin, development economics—we do not have an easy time modeling or measuring anything close to the complete list of such effects. In part this is because the raw input we use to generate the demand and supply schedules in such models is, respectively, "willingness to pay" and "marginal cost." When private and social valuations diverge, neither valuation is a good guide as to what society really wants, or the costs it will incur.

This is all complicated, but it is not complicated enough. If changes in the spatial organization of production have a significant quantity of the possible effects mentioned above, then in addition, the *temporary* adjustment costs to the individuals affected can be big—just as they are with trade displacement. These effects can become permanent on the people and places affected, both positively and negatively. Dani Rodrik (2011) argues that when trade has big aggregate gains, it is also highly likely to have big negative distributional impacts; the ratio is a strong one. The same is likely true of the analogous process of agglomeration: the greater the gains to agglomeration, the greater the probable increase in inequality among persons, and the same could be true for rapid deagglomeration. Today's extraordinary wave of city building is likely to have these sharp distributional effects.

In recent years, then, there has been widespread consensus about the benefits of agglomeration, including across national borders (world cities), and the spreading out of activities, as the two spatial versions of "gains to trade." But the state of knowledge about the reality of these gains along with the inevitability of their spatial or urban underpinnings is light-years away from a solid scientific proof. I will return to the normative implications of urban systems and spatial arrangements in greater depth in chapter 13.

Taking Stock

NEG, building on a long tradition of work by economic geographers, industrial economists, and development theorists, has rightly placed the geography of production at the heart of the development of cities and urban systems. Jobs and firms are the motor of city and regional development, and so we need to know what structures the location of jobs and firms. The agenda must start from the concentration and spatial deconcentration of sectors; it integrates forces such as different types of scale economies, the variety and quality of products, trade costs, and the different effects of the uncertainty generated by innovation and competition as well as the counteracting effects of greater stability that comes from standardization and maturing markets and technologies. Then it incorporates issues such as the inertia of history plus shocks to technologies of production and technologies of transport and communications.

Moving upward from all this to the urban/regional scale is an aggregation problem of daunting complexity. The response is not to try to create an NEG version of a general spatial equilibrium for cities, in which we would have perfect knowledge of the scale, scope, and locational parameters of all industries, allowing us to project them upward to cities and city-systems. This would be unrealistic because of the amount of primary data needed (industry scale, scope, product variety, elasticities, factor costs, etc.), and because there are other noisy influences on what happens to cities, notably from the secondary effects of home markets, the feedbacks from local actors to innovation and industry development, and massive policy influences on location costs and trade costs. There is a messy composition problem of industries, people, and places with some general lessons about each one that can only be brought together using a lot of good sense to combine the partial insights from different specialized tools. This would enable us to get much further in understanding city sizes along with the types and levels of city specializations, and get a baseline for modeling change. We need to create these data in order to begin constructing an economically rigorous view of city building and urban system change.

A first step in an economically rigorous view of change is to consider the economics of innovation in a geographical context. Innovative places have local economic dynamics—their price systems—that are different from the economy as a whole. Innovative places relate to noninnovative places in many ways that I examine in the next chapter.

Disruptive Innovation

GEOGRAPHY AND ECONOMICS

Why Are Some Cities So Rich?

At any given moment, some cities and regions are much richer than others. Currently, city-regions with high per capita incomes include places such as San Francisco, Washington, DC, and Zurich, whose incomes are about a third higher than their respective national economies' average, and those national economies are already rich in the hierarchy of world economies. Within countries like the United States, San Francisco's per capita income is about three times that of the poorest metropolitan areas. And as I noted in chapter 2, these differences are not just in money terms; they persist (though reduced somewhat) even when we take into account different costs of living and quality of life among regions.

Some of these differences at the international level are simply a matter of catch-up dynamics. For instance, Shanghai and São Paulo have been closing the gap with the United States, and one day they may even reach the levels of the richest city-regions in the United States or Europe. In the past, places like Buffalo, Syracuse, and Cleveland had extremely high per capita incomes. Great fortunes were made there, some of which can be seen in the beautiful big houses, theaters, and other public buildings dating from these cities' heydays; many cities of relatively modest income levels in the Old World today also bear the marks of past riches in the form of palaces, theaters, and historical monuments. Often, visible past riches reflect both high inequality and the high average incomes once enjoyed, as in Venice, Istanbul, Seville, or Lisbon in their heydays.

Oddly enough, urban economics is quite ambivalent about the existence of these rich cities and regions. Most urban economists hold to the view derived from general spatial equilibrium theory that the party cannot go on in these places; instead, their own excessive housing and labor prices will bring these cities down. In the United States, as I noted, at first glance this seems to be true for some expensive cities like New York whose populations haven't grown nearly as fast in recent decades as those of the cheaper places like Dallas or Orlando. But actually New York has done well in real income terms. And there are other high-income cities—such as San Francisco and Washington, DC—that have added considerable population while maintaining high incomes. The relationship between high incomes and prices, on the one hand, and changes in population, jobs, and incomes is, as we will see, a complex one. Nonetheless, most policymakers and commentators, like economists, subscribe to the notion that many cities are "too expensive" for their own good.

Let's reformulate this debate in terms of economics. First, if the average prices (cost of living) are high, and the difference in prices between a given region and other regions is greater than their difference in average productivity, then the region is likely to be in trouble, especially if the trade and relocation costs for the existing activities are low; this is what is realistic in the commonsense view. A second possibility, more sophisticated, comes from the general spatial equilibrium NNUE model. If the average price levels (cost of living) for immobile resources are high, they could reflect many things (such as building restrictions). They will serve to drive away people and firms that don't have the high wages or productivity needed to live in these places. The region's comparative advantage, in this view, is defined by the local cost of living, causing firms and people to sort and select themselves in or out, and hence driving the area's population change. These dynamics are supposed to lead to the equalization of utilities between regions, which I looked for but failed to find in chapter 2. A third possibility is that prices for immobile resources such as housing and local services like hair salons are high compared to other regions, but average wages and real incomes are also higher. In this case, wages and incomes in the primary tradable activities of the region reflect innovation rents. These rents are in part shared out, as an externality, to other wages and prices in the nontradable sectors in the region. The hair stylist earns more because the hedge fund trader shares some of their innovation rents with their hair stylist, and both in turn spend some of this in the home market, further stimulating it. This latter dynamic impedes the mean reversion in prices and equalization of utilities across regions.

What Kind of Economics?

Most spatial economics favors a combination of the first and second perspectives mentioned above. This leads to a distinctive view of long-term change: cities with high real prices cannot do that forever; there is something wrong with them. I will argue for the third view in this chapter, holding that disruption is a key force in the economic process. In order to arbitrate this debate, we need to consider what kind of economic assumptions about the geographical-economic process to employ.

Economics uses the equilibrium concept in two ways. The first way is as a heuristic device to solve for a possible empirical distribution of prices and quantities; in the case of geography, this means the territorial distributions of supply and demand for factors (hence people, firms, and capital) that underlie these prices and quantities. This heuristic device is useful because it allows us to see what-if scenarios as a consequence of change in the underlying structural (causal) determinants. Used in this limited way, almost any configuration of prices, wages, output, and population can be subjected to a shock, and we can shed light on the way cities will change in response to it.

A second way that equilibrium is used is much more ambitious, and it occupies a central position in the theoretical edifice of economics. Particular empirical aspects of the economy—in our case, the spatial distribution of population, output, and incomes—are claimed to fit into the general equilibrium of the economy, in which all markets clear according to a "zero-excess rule." The general spatial equilibrium model considered in chapter 2 is an example of this use of equilibrium. Households, builders, and industries are all said to be part of a single economy-wide set of price-quantity interactions with one another, with causality multidirectional, and affording possibilities for substituting labor, housing/land, and wages for one another in meaningful ways.

The contention in this chapter is that such models represent only one side of the economic process. These models emphasize only the (long-term) tendency of prices and wages across places to revert to some mean, and the tendency for some equalization of utilities long after shocks. They de-emphasize the normal operation of the economy to generate its own shocks in the form of innovations. These innovations generate geographical concentration and must be compensated with rents in order to exist—in turn generating high wages and prices in certain localities, and divergence between places.[1] Without such innovations, there cannot be long-term economy-wide increases in average wealth and income—that is, development (Aghion and Howitt 1997). Innovation will always be reflected in the creation of high-income cities and regions. The day that this phenomenon stops and all places have the same incomes is the day that the economic system's progress grinds to a halt. So disruption—economic and geographical—is the permanent norm and necessary condition of development.

The Space-Time Dynamic of Rents from Innovation

This latter view does not fit comfortably within the edifice of economics in general or—as we have seen throughout this book—urban economics. And yet with some clarification of the ways that the rents from innovation are enjoyed by particular city-regions relative to the economic process as a whole, this perspective actually is part of a more internally consistent view of how cities contribute to economic growth overall (cf. Lundvall and Johnson 2004).

To investigate these complex theoretical issues, we first need to pull back from the strictly local dimension of possible positive externalities. The economics of growth, and in particular the Romer (1986, 1994) growth model, establishes economy-wide increasing returns as the principal source of long-run economic growth under resource constraints. In endogenous growth theory, knowledge and technology are different from other types of inputs into the economic process. They are nonrival and generally only weakly excludable over time. If I use a chair, I am a rival to you in sitting in that chair, and moreover, I will wear the chair out by extensive use of it over time. Knowledge is different: true knowledge can be used at the same time by both of us, and it can be infinitely reused without loss. I also can exclude you from using my chair—by locking it up physically, or asserting my ownership right over it and using the law to punish you for using it. Knowledge is poorly excludable over the long run; it leaks out from inventors to wider communities of users, and legal restrictions on its use are temporary. True knowledge also tends to be cumulative in the sense that each step in understanding a biological, physical, or mechanical process leads to technological manipulations of it. And each such capacity generally can be built on to be incrementally better, or it can be replaced by a much better substitute as the incremental knowledge of a past phase of understanding attains a new phase that brings together new synthetic understanding of the domain of inquiry at hand.

In formal terms, this means that the productivity of the R & D/innovation sector of the economy is not subject to diminishing returns. It becomes, on average, cheaper and cheaper to generate additional increments of useful knowledge. This isn't true of every single domain of science and every moment, since sometimes barriers are encountered, or past achievements generate technological, environmental, or socially unanticipated and expensive side effects (negative externalities). But for the past several centuries, on the whole, the average cost of intellectual and technological progress seems to have been getting cheaper in real terms (Mokyr 1991; Rosenberg 1982).

The implications of this simple idea are enormous: innovation can become a source of long-run unlimited growth. If returns to all additional factors are diminishing, they help firms and individuals allocate a given set of resources efficiently. Yet they are rather dismal for the economy as a whole. If knowledge and technology are subject to diminishing returns, then productivity improvements are hard to come by in the long run (they are costly, and possibly increasingly so). As a result, humanity will be locked in a dismal Malthusian struggle for resources of the kind that kept world incomes stagnant for a thousand years prior to the Industrial Revolution (Maddison 1982). The existence of increasing returns explains why an economy can grow from its own internal dynamic. In this way, growth does not depend exclusively on fortuitous events such as better climate leading to expanding population or miraculous exogenous increases in knowledge (the "knowledge drops like manna from heaven" idea).

But as the reader can see, there is a tension between this growth dynamic—based on increasing returns—and the efficiency, or allocation, mechanism of the economy. The allocation mechanism must be based on diminishing returns, which allows it to find the last, or marginal, quantity of a resource to be allocated to a given activity, and then allocate it to other activities. Endogenous growth theory reconciles these two principles, almost if by a miracle. It shows that even though the different specific activities (products, industries, and activities) to which innovations are applied are perfectly competitive (due to diminishing returns), in the long run the economy as a whole is freed from the dismal state of diminishing returns via the cheapening, diffusion, and cumulative nature of productivity-increasing innovations (Romer 1986, 1994).

Notice that we are now a long way from our interest in local clusters. The link can be made by asking the question, What is the mechanism, in time and space, that links the specific sectors to the economy as a whole in this way? We can begin with time. The first movers or inventors of newness reap extraordinary benefits from them in the form of monopoly rents; that also means higher wages for people and higher prices for products than would normally be the case. The economy rewards newness because it is scarce (it takes time for others to unlock its secrets, imitate, and increase the supply), and also because investors anticipate the future applications of the innovation to raise productivity elsewhere through rent payments. Nevertheless, and this is the paradox, these motivations to raise prices and wages only exist because of their temporary character. Ultimately such high prices and wages will be erased through the diffusion of the innovation (nonexcludable, nonrival, and cumulative in the long run) to other firms, industries, workers, and consumers.

And now comes the second big effect: it is precisely this diffusion, through the economy-wide recombination and reuse of technology (across firms, sectors, and users) that creates the increasing returns of the economy as a whole. Innovation is temporarily expensive and thus provides great rewards to innovators. But it is in the long run relatively cheap—not subject to diminishing returns—and offers the economy freedom from the dismal trap of such diminishing returns.

So what does all this mean for the spatial dimension—cities, regions, and even countries? As noted, when it is applied to the geography of economic growth, the Romer theory is frequently allied to earlier contributions from Marshall (1919) and Kenneth Arrow (1962), respectively, about technology spillovers at the regional scale ("the secrets of industry are in the air") and "learning-by-doing." There is widespread use of the concept of "Marshall-Arrow-Romer" (MAR) externalities at the regional scale.[2]

But if the only source of increasing returns were technologies with restricted local access, then in effect the insiders would price their outputs to capture all the returns to innovation in the form of localized technological or knowledge rents.[3] If this were the end of the story, then there would be no way to account for the sustained economic growth that the West has experienced since 1820. Rather than increasing returns at the economy-wide level, there would simply be a long-term accumulation of rents in certain lucky regions or people (Mokyr 1991). Knowledge would be economically excludable because geographically excludable. The defining pillar of the theory of Romer externalities would be broken. The nonexcludable, nonrival, and cumulative character of knowledge would be nipped in the bud, somewhat in the way that Chinese emperors did in the fourteenth century for certain inventions there.

A geographical view of the Romer theory, with both localization and diffusion, is necessary to account for the findings of economic historians about the Great Divergence between Europe and the rest of the world in the seventeenth and eighteenth centuries. Rents accrue to some firms and places for some periods of time, and then slowly break down, as the *potentially* nonrival and nonexcludable character of technology progressively becomes real, allowing the economy-wide increasing return to become real in turn.[4] Increasing returns are only realized through the geographical and organizational process that leads from localization and monopoly rents to the geographical (hence economic) diffusion of technology as well as the breakdown of those rents. This point was also central to classical studies of the geography of innovation diffusion (Pred and Hagerstrand 1967).

A major consequence of this point is that strictly speaking, there are no so-called MAR externalities. Instead, there are M-A sources of *local* technological externalities and possible local monopoly rents, but the true R-sources of *economy-wide* increasing returns cannot remain localized. The economic (price) effects of localized externalities and rents thus must be seen in a wider context as part of a disruptive growth process that spreads the wealth around after it first concentrates it.[5] In this wider view, the externalities that are locally good for, say, London, are also good in some ways for Manchester, even as they detract in other ways from Manchester's long-term well-being.

A reformulation of this process looks as follows. In t1, innovations emerge in certain, specific places and organizational settings (firms). The geography of this innovation often reflects M-A effects of proximity and tends to be localized. There are monopoly rents to such innovations for a certain amount of time. These monopoly rents last as long as there are barriers to imitation, which include both knowledge barriers and the trade/communication costs associated with using the technology—it is effectively, if not juridically, excludable. Indeed, some research shows that the regional concentration of patenting communities has strengthened, rather than weakened, in recent years (Sonn and Storper 2008); the time during which local clusters can enjoy rents thus may be lengthening (see also Moretti 2012; Malecki 2010).

In t2, these innovations can diffuse to a wider set of places. The knowledge is more amenable to imitation and copying because as it becomes more widely used, it tends to be codified, enabling more people to learn the ways to use it, and hence the costs associated with deploying it to other uses and places decrease. On the ground, innovation-based Schumpeterian-like competition is replaced by standard efficiency competition, with widespread access to the technology and imitation driving prices down to average costs. The locational dynamics of this are described by the spatial versions of the product cycle, but as noted in chapter 3, it captures only some cases (Norton and Rees 1979). Simultaneously, geographical diffusion and increasingly nonexclusive application of the knowledge emerge through its recombination into further rounds of innovation. These drive long-run growth in the Romer model.

The process repeats itself over an unlimited number of cycles. The precise parameters for technology creation, trade costs and barriers to imitation, and Romer-like diffusion and reapplication of technology will determine such things as the spatial hierarchy of incomes at any given moment, the amount of time it takes for a shift away from the rent-earning (first-mover) part of the innovation cycle to economy-wide increasing returns, and the amount of increasing returns in the economy as a whole. Underlying all this is the geography of innovation: additional innovation processes get started, and new rounds of monopoly rents are earned. Locally high prices and wages are therefore not signs of a dysfunctional or unsustainable city-region. In a dynamic economy, even the congestion costs associated with them are reflections of the demand for locations that have positive externalities and so allow them to earn rents. These expensive places are not only good for themselves but they also are good for the economy as a whole—a manifestation of a dynamically disruptive economy.

But wait. Did we not admit that such rents must be temporary in order for the M-A (localized) externalities ultimately to yield economy-wide benefits (R effects)? And if so, is this not just another way of saying that the urban system is simply a gigantic mean-reversion mechanism, in the same way that the standard general spatial equilibrium theories claim? All this depends on what we mean by temporary. In the next two sections, I argue that even though innovation rents must be temporary, they seem to have certain long-term effects on prices and real incomes of places. I discuss this first empirically and then supply the theoretical reasoning behind it.

Convergence Revisited

Most research on the incomes of cities, regions, and countries from standard trade theory to NEG and NNUE—searches for long-term interregional income convergence (Sala-i-Martin 2006; Pomerantz 2000; Barro and Sala-i-Martin 1995) as a matter of theoretical conviction. When convergence is not in evidence or slower than anticipated, research concentrates on whether there are barriers to it. In the international development literature, barriers to factor mobility figure prominently in standard accounts (Helpman 2004), since international trade is now so widespread and deep as to not constitute a barrier to convergence.

Within countries—with the United States as the standard example—most literature calls attention to the long-term trend to interstate income convergence, and takes it as proof of the convergence hypothesis in the presence of high levels of factor mobility (Hammond and Thompson 2008; Carlino and Mills 1996). Yet on closer examination, the dynamics of income convergence among metropolitan regions do not confirm this interpretation. Matthew Drennan, José Lobo, and Deborah Strumsky (2004), Drennan (1999), Drennan, Emanuel Tobier, and Jonathan Lewis (2006) show that while there is beta convergence (a tendency for gaps among pairs of regions to diminish) among regions, there is no sigma convergence (an overall reduction in the dispersion of per capita incomes). Enrico Moretti (2012) reveals that a new Great Divergence in wages among US metropolitan areas for both highly skilled and less educated workers began in the 1980s, and has steadily increased. Theory instructs us that there are two reasons why beta convergence does not line up with sigma convergence. On the one hand, the tendency for initially poor metro areas to close the gap with much richer ones is the initial advantage of backwardness, or the Gerschenkron effect of initial catchup. But such effects cannot be projected onto convergence, because the backwardness advantage diminishes on the margin, and economies often fall into a middle-income stagnation trap. This is why Brazil's 10 percent annual growth rates in the 1950s and 1960s leveled off in the 1970s; if they had not, Brazil now would have the per capita income of the United States today. Analogously, it is far from sure that El Paso will be as rich as New York on day, or that similar cities in general will ever be as well off.

Their aggregate divergence reflects complex patterns of turbulence in the fates of individual cities. In the United States, some old industrial cities such as Buffalo and Detroit have fallen down in the real income ranks, while Boston, New York, and Washington, DC, have stayed at the top; some new Sun Belt cities like Houston have moved strongly up, while others such as Brownsville, Texas, have not. On average, then, the spread of capitalism in the United States (or other countries or world regions) tends to generate an initial beta effect that looks like convergence, but middle-income traps plus the selectivity of development level it off and preserve the sigma effect of divergence. Convergence is in many ways an averaging illusion, reflecting the way that capitalism has spread (among nations) or industrial composition has converged across national territories. The reality involves finer and finer functional distinctions (intrasectoral, by task and skill composition) among territories, creating powerful income divergence effects (Yamamoto 2008).

If M-A rents are the principal force for divergence in incomes between high-level innovative places and other economies that are places to which innovations subsequently diffuse, then only if and when these latter cities are able to move up the quality and technology ladder to become M-A cities will they be able to close the gap with the Bostons of the urban system, and only if Boston keeps reinventing itself—through its innovation and nursery functions—will it be able to outrun the possible catch-up of newcomer cities. Under some circumstances, not only will innovative places have M-A rents; the economy could well pull resources into them more deeply, and penalize less innovative regions through unfavorable terms of trade intimately tied up with the diffusion of these same innovations (the innovations are embodied in standardized, routinized practices, whose prices diminish, as in today's legendary story of the iPhone, designed in California and manufactured in China).

But this is not the only possible outcome. An innovation spark that is initially localized in certain cities can renew other local economies, as seen in the capture of certain second-order innovation positions by Pittsburgh, Boston, or Orange County in the United States, and Toulouse in France. It can also be built in catch-up economies; just like Taiwan and South Korea broke out of their structural categories in the world division of labor, so have Houston and Dallas in the postwar period in the United States. Yet just like all developing economies have not been able to perform as well as Taiwan, so it is for many Sun Belt or lagging city-regions. The process of spatial economic development is riddled with these dynamics, rather than the smooth substitutions and mean reversions around which most models of NEG and NNUE are built.[6]

What about convergence within structural classes of regions as opposed to between them? I don't expect the incomes of San Francisco and Phoenix to converge anytime soon, yet I might expect there to be convergence within the similar structural classes of cities in the United States, such as between New York and Boston, or between Phoenix and Las Vegas. But the results presented above suggest that even within structural classes, there is some kind of residual. The rich, innovative, high-skill cities do not have perfect convergence. Why might this be the case? In economics terms, it might be that the localized rents for, say, the information technology industry in San Francisco are greater than those for finance in New York, or that in the former case they are proportionately greater in the local economy at least, due to a higher degree of specialization.

Convergence patterns are also uneven over time. There are periods of low innovation in which interregional convergence is stronger than in other periods. A good example of this is the 1970s in the United States, corresponding—in retrospect—to a major transition between the postwar mass production economy and the New Economy. These periods are worrying, since when we are in them, regions may be converging because the economy is doing poorly at reinventing its upper end, manifested by a slowdown in the innovation-driven MA-to-R process that I identified above.[7] Interregional equity is not always a good thing, even if divergence creates its own problems.

Prices and Wages in Time and Space

Why should temporary innovation rents cause us to think about urban and regional economics in terms other than general equilibrium processes, and in relation to some combination of mean reversion or utility as well as wage or price equalization over space? The response to this question is technical, and the generalist reader or noneconomist may wish to skip this section.

In general equilibrium analysis, the big problem is forward uncertainty. There is no pervasive mechanism that allows agents to know how to transfer their wealth perfectly from one time period to another (and all the promises of perfect financial market mechanisms for doing this have come to naught). Forward uncertainty is complicated when there is a spatial location to wealth in the form of sunk costs, social relationships, or externality effects. This often makes it impossible for the price ratio of factors to reflect their marginal rate of substitution over time and space. Moreover, there are not only price effects but also wealth/endowment effects of each equilibrium, such that each "local" equilibrium is no longer unique. Future equilibrium possibilities shift at each instant and are unknowable at the present. The end result of all these aspects is that the economy does not, at any given moment, and possibly even over the long run, allocate resources according to the canonical zero-excess rule, and that means that there are markets where there is excess demand (Sonnenschein 1972, 1973; Debreu 1974; Mantel 1974). Innovation, in the view advanced here, is the built-in force that generates pervasive excess demand in the economy with concomitant effects on prices—and some of these effects are spatialized.

In addition, future equilibrium possibilities can be manipulated, since the owners of wealth can cause factor prices to go higher or lower through nonhomogeneous rates of the substitution of outputs. This in turn means that the agents in the economy, such as the owners of factors, are not always competitive price takers; or to put it in more common terms, there is room for factor prices in the present to be manipulated. In any case, subsequent equilibriums do not reflect those that can be analytically derived from the initial endowments.

If urban and regional economics wishes to better capture the adjustment to change—the most important source of which is innovation and the MA-to-R process—it therefore needs to develop models whose excess demand functions are not overly restrictive, where rationing rules for these situations are specified correctly, and that ask how local factor endowments change along the way and hence how pathways to geographical outcomes are really traced out. This is the context of the medium-term "where" of the pattern of prices, quantities, and incomes over space.

Closely linked to the rationing problem alluded to above is the need to achieve more behavioral realism in considering how heterogeneous agents behave in heterogeneous space. Up to now, those who recognize how thorny it is to try to model dynamics tend to conclude that we cannot introduce forward-looking agents, because they need to be omniscient for models to work. They then turn to introducing restrictive conditions to make future decisions equivalent to static situations by making expectations of the future irrelevant (Desmet and Rossi-Hansberg 2010). In contrast to this, Thisse (2010) suggests that we can understand the creation and destruction of spatial equilibriums by identifying sensible selection rules, including evolutionary and learning processes, and heterogeneous agents. Going further down this pathway would make urban and geographical economics much more realistic.

Indicators and Methods

The study of urban and regional change is saturated with claims made with numbers. But the use of evidence is heavily influenced by theory, so the results are sensitive to whether the right questions are being asked. The results are also sensitive to the natural desire of academics, consultants, and governments to be clear as well as assertive in their claims.

Imagine a typical report on urban growth. It starts by identifying growing and declining cities, and then—in more subtle academic versions of it—reads back from the differences between these two kinds of place to infer something about causality (DeVol, Bedroussian, and Klowden 2011). In this example, growing cities have some combination of population growth and gross domestic product (GDP) growth, while those that are declining have slow-growing or declining populations along with GDP growth rates or GDP shares of the national economy. This type of exercise provides a picture of a few raw magnitudes of the system. If we read into it, for instance, that the growing places are warm and cheap, and the other places are cold and expensive (or that they have amenities, good or bad business climates, or whatever), we are making causal statements about growth and change. Growing places might, however, be in two different groups: those where GDP per capita is growing, and those where it is not. Adding this datum tells us that there is a further pattern of productivity. Moreover, some places with declining populations could have a rising GDP per capita. With a growing population, a rising GDP per capita indicates that high-productivity activities are locating in the city-region; with a declining population, it could mean the same, or that the population is declining faster than employment, but without growth in productivity per se. A growing population with little GDP growth per capita could easily be combined with a big absolute growth in the GDP or GDP share.

Notice that different stories can be teased out from a sensitive conversation with the data—stories that combine people (households and labor force) and industries. But let's go a step further. The GDP per capita can increase when a regional economy becomes more capital intensive and creates few jobs, and when in-migration does not increase the denominator too much. It can also increase when the economy becomes more labor intensive, but in industries where the labor costs are passed through in the form of output prices, due to the quality of the outputs or rents on innovations through scarcity—as in the M-A economies described above in this chapter. In the former case, the per capita income will not be relatively high; in the latter case, it will be high. Going further with this last indicator, if the per capita income rises, it could be in part due to the population declining faster than the workforce without a concomitant out-migration of jobs, or it could be due to a shift in the jobs/industries up the economy's hierarchies of innovation, quality, or productivity.

These many facets of performance must be considered in order to begin to detect the patterns of shifting jobs and people, and the many possible causal stories behind these shifts. Even these combinations are just the beginning of the hard work of teasing out the causal stories and development dynamics. As noted above, urban and regional systems can really only be understood against some kind of benchmark or notion of where they stand in a system, and this is generally done by thinking about convergence or divergence, or in a simpler version, how cities stand on any indicator in comparison to some class of cities (such as all cities in the reference country). Any such overall system benchmark itself, though, can be dealt with by the analyst in beta terms (how fast is one place changing relative to another, or a rate of change indicator) or top down, as a sigma indicator of whether any descriptor of the system is itself compressing or enlarging its variance. Thus, population, the GDP, the GDP per capita, income per capita, the distance of these to system means, and so on, all have beta and sigma dimensions that shed additional light on the causes as well as patterns of change, but only in association with one another.

Mean reversion across regions in prices and quantities is partial, time dependent, and nonlinear because it is subject to glass ceilings as well as additional, spatially selective "upward" (innovation) shocks. The spatial selectivity of upward and downward shocks has to do with systemwide dynamics such as factor mobility, but also local factors such as learning-by-doing and congestion costs, on the one hand, or downward spirals, on the other. The many possible combinations of development indicators for cities exist because there are so many possible interactions. As a result, urban and regional growth is potentially a *twelve*-dimensional statistical problem with four main aspects: population, output (GDP), GDP per capita (productivity), and incomes. These, in turn, have three ways they can be manifested: levels, rates of change, and mass of change.

Introducing more such dimensions will take us further into the land of finite samples; there is no way around the hard work of using not just internal consistency with a limited number of data but also external validation and consistency once we increase the number of dimensions we use to cross-check one another. External validation, in turn, requires information about time sequences of change as a plausibility test on the observation of trends in relation to "breaking points," and both in relation to their possibly different causes. In the urban and regional field, as in much of the economics of development in general, we have data that indicate large-scale (but still finite) sets of repeating processes (many people making migration decisions; firms responding to factor prices; etc.), and we are best at detecting large numbers of mutual marginal readjustments of these actions. But NEG and some historical knowledge suggest that there may be decisive events as well as turning points in the geography of the economy—as I argued in chapters 2 and 3 in interpreting the beginnings of the modern Sun Belt. Agglomeration economies tend to be circular and nonlinear, until some dramatic new force such as technical change in products or transport suddenly undermines them. Our data sets do not have the category of "events and shocks" in them; only if we pay consistent attention to these disruptive forces can we get beyond the tendency to put turning points in the black box of "nonnormal shock." An ideal data set would combine information on the establishment and lock in of agglomerations along with other time-and-place-specific shocks, breakthrough technologies, sharp switches in preferences, and such—which are "key events"—with large-scale, large-number processes of adjustments and reactions to these forces (Davis and Weinstein 2002).

No data set is going to do that, and even with it, there is no econometrics that could process such multifaceted finite numbers without a lot of hard work, sensitivity conversations, and tolerance of messiness (Morck and Yeung 2011). These are techniques for winnowing out implausible alternatives and guiding the data-driven researcher through the messiness in a powerful way. Edward Leamer (2010, 1983) has long eloquently pleaded for realism in the use of econometrics and especially the interpretation of results as well as their robustness. He argues that a succession of ever more powerful techniques—instrumental variables, nonparametric methods, consistent standard errors, and randomized experiments—have in some ways just contributed to a deeper problem. This problem is manifested in the use of these techniques with limited and finite data in an attempt to extract conclusions that try to confirm the researcher's underlying bias that the underlying world is asymptotic, behaving in a regular way according to secure laws. In the past few chapters, by taking a broader look at the underlying processes and stories that the data can tell us about urban and regional change, I have argued that the spatial development of the economy does not work that way. As called for by Leamer and others (e.g., Abrams 1982; North 2005), building a realistic framework for explaining change involves using theory, models, and data, but also triangulating them with external validation, using broad knowledge of the processes at work that may go beyond the strict limits of the data set, and most especially, being attentive to using realistic assumptions about human behavior.

Conclusion: Disruption Is Development

The developmental perspective—with its focus on disruption—that is outlined here has a long lineage in economic thought from Joseph Schumpeter to, most recently, Douglass North (2005; Aghion and Howitt 1997). It is clear that any market economy is actually both generating its own disruptions—innovating and creating agglomerations full of expensive labor along with high factor prices, expensive land, and high incomes—

and trying to revert to the mean—expelling firms, pushing people to migrate, and trying to disperse them both away from expensive places. The combination of these two forces gives us the noisy reality of cities and regions at any given moment. As we have seen, the choice to emphasize just one side of this process is epistemological; there is no "positive" basis for it. The overarching methodological challenge is to link epistemology, theory, modeling, and data together in a way that enables plausible stories about change and development to be told.

Cities and Individuals

HOW WE SHAPE CITIES, BUT NOT THE WAY WE WANT TO

The Gap between Choices and Outcomes in Cities

I am now going to step down a level in geographical scale from examining the interregional pattern of urban economic development to look inside the space of the city-region.[1] The internal arrangement of city-regions has a lot to do with how they look and feel, and may have something to do with their economic performance, although this is not any solid proof yet for this latter notion. The space of many metropolitan areas is highly coveted by firms, households, and interest groups, and as such, the preferences and choices of individuals—firms, workers, consumers, and households—are a force in shaping cities.

Urban land and buildings have characteristics—supply inelasticities and inherent externalities—that make them different from the other inputs to the economy. As a result, space in metropolitan areas is subject to competition, and there are many potential zero-sum outcomes for different users and how it is used. Because of its two unusual features, there are almost always wedges between the social and private costs and benefits associated with urban form and land use.

Moreover, there is a gap between the intentions and preferences of individual agents, and what they actually get when their choices interact with those of others, giving them a world they often don't recognize and wouldn't necessarily have wanted. The classic example of this comes from Thomas Schelling's (1978) work *Micromotives and Macrobehavior*. Schelling sets up a realistic residential choice game where individual agents are not racist but instead exhibit a slight preference for having a small minority of people "like them" living close by. Their incremental choices lead to extremely high levels of segregation by color in a perfect illustration of unintended consequences as well as the gap between individual preferences and collective outcomes.

Urban choices and outcomes run throughout contemporary debates about the nature of the city and the ways of life it harbors. There are, for example, pitched debates between those who believe that density is better than suburbanization; those who support homogeneous zoning and neighborhoods versus those who believe in mixed-use and mixed populations; the partisans of old, irregular cities and new, geometric ones; high-rise and low-rise buildings; and private cars and public transit. These disagreements are often cast in terms of utilitarian efficiency considerations nowadays (Is density a way to reduce greenhouse gas emissions? Is public transit more efficient than private cars? Is public transit more "sociable" than private cars?). Sometimes outcomes are alleged to be the result of ignorance: if people only knew better, they would choose different kinds of cities, transit, and neighborhoods; it's just that they don't know what they "really want." People would "prefer to prefer" something else if they only knew that such different outcomes were possible. For others, the idea of a different organization of urban space is what insensitive technocrats would like to force on normal people who vote with their feet.

In many ways, these debates are simply public charades that hide intense conflicts over basic values and desires. But they are also about the nature of the wedge between individual preferences and collective outcomes in the organization of metropolitan space and land use. The extent to which cities satisfy the preferences of individuals, firms, and households also defines whether the role for possible alternatives will be narrow or expansive. How well such alternatives can reconcile individual and social costs also defines the role for public policies that might be used to try to make these alternatives reality.

A Thumbnail History of Urban Doom and Resurgence

In 1990, Saskia Sassen prominently called attention to the reigning trio of London, New York, and Tokyo as "global cities." Since then it has become commonplace to analyze the resurgence of older cities, once thought of as economic basket cases. Notice that a double choice is said to have been made: interregional (old and cold cities) and intraregional (center versus suburbs). Most of the cities that are claimed to be resurgent are big, dense, former manufacturing cities in colder climates that starting in the 1990s, once again added jobs, enjoyed high levels of per capita income growth, attracted significant new investment in central cities, and saw steep increases in population and/or housing prices. The revival of US urban areas like Boston, New York, and Chicago along with European centers like Paris and London belied the idea that old, cold places could live only in the basement of the New Economy.[2]

There is nothing so new in these claims. In the final chapter of his history of US urban revitalization, John Teaford (1990) notes that in 1955,

Time magazine devoted a cover story to "The Rebirth of the City." In 1962 it published a similar story on urban rebirth, titled simply "Renaissance." In 1981 the magazine gave a cover to developer James Rouse, king of the festival marketplace, and titled it "Cities Are Fun!" Six years after that, in 1987, the cover went to "Bringing the City Back to Life." The urban comeback has been in motion for some time now.

And yet so has the urban crisis. Eight decades of boosterism for the city have been matched by decades of despondency as well. "The city is doomed," Henry Ford declared in the 1920s. "Is the Inner City Doomed?" *Public Interest* asked in a 1971 symposium. The answer was yes, at least according to the symposium's contributors: US cities were now "sandboxes" (Sternlieb 1971) or "reservations" (Long 1971)—museums of themselves, to be photographed by tourists, or containers for a permanent underclass. In 1987, just as *Time* was bringing the city back to life, Anthony Pascal (1987), with his "vanishing city" thesis, was claiming the opposite. New Economy capitalists in the 1990s declared urbanity obsolete; older cities were vertical settlements in a horizontal world, artifacts of a time before distance died (Garreau 1992; Downs 1997; Glaeser 1998). Los Angeles burned in 1992, as did Paris in 2005, and London in 2011, rekindling fears that dense big cities were too dangerous to contain the social tensions of an urban age characterized by mass migration as well as increasing chasms between the rich and poor. In 2011, it was confirmed that neighborhood income gaps had greatly increased in the last thirty years in the United States, but that the increases were greatest in the biggest cities (Russell Sage Foundation 2011).

Moreover, the presence of these resurgent cities does not suggest that people have suddenly abandoned the suburbs for a renewed love affair with downtown life. The trend lines of urbanism in the United States since World War II have been fairly constant. In the United States, population has shifted from the Northeast and Midwest to the South and West, and from cities to suburbs. Center cities are, on balance, healthier, less populous, and better governed than they were in the first half of the twentieth century. Metropolitan regions have continued to grow outward, though, and center cities play a smaller role in the everyday lives of most people. European center cities remain as important as ever, but most European cities are also growing outward, albeit with higher average density than in the United States. But wait! For the first time in decades, in the course of the recession that began in 2009, some of the old, cold expensive cities of the United States, with New York at the top of the list, had more income and population growth than the Sun Belt cities (Brookings 2010). It is a confusing picture. Are people simply frivolous, changing their minds about what they want?

Why Did Urban Resurgence Take Place?

Boston's economy has collapsed three times in the twentieth century and recovered three times as well, and the common thread in its upswings seems to be its supply of skilled workers (Glaeser 2003). Why do skilled workers go to or stay in old, cold places like Boston? Richard Florida (2002) has famously argued that the "creative class" follows particular packages of amenities, including cafés, galleries, music, and a generally bohemian, tolerant atmosphere (which he measures via the numbers of gay people). These factors are strongly correlated with the presence of knowledge workers coupled with the geography of high incomes and high population growth. Leading urbanists also now claim that London is a playground for the new global rich, and that's why London is a world city (Glaeser 2010). Resurgence is thus represented as preference driven: a new generation of young people rejected the suburban tastes of their parents, and instead opted for old, cold, and dense cities.

The Florida-Glaeser perspective has had significant influence on policymakers around the world. The mayors of a number of declining US cities are building economic development programs around luring gay twenty-five-year-olds to their cities (Swope 2003; Shea 2004). The governor of Michigan, after reading Florida's (2002) *The Rise of the Creative Class*, urged her state's mayors to form "Cool Cities" advisory boards to help them lose their Dullsville image; Detroit's mayor responded by proclaiming himself "hip-hop." In Europe, the mayor of Berlin has touted his city as "poor but sexy." Florida alone is not responsible for such strategies—New Labour politicians had never heard of him when they rolled out their "Cool Britannia" initiative years ago—but his work unquestionably led to a spike in cities marketing themselves for their "coolness" (Shea 2004; Kotkin 2005).

One reason that consumer-preference explanations are appealing is that they require few logical leaps; in essence, they just extrapolate some generally agreed-on microeconomic principles. The benefits of innovation in consumer goods and services accrue most to those individuals who have high elasticities of substitution, low aversions to risk, and high levels of disposable income. A high elasticity of substitution, in turn, implies a substantial willingness to search, because the discovery of new goods and services is impossible without searching. And a willingness to search generally requires long time horizons. The individuals who meet these criteria are young, educated, upwardly mobile, and still developing their tastes for a wide variety of goods. They look, in short, a lot like Florida's creative class (Tabarrok and Cowen 1998).

As I noted in chapter 2, one disadvantage with such an explanation is that, again, many of the consumer amenities said to be preferred by individuals do not vary much between metropolitan areas of similar sizes. So while consumption can explain why the young and college educated would live in urban areas rather than rural ones, it has a harder time explaining a decision to live in one metropolitan area over another. The Boston, New York, and Chicago Metropolitan Statistical Areas (MSAs) all saw a net in-migration of young, college-educated people from 1995–2010, but not nearly as much as Charlotte or Atlanta. And Las Vegas outpaced them all (Franklin 2003). In his list of creative cities, Florida includes not just San Francisco and New York but also Austin and Orlando. So now the explanation is not merely about old, cold, and dense cities but about warm, sprawling, and new ones as well. But aside from the presence of these individual cities, the commonality between them is hard to find. The mixing of people in Orlando does not happen in the same manner as it does on the streets of London or New York; Orlando lacks the tradition of bohemian tolerance (as well as the same pattern of narrow streets and short blocks) that characterize the bigger, older cities. Nor is Orlando known as a place where people move to have café culture and spontaneous interaction, fix up charming old houses, have loft parties, or hang around Prada stores. Lest this be considered an exclusively US story, there are parallels in Europe, though less stark.

Even if the criteria are tightened, however, they will include both cold, old and sunny, sprawled places, not one or the other. Think about different types of places, such as Jane Jacobs–style cities of serendipity and diversity; homogeneous, neighborly, traditional, and confidence-based enclaves that look like Robert Putnam's (2000) places of "high social capital"; and the "leave me alone" places offering anonymous suburban living. Abundant cases of all these types of places exhibit high income levels and concentrations of highly skilled people. Notice that we have just lost a way to discriminate between resurgent and emergent places. It is also telling that the categories above not only describe both Phoenix and Boston; they also aptly characterize Boston by itself, where a dense central city is surrounded by a sprawl that is less dense than Phoenix's suburbs.[3]

In this closer look at the pattern, it seems that the preference theorists have gotten their causality reversed: in the old and cold cities, the concentration of skilled workers creates a market for their amenities. But the amenity preferences of these workers do not account for why some of these places have grown and become richer. Research on "power couples"—couples in which both individuals hold highly skilled jobs in the New Economy—shows that many choose to live in large metropolitan areas because doing so maximizes their joint access to jobs, and allows them to adjust, at relatively low cost and risk, to changes in or losses of employment (Costa and Kahn 2000). Power couples can certainly do just as well in places like Silicon Valley and Orange County, with their sprawled residential patterns and automobile-dominated transport system, as they can in dense cities such as London or New York. The advantage of refocusing the "skilled city" explanation away from the preferences of the skilled and back toward the economic base and its associated demand for labor is that it encompasses both the resurgent old, cold, and dense cities, and in a discriminating way, some of the new, warm, and sprawled cities, and enables us to judge claims about the link between urban form and urban economic performance.

Certain observers have noted that manufacturing's location in central cities in the twentieth century had been an aberration—one that provided a temporary surge of growth at the cost of misallocating valuable land. Historically cities had been centers for the exchange of ideas, and with manufacturing's exit they could be expected to reassume this powerful and more durable role (Cheshire and Sheppard 1995; Drennan and Lobo 2007; Frey 1993). The reason that older cities were said to be doomed is that they suffered from the deagglomeration of manufacturing away from them—first to their suburbs, then to the Sun Belt, and finally to developing countries. In this regard history may have played a trick on us, for we poured our efforts into understanding manufacturing as the basis of urban economies just as manufacturing was ceasing to be the basis of many urban economies.

The decentralization of manufacturing essentially ended central cities' role in it. But did not put an end to urban concentration. Manhattan's business advantage is no longer a function of its waterways, and Boston's harbor is no longer its prime economic asset. The New Economy's demands for proximity are instead stimulated by information, which often requires that people work in close quarters with one another.[4] Information is not scarce, and indeed the modern world teems with it, so it seems counterintuitive that information access requires proximity, particularly when we can move it at ever-increasing speeds. The proximity advantage lies not in information's quantity but rather in the ability to mediate it. The mediation of this information, because much of it is new and not standardized, often requires face-to-face interaction, which is crucial for learning, building trust, and reducing risk. Face-to-face contact, as I demonstrate in chapter 11, is a "soft" exchange: it allows information to be mutually understood and placed in context, and creates the human relationships necessary for innovation. Thus, it makes perfect sense that old, cold, and dense cities can flourish in the New Economy, just as can some new and sprawled suburban environments. The key to why both of them can flourish, under the right circumstances, is not their appearance or built form, nor their superficial sociological characeristics, but their economic bases.

In order to deepen this analysis, I will now examine many of the social and amenity features of urban areas today. I will show that these features are outcomes of the process of urban economic development, not causes. In so doing, I will deepen the critique of the amenity- or consumer-driven theory of urban growth that I began in chapter 2.

Diversity as Outcome Rather Than Cause

In the United States, many of the highest-income metropolitan regions are also those that have the highest proportion of foreign-born residents—a list of cities that includes New York, San Francisco, Washington, DC, Los Angeles, and Chicago. There can be little doubt that increases in immigration (which is usually diversity's source) have contributed to an urban resurgence. If nothing else, immigration increases the supply of capable people and can tighten a slack housing market.[5] Indeed, in the United States in the 2000s, metropolitan areas such as San Francisco, Los Angeles, New York, and Chicago had net domestic out-migration—compensated for by foreign immigration (Brookings Institution 2010).

Florida (2002, 2005) argues that creative, high human-capital people thrive in and therefore go to places of diversity and tolerance. Leaving aside for a moment the difference between the two terms, we can speculate as to why a diverse urban area might fare well in the information economy. Taking a different approach, Gianmarco Ottaviano and Giovanni Peri (2006) contend that ethnic diversity can increase the human capital of native-born people as a result of mutual learning.

Diversity can be approached in the same manner as density: by viewing it as both an amenity in itself and a vehicle for accessing other amenities. It may be that people welcome (or tolerate) ethnic fragmentation because of the consumer benefits it offers. Edward Glaeser, Jed Kolko, and Albert Saiz (2001) point out that one of the values of diversity is its ability to increase the array of available consumer goods—and certainly the Mexican markets, Korean and Persian restaurants, and Chinese-language newspapers of Los Angeles lend the city some attributes that other places lack. A corollary to the ethnic diversity and consumption hypothesis is the relationship between "lifestyle diversity" (i.e., the presence of gays) and urban consumerism. Because most gays are childless, they have a different demand for housing than families with children, more disposable income to spend on consumer goods, and are unburdened by concerns about the quality of poor urban schools, possibly increasing their willingness to live in central cities (Molotch 2002; Black et al. 2002).

It may also be that diversity in the form of immigration provides cheap labor, which effectively increases the spending power of affluent residents. Those with high incomes and high values of time can use a low-wage service class to emancipate themselves from tasks they would rather not do, and instead devote time and money to activities they enjoy. Diversity therefore may increase the productivity of high human-capital people by letting them outsource the mundane aspects of everyday life.

So-called world cities, which are centers of immigration, are better positioned to offer all these features than are suburbs or smaller metropolises. Some empirical research is consistent with this view. Alberto Alesina, Reza Baqir, and William Easterly (1999) show that in the United States, the level of ethnic fragmentation in a city varies inversely with its spending on public goods, suggesting that white majorities might like the returns they gain from diverse populations (an increased array of private goods), but do not want their tax dollars spent on amenities for people different from themselves.

Evidence of this sort suggests that tolerance, which is the extent to which different groups embrace diversity, depends on each group's ability to manage diversity's benefits and costs. A further implication is that tolerance can be a function of segregation.[6] Regions or cities that are statistically diverse are often quite segregated at smaller scales, be it the neighborhood or even block level. Affluent residents of Los Angeles are able to isolate themselves from people of other cultures via the relatively low-density neighborhoods of that city as well as the schools they send their children to, and their use of private automobiles rather than public transportation.[7] For these elites, the costs of diversity are low and the benefits are high, which could explain why tolerance is a value usually associated with people of high human (and financial) capital. For less wealthy members of the majority the opposite is the case; they can afford fewer of the goods and services made available by diversity, and have a higher risk that diversity will generate problems for them at home and school as well as during their leisure time. So they may choose to segregate themselves via suburbia because it helps them manage the potential costs of diversity by increasing the spatial distances of interaction. All this may have little to do with the level of diversity fundamentally desired by each group.

Tolerance, too, is more likely to grow out of economic development than it is to ignite it. At the institutional level, a certain amount of economic integration is often a necessary precondition for the passage of laws designed to protect minorities. As regional economies become less self-sufficient, business and government leaders become increasingly unable to ignore the opprobrium of other regions. Lynchings in the South declined rapidly when the southern economy became more dependent on investment from other places and thus more sensitive to the "frown of the world" (Fischel 2001). Similarly, corporations in Cincinnati have crusaded to overturn the city's ordinance barring equal protection for gays and lesbians on the grounds that such laws inhibit the recruiting of top-flight personnel (Swope 2003).

On an individual level, psychologists and behavioral economists view tolerance as a benign reaction to the inherent desire to influence those behaviors of other people that impact their own happiness. As a population becomes larger and more diverse, however, the sheer number of these behaviors outstrips the capacity of the human mind to monitor and interfere with them. Tolerance is a value that develops to suppress the unattainable desire to meddle (Kuran 1997). Such a view would explain why cities are more tolerant than small towns. It also explains why tolerance, while frequently valued in the abstract, often breaks down in the case of an individual's most deeply held convictions. With these convictions the desire to interfere is the least easy to suppress. The person who values tolerance but is also fiercely patriotic will support free speech even as they condemn the activist who burns a flag.

Where does this leave us? Tolerance, like diversity, is a necessary but not sufficient condition for urban or regional growth. It is unlikely to generate resurgence, although its absence—by dissuading people of high human capital—may well prevent it. A growing urban area will likely become more diverse, and to continue growing it will need to become more tolerant. But as explanations for resurgence in particular, or urban growth and performance in general, diversity and tolerance fail the test.

Density and Beauty as Causes of Urban Growth

As noted earlier, there seems little in the way of amenity packages that separates the resurgent cities from newer growth centers; there are restaurants, art galleries, shopping, and museums enough for most people in both Atlanta and New York, Lille and Paris. Except for the serious culture vultures, who are a small minority of people in the world, it is not essential to live in the biggest cities.

A more promising approach might be to focus less on the amenities themselves and more on how they are obtained. What does differ across metropolitan areas (and to some extent within them, between cities and suburbs) is how amenities are spatially packaged, and the modes of transport used to access them. The density of Hong Kong, Paris, and Manhattan might be exciting in and of itself—i.e., for some people the density may *be* an amenity—but it also provides *access* to a large number of amenities in a small geographical area. A half-hour walk or subway ride in New York might take you only from Lower Manhattan to Midtown; a half hour of driving from downtown Los Angeles will bring you to Santa Monica beach. A more powerful comparison is between New York, London, or Paris, on the one hand, and Los Angeles and London, on the other: a half-hour trip in the center of the first two, on foot or by public transportation, will give you access to the same amenity package (movies, museums, galleries, concert halls, and architecture) as a half-hour car trip in a comparable area of Los Angeles or forty-five-minute tube ride in London.

Comparing places by access is more promising than a "skyline versus sunshine" story, and gets us closer to a microlevel explanation of urban resurgence. Individual preferences will always vary, and rising incomes, falling prices, and technological advances might accelerate the rate at which our preferences change. Increased exposure to foreign cultures—via trade, travel, and immigration—can alter our conceptions of beauty, change our aesthetic preferences, and broaden the array of goods and services we want at hand (Postrel 2003). Resurgence, then, may have less to do with any particular bundle of amenities (cafés, sunshine, old buildings, or new architecture), which in any event will be unstable, and more to do with the ability of certain places to provide particular forms of access to whatever preferences we may have, in an age when preferences are rapidly changing. If we prefer to gain access through density, or if we consider density an amenity in itself, then places like New York are desirable. If instead we consider a smooth-flowing road system an amenity, we might like Orlando; if we prefer to access amenities by car, then we might like Los Angeles (or New York's suburbs).

Another major explanation put forth for urban resurgence is that households and individuals increasingly favor the unique amenities of old, cold, and dense cities because they are beautiful. This theory applies more to center cities (and certain older suburbs) than to entire regions. Firms are unlikely to choose an urban area based on its aesthetic qualities. Silicon Valley overflows with business, but is no one's idea of an architectural treasure; Savannah, Georgia, or Venice, Italy, are a preservationist's dream with despondent economies.

Individuals who locate in an urban area for other reasons (e.g., access to jobs), however, can choose from a number of jurisdictions within that area to live, and the aesthetic appeal of the center city—combined with a desire to walk or use public transportation—may influence intraregional location choice. Skilled in-migrants tend to concentrate in a few neighborhoods such as loft districts, near well-publicized redevelopment projects. Out-migrants, by contrast, tend to depart from neighborhoods throughout the city and arrive at equally scattered destinations throughout the region (Kasarda et al. 1997). Just as the graphic images of closed factories may have made decline seem more far reaching than it was, so too can the photogenic nature of new loft districts make the renaissance seem grander than it actually is.

Nevertheless, while it is important not to overstate the rebirth of center cities, it is equally crucial not to trivialize it. Part of the *cachet* of these resurgent cities lies in their beauty; the urbane lifestyle is built in no small part around the architecture and urban design of the central city, and the beauty of dense cities can offset the numerous difficulties of living in them. But the concept of beauty is elusive and subjective. In practice, "beauty" usually seems to mean "oldness."

Accepting the qualifier that beauty is a subjective notion, the aesthetic advantage of old areas probably has multiple explanations. The first is simply selection bias: in general, the worst of the past gets destroyed and the best gets preserved. William Shakespeare had no shortage of contemporary rival playwrights, but his work alone persists. The same mechanism is at work with buildings. Some wonderful old buildings get demolished, yet few ugly old buildings get saved. At any given moment, a city will be comprised of old buildings that have withstood the selectivity of the wrecking ball, new buildings that are charming but have yet to face time's judgment, and new buildings devoid of charm that are equally untested. The old will thus look good relative to the new, and the bigger the proportion of old buildings there are, the more aesthetically pleasing an area is likely to be. Other explanations for the comparative charm of older structures include the rise of property taxes—which create incentives to improve the interior rather than the exterior of buildings—and advances in construction technology. New technology enables not only some stunning architecture (the graceful, computer-designed curves of Los Angeles' Disney Hall, for instance) but also function without form. There was a time when a wall, in order to be sturdy, needed to be made of brick; its arresting appearance was part of its utility. This is no longer the case, as long rows of durable though unsightly tract homes can attest. A final factor in the decline of urban architecture may be the rise of business regulation. In the days before insurance and sophisticated contract law, the aesthetic grandeur of a building was often used as a signal of trustworthiness and stability—particularly for banks, which had to convince citizens to deposit their money. With the advent of federal deposit insurance (and other laws protecting customers), however, stability became more of a given, and aesthetic signals became less important. Certainly US bank design has plummeted in quality since the Federal Deposit Insurance Corporation was established. It is not hard to spot a handsome old bank building, but most contemporary banks are nondescript boxes (Benedikt 1997).[8]

All this begs a further question, though: If beauty is oldness, why has oldness only recently become so valuable? The most immediate answer is that oldness is scarce. Good oldness cannot be imitated (even by Las

Vegas), so it is supply inelastic and hence earns rents. But scarcity alone cannot account for people's increased willingness to live in and pay for old environments. Oldness has not always earned rents, after all. For a long time the old neighborhoods of many cities languished unwanted, and in many cities they continue to do so. The disappearance of manufacturing untethered oldness from one of its great costs: dirt and pollution. The effect of unbundling old neighborhoods from dirt is nowhere more evident than in the redevelopment of urban waterways. For much of the twentieth century, urban architecture in dense cities turned its back to rivers and lakes, because the waterways were unsightly industrial landscapes. Cleveland's Cuyahoga River, once so polluted that it caught fire, is only the most infamous example. The Cuyahoga today is much cleaner, and residential properties now line its banks. The departure of heavy industry allowed waterways to become an aesthetic amenity rather than an aesthetic liability.

But more important, the departure of manufacturing freed old buildings and neighborhoods to overcome some of their technical obsolescence, and become places for production in the New Economy—returning the city to the function it had prior to the heavy industry interlude of the mid-nineteenth to mid-twentieth centuries. Dense city neighborhoods had serious functional weaknesses in the late twentieth century: designed in pedestrian eras, they were deeply unpleasant places to drive and utterly horrible places to park. City living was thus bundled together with a car-free life, and a car-free life was something that few people wanted, and fewer still could afford. Eventually old cities took steps—some desirable and some less so—to remedy this functional obsolescence of their designs and make a car-urbanity bundle possible.[9] Neighborhoods like Boston's Beacon Hill sold curb parking spaces at market rates. More commonly and regrettably, cities invested in or required developers to provide off-street parking spaces. Off-street parking surmounts the technical obsolescence of the urban core, but it also supplies incentives to drive, undermines density, and debases the city's aesthetically advantageous urban form (Shoup 2005). Most recently, and to the delight of transportation economists worldwide, London introduced cordon tolls for vehicles entering its central business district. The pricing of roads is frequently applauded on efficiency grounds, but in dense cities it has aesthetic benefits too. Congestion is often a product of density, and the use of market-clearing prices on the roads makes old areas more amenable to driving while preserving their pedestrian-orientation and the visual appeal of their built environments. Just as the new functional obsolescence of urban waterways and manufacturing districts has allowed them to become beautiful, the proper pricing of beautiful urban streets has once again allowed them to become functional. And this aestheticization of what was once considered ugly corresponds, not coincidentally, with its new usefulness in consumption (shopping, restaurants, and entertainment), production (work sites for the innovation-based economy's clusters), and residences (living near work).

The steps taken by central cities to become more car friendly, combined with well-publicized redevelopment and crime-fighting efforts, highlight a larger point about both central-city rebirth and region-level urban resurgence: many preferences are quite similar across places, in spite of different appearances. Central cities are becoming more like their suburbs (and vice versa). Urban life has now adopted some of suburbia's trappings, and suburban life has become more urbane. Suburban-style malls and supermarkets now proliferate in central cities. Target and Walmart have begun building multistory urban discount centers in places such as Manhattan. A sporting goods chain store is now behind the elegant facades of the old Trois Quartiers store at the Place de la Madeleine in Paris, and in my neighborhood of Paris, mini versions of chain grocery stores now compete with the local *artisan commercants*. Times Square in New York has been cleaned up and returned to mass retailers, and in many ways looks like a denser version of the culture one can find in any suburban mall. Megamalls like South Coast Plaza in Orange County or even Les Arcades in Noisy-le-Grand in suburban Paris offer a lot of what you can find on major center-city shopping streets, albeit in a less historically distinctive container.

The same observation can be made at an interregional level. Traditionally, urbanists have held up the US Southwest as an archetype of sprawl, and pointed to the old, cold Northeast as a model of dense living. By 2000, however, something closer to the opposite was true. The northeastern cities have compensated for their high-density centers by developing some of the most sprawling suburbs in the nation while the Southwest's lack of strong urban cores is now counterbalanced by its extremely dense suburbs. The monotonous density of Los Angeles' urbanized area is the highest in the United States at 7,009 persons per square mile, compared to the second densest at 5,239 in the New York region's urbanized area. The difference is that New York City has a density of 26,343, while the city of Los Angeles, the urban core of the Los Angeles metropolitan region, is only slightly denser on average than the whole region at 7,828, even though there are neighborhoods within Los Angeles that have almost 50,000 per square mile (still only a quarter of the peak Manhattan densities). The suburbs of New York are only 12 percent that of their central city, and New York's suburbanites occupy, on average, 155 percent more land than Los Angeles (Manville and Shoup 2005). The New York, Chicago, and Boston regions will never outdo the Southwest in the sun department, but they are now competitors when it comes to sprawl.

At the intraregional—center city versus suburb—scale, then, the qualities of the built environment might play a significant role in residential choice. Yet this discussion has showed that preferences (the demand side) do not operate in a vacuum. There were structural transformations of the center cities that allowed them to become more attractive. These "supply-side" changes were generated principally by the economic transformation of center cities—the emptying out of manufacturing, the lower incidence of crime, and the "suburbanization" of their consumption opportunities and transport modes. All these latter changes were driven mainly by the shifting structure of the economy, from one dominated by manufacturing to one dominated by services and knowledge-intensive production—activities that need center cities in general, and do not particularly favor the Sun Belt, as manufacturing does.

Why Our Choices in Cities Do Not Reveal Our Preferences

Urban economics has long recognized that land has features that make markets in it different from standard markets, and one of these is that land has some inherently monopolistic attributes. Land exists in a more or less fixed supply. For the most part it neither can be created nor moved, and it is largely indivisible. Densely built environments impose unusually strong trade-offs on choices that are made. As a consequence, such choices do not reveal preferences as well as those made in standard types of markets (Thompson [1968] 1996). Amenities come in bundles (nice trees, lots of space, low crime, and highly educated neighbors would be one such grouping), not as sovereign, mix-and-match features. Bundling is not unique to land or cities. Many people who like to watch sports on television buy cable television packages that have hundreds of channels they don't want in order to get the one or two sports channels they do want. The standard approach to dealing with bundled goods is to argue that preferences for them, like those for many private goods, are "revealed"—that in the end, we know what people want by observing what they have done. If a majority of people buy single-family homes on large lots and drive a lot as a result, then we can conclude that this way of life expresses majority preferences for both land use and transportation. The person in the large suburban house may like the space they have but dislike the amount of driving they have to do because of it. If they like the space more than they dislike the driving, they will choose to live in the house. For this person, the package of amenities, even with its drawbacks, is better than the available alternative bundles.

If some external shock alters the available alternatives (if the amenities become unbundled from each other, and it becomes possible to have lots of space without driving), though, these revealed preferences could change, even if this person's latent preferences do not. On the other hand, it might take some time for the revelation to occur. If the external shock impacts their house specifically (if a commuter rail line opens nearby that can take them to work and leisure), their behavior might change right away. If, however, the market just creates more spacious central-city apartments, the process of change will be much slower. This person has already purchased their house, and people do not upgrade homes the way they do cars or notebook computers. So they stay put longer than they might prefer, because they have sunk costs into their property. And when they do move out, their house doesn't disappear; it remains for the next occupant of the house with a lot of space and a lot of driving, regardless of the tastes of that occupant. Lastly, our suburbanite may not move at all, but someone else in the future who has similar preferences may move to the spacious apartments in the center city. All this adds up to a subtle and slow-moving process of change.[10] The time lag between shifts in transportation, land use, and lifestyle options and the population's locational adjustment to all this makes change difficult to foresee, and obscures the link between behaviors and the preferences they supposedly reveal.

Urban economics has long considered one dimension of this problem through the theory of externalities. It argues that many positive externalities are capitalized in land prices; thus, when good schools are obtained by living in a certain location, the land value will capitalize on not only the nice quality of the neighborhood but also the school access. The same will happen in reverse for negative externalities. But notice that this does not deal with the problem of bundling in relationship to preferences. If externalities are priced in, all they then do is make the effects of bundling even more powerful, and drive a bigger wedge between what we would prefer to prefer and what we can actually get in the urban environment. There is, if anything, an even bigger market failure at work.

What Do People Want in Cities?

There are, of course, a number of hypotheticals in the example given above, although the basic tension—between the desire for space and the desire to drive less—has been reported in more than one survey of US and European homeowners. The standard view of preferences is that they are fully rankable and not lumpy, but smoothly continuous in their rankability. In the short run, this may indeed be what people do, choosing a flat in central London's Covent Garden rather than a small house in hip, upper-middle-class Islington, a larger house in Crouch End, or even a detached house way out in Suffolk.[11]

Economic theory generally has little patience for the idea that people's internal preferences might conflict or that preferences can't be perfectly ranked.[12] Yet recent work in behavioral economics has begun to lend such ideas more credence. David George (2001) introduces the idea of "second-order preferences," which he defines as those things we would "prefer to prefer." Our second-order preferences can differ from our revealed preferences, because the second-order preference is subordinate to a conflicting preference for another good (as often happens with bundling), or because other external incentives are aligned against it. If a second-order preference has distant benefits and immediate costs while a competing option has immediate benefits and distant costs, then the competing option is likely to prevail. George's example is his tendency to eat fast food when he is hungry—he would prefer that he did not, but the extra increment of immediate satisfaction that he gets from McDonald's shifts the balance in favor of it. His revealed preference may not be stable, however, because it is accompanied by dissatisfaction. Or to be more precise, the satisfaction he gets, although immediate, also decays faster, while the foregone option—eating healthier—involves delayed but longer-lasting gratification (Frank 2001).[13]

Latent dissatisfaction makes choices prone to change, even in spite of an outward appearance of firmness in underlying preferences. If the external incentives shift, what seemed like a stable equilibrium can quickly unravel. In a standard goods market, when this happens, output can adjust relatively quickly, and within a short time the market is stable again. But this doesn't happen in the built environment because the adjustments are so slow.

How do these changes manifest themselves? In the narrowest sense, people living within fixed budgets who demand both space and access have to cut back on other items of consumption; they make a lifestyle shift. Or the increased demand for space and access could encourage innovation in how they are supplied, breaking down and transforming the old links with density and accessibility as traditionally defined, and in the process, possibly giving rise to some new negative or positive externalities.[14] The upending of traditional trade-offs between space and access could come in the form of government intervention through, for instance, the zoning laws that require off-street parking spaces for every new development. Preferences emerge against a dynamic backdrop not just of what has historically been supplied but also in light of emerging new lifestyles, expectations, income levels, and technologies. They emerge institutionally from "outside" the urban environment as much as from within it, yet they have to find a concrete material expression within it. The sudden (unlikely) absence of all fast food might make George less likely to surrender to his cravings; the new (quite likely) presence of off-street parking in a central business district might allow a person with a low demand for space to satisfy their high demand to drive. So the demands from imperfect substitutability create situations that are contradictory. Thus, housing and transportation choices can be motivated by relaxed income constraints or new income trade-offs outside the housing-transportation budget. The consequent effects on transport use and pricing, or house prices, can be enormous as well as unanticipated, and in turn can provoke further unanticipated reactions.

You Can't Always Get What You Want

The example of the suburbanite trading space for more driving can now be extended. If this person lives in the United States, it is entirely possible that they want neither as much space nor as much transport as they have. What they may want instead is good public education for their children. If the local schools are funded by property tax, then exclusive communities will likely have better schools. Exclusive communities are generally exclusive because they practice fiscal zoning, usually in the form of large minimum lot sizes. One "buys" one's way into the community by being able to afford a large house, which is made valuable not just by its size but also by the fact that the quality of local schools get capitalized into the home value. In essence, then, my hypothetical resident buys more house *and* more transport than they want in order to get the schooling they covet for their children (Fischel 2001).

Land, complicated as it is, is not the sum total of the supply side in cities. The supply side also involves public goods, like education, and the public goods are often bound up in what occupies the land (sometimes referred to as "place"). Almost no one can create land, but the making of places is a joint project of architects, developers, engineers, regulators, and others. Although prices play an essential role in coordinating these disparate sectors, the coordination is highly imperfect, and a tremendous amount of information is still lost by the resulting prices. For example, my suburbanite might be enticed to move not by spacious city apartments (built with required parking) but rather by an increased number of urban private and parochial city schools, which allow city living yet suburban-quality education. Or they could be enticed by school vouchers, which detach school quality from residential location, but also sever its connection to property values. School vouchers, intended to increase educational quality, could actually diminish it, if they remove the incentive for childless homeowners to fund schools in order to maintain their property values (Fischel 2001; Hilber and Mayer 2004).

Thus, public goods suffer from their own revelation problem in that an individual's taxes depend on their demand for public goods, which creates an incentive for them to falsify their preferences and free ride. If a majority of people free ride, of course, the public goods will be underprovided, and revelation will supply an imperfect reflection of the public goods package that is actually desired (Stiglitz 1982). Charles Tiebout (1957) offered the classic solution to the revelation problem for public goods. The Tiebout hypothesis is that competition between local governments will create a market in public goods, and this in turn will let people reveal their preferences for public goods by moving to those communities that offer the package they like. Politicians, like the producers of private goods, will have an incentive to provide the goods demanded because the value of public investments gets capitalized into residents' homes. For most homeowners, the house is their most important and least divisible asset, so residents have an incentive to closely monitor city hall and turn out those politicians who fail to deliver the proper package of public goods.

The Tiebout hypothesis has never lacked for criticism (Stiglitz 1982; Rose-Ackerman 1983; Donahue 1997)—some of it spurious.[15] For my purposes here, a valid criticism of the Tiebout model is that it responds only somewhat effectively to the inertia of the built environment. People make their choices, but they are still choosing from a limited number of bundles, and the bundled choice sets are typically of limited convexity. People cannot in general consume half a house in central London and then another half out in the suburbs.[16] Yes, a few wealthy childless people— the pied-à-terre brigade—might buy a flat in the Barbican and a substantial house in Gloucestershire or Somerset, and a few extremely wealthy people might buy a substantial apartment in the seventh arrondissement of Paris along with a country house in the Lubéron, a Manhattan apartment, and a place in the Hamptons. But these are not typical individuals. And as always, the hobgoblin of distorted prices rears its head. When the costs of one sector are externalized on to another one—if by choosing, say, a house with a lot of transport, some of the housing costs end up being dumped on to the transportation system, and some of the price of a home is reflected not in its mortgage but rather in the congestion at the end of the street—our understanding of preferences is obscured.

People often don't recognize that they have conflicting preferences, and frequently do not link their individual preferences, whether first or second order, to the social outcomes that result (if they do make this link, they generally try to reconcile the conflict). Although the options are generated through decisions made in separate institutional spheres (housing, transport, work, and firm location), they come together in bundles. The tourists who are dragging their kids around beautiful historic neighborhoods in European cities usually cannot help but yield to the temptation to feed their children at McDonald's, and the property market obliges. It is not clear that this outcome—the Piazza Navona decorated with the Golden Arches—is desired either by the tourists, residents, or perhaps even landlords.

Unstable Preferences and Frustrated Urbanites

Where preferences are intransitive, there can be unresolved tensions that express themselves as "untapped markets," and generate demand for innovations in architecture, transportation, location, and lifestyles. Where such innovations are not possible, though, they may lead to exit or a search for better ways to live; where neither is possible, they may lead to collective voice—that is, politics to influence the urban environment. Even without considerations of political power, the range of current preferences is limited by past choices. The built environment constructed by one generation remains the built environment for the next. The density of central-city Boston is both its status quo and a function of its past; most new construction in the Boston area after World War II has been at a low density. Individual preferences do aggregate to social outcomes, but those social outcomes in turn constrain future preferences. New preferences can only be revealed on the margins, in the form of new construction, and of course new construction today will further constrain preferences tomorrow. Were cities wiped clean with each new market adjustment, this certainly would not be a problem.

Nor is the built environment just an aggregation of past preferences. An argument can be made that it is an aggregation of past *minority* preferences. The amount of new housing construction in any given year is generally a small portion of the overall housing availability. In California, for example, only 1 percent of the housing is constructed new each year; the *American Housing Survey* shows that only 2 percent of homeowners and less than 1 percent of renters on average live in dwellings constructed the year before. If the people who choose new construction have significantly different preferences than those who find housing on the resale market (and there is some evidence that they do), then the development industry will be catering to a minority, and this minority will in turn have a disproportionate influence over not just the development industry but also the options available for future home buyers (Myers and Gearin 2001). The physical results of people's past preferences for housing last longer than the people themselves do.

Similar dynamics are at work in the political arena. Just as past individual preferences inhibit current and future choices, so too do past government interventions. Most theories of urban politics see the city government as an instrument for manipulating the externalities of growth, seeking to capture elevated land values as well as repel problems like traffic and homelessness (Peterson 1981; Swanstrom 1983; Logan and Molotch 1987). Tiebout assumes away many of the problems associated with this calculus, but as I mentioned above, the Tiebout mechanism is derailed in the case of large cities. In large cities homeowners have a hard time monitoring city hall, and there are fewer homeowners and more renters (who suffer from the "renter's illusion" that they pay no property taxes). Larger cities also have larger pots of intergovernmental money at stake, increasing the incentive of special interests to meddle in public policy. Tiebout's great insight was that in some instances, public goods could be supplied without politics. But in complex and big metropolitan regions, the politics is still likely to impinge strongly. To the extent that politically supplied public goods are produced in the interests of a powerful minority (i.e., large landowners with a disproportionate influence over city government—especially in big-parcel, low-homeowner areas—politicians who see reputational benefits from overseeing spectacular building projects, or bureaucrats who desire expanded power), the built environment reflects a combination of aggregated individual preferences and the material remainders of a vision imposed by people who were able to control the agenda of city building.

We see this best with the construction of geographically immobile resources such as infrastructure, which like many public goods are often conceived in a context of misaligned costs and benefits, and hence distorted incentives. Urban highways were oversupplied in the United States (and many other countries) in the postwar period because the cities that built them did not pay for them; the federal taxpayers who did pay for them did so at small individual burden to themselves, and the contractors who built them did so at massive gain. The oversupply of highways contributed to driving, which itself was underpriced, and the highway oversupply soon became a peak period undersupply, as congestion resulted. Congestion, because it disproportionately impacted the city center, in turn led to the devaluing of downtown real estate and probably also to an excessive dedication of downtown land to auto infrastructure (Anas, Arnott, and Small 1998). Congestion also fuels the migration of people outward, because dispersal lowers commute times for some. Yet rather than take steps to correct the price mechanism through congestion charges, many cities have turned to rail systems, which are themselves public choice problems (paid for by federal taxpayers and supported by construction unions), and parking requirements, which are de facto fees on developers in order to subsidize automobility (Shoup 2005). Thus we have urban transport systems with an excess demand on some auto infrastructure (roads and highways), an excess supply of others (parking spaces), and a supply of public transit that wildly outstrips its current demand, in part because this demand is suppressed by these other distortions.

In the Paris region, abundant but radial-style public transport so increases the value of the center city and near-western suburbs that it has historically devalued the rest of the suburbs, since this system means that they are relatively poorly served and have low levels of amenities compared to the privileged areas. This leads to both the extreme peak-time congestion of public transport as well as roads and underinvestment in potentially attractive suburban locations. There is a circular and cumulative process of spatial sorting of elites into the center, followed by more investment in it (and a better tax base), more gap with the lesser areas, and so on. As a consequence, it has proven almost impossible to break the value of centrality in both practice and perception. Although high housing costs have induced some movement outward, mostly what has happened is the readjustment of budgets on the part of those who want the good central and near-western locations. This is quite different, of course, from what has happened in London, New York, or Los Angeles, where the distribution of amenities is more even and land values are more polycentric.

Robert Dahl ([1961] 2005) noted in his classic study of city governance that an election reveals only the first preference of a majority of voters with regard to those preferences they can choose from. Knowing who won an election is therefore quite different from knowing what people want. Candidates are also bundles—assemblages of positions and issues that cannot be disaggregated—and for this reason many votes are reluctant ones. It is also for this reason that electoral politics are prone to sudden reversals. The problems with the political option are well known. A long-standing tenet of political science going as far back as the eighteenth-century insights of the Marquis de Condorcet is that in instances of cyclic preferences (that is, where A is preferred to B, and B to C, but C is preferred to A), it is impossible to generate a single "winning" option; there will be conflicting majorities instead, and the electoral winner will be determined by who sets the agenda (because the difference would lie in which options were voted on first). But the winning option may not endure, because a latent majority will always be capable of overturning the decision.

In choices on how to build a city, however, unlike in an election, the reversals are not as smooth. In electoral mathematics, the problem of decisive influences tipping political decisions is offset by the fundamental instability among conflicting majorities: political decisions often "tip back" to something close to the optimum. The volatility of preferences leads to a volatility in governing coalitions and prevents any one vision from dominating. Yet in urban space, the winning decision is frequently written in asphalt and steel. Support for programs thus may ebb and flow, but taking down a highway and building something new is slower as well as more durable than winning the next election.

Conclusion: Better Social Choices, Happier Individuals

Research and technical advice to policymakers remains remarkably concentrated on optimizing choices. For some, this is brought about through Tiebout-style competition; for others by correcting market failures and internalizing externalities; and for still others through government regulation. These positions represent, roughly, the range of the political spectrum. These are all potentially useful up to a point, but the analysis in this chapter also suggests that none of them will ever solve most of the problems of jockeying for urban space on the part of different agents. They obscure the nature of what is being chosen and what choice can do. Most important, they dress up complex and messy processes in the language of optimization or procedural correctness, and by so doing, they fail to face up to the inherent complexity of agent interaction in urban space.

There certainly are many experiments at work in metropolitan areas—under the fuzzy terms of "governance" or "civic participation"—that try to respond to the contentious process of making collective decisions that intersect with heterogeneous private preferences and costs. This is not the place for a full-fledged consideration of these experiments, but several points can be made in light of the argument of this chapter.

First, even with regional authorities, the ultimate power for making decisions is usually unchanged and hence continues to reside in extremely fragmented local governments. No country has established sovereign metropolitan governments, whether unitary (a single authority) or federal (linking all local governments constitutionally). Moreover, even when complex decisions are moved to special-purpose, regional-scale agencies (such as transportation commissions), they end up in bodies that are basically intergovernmental authorities, not new levels of government per se. In any case, in terms of the contentions presented in this chapter, it is not clear that kicking formal decision-making power upstairs would solve the problems of preference satisfaction, though it might change Tiebout competition significantly as an element of the process.

It is precisely by taking seriously the built-in conflicts over urban space and impossibility of satisfying most preferences that we could further more innovation, which would concentrate on changing the possible bundles along with unbundling what we don't want. The frontiers of such innovation today are in areas like combining density, privacy, and access, and overcoming the cleavage between suburbs and the central city, combining urban villages and exciting cities, or combining production, consumption, and leisure in better ways. But some conflicting, hard-edged, undesirably bundled aspects of the city will remain, and therefore so will some hard trade-offs. Economics cannot solve them. In this case, rather than continuing to tell the public that we can find optimal solutions for bundling or pricing their effects, scholars and policymakers instead need to shed more light on the bundles that are possible and those that are not, and their mixes of desired and undesired impacts. We should tell the public what is possible, and we should tell the public more clearly about the nature of the bundles they are currently getting. This would enhance our society's ability to make informed social choices about our cities, possibly getting us closer to what we would prefer to prefer. I tackle the social choice framework for cities in chapter 13.

PART II

The Institutional Context
of Cities and Regions

Winner and Loser Regions

THE "WHERE" OF DEVELOPMENT

The origins of the economic specialization of particular places are in some ways the elusive holy grail of both urban and development economics. The economy consists of a ladder of specializations from more to less complex and skilled. Development clubs form around positions on this ladder. This then tells us about the specialization of an economy, and we can tell you much about its level of wages, prices, and per capita income.

Specialization changes; it is pushed along by the forces of technology, trade costs, and innovation and learning. This shifts the positions of national and regional economies on the ladder of development. In some ways, interregional development within a country can be more turbulent than nations in the global economy. We saw this in table 1.1, where US metropolitan regions have moved up and down the ladder of incomes, and then combined that with radically different population changes in just a few decades. To take just one pair of regions, the San Francisco Bay Area has a per capita income fully one-third greater than its southern neighbor of Los Angeles, even though they were virtually identical in 1970. No equivalent gap has opened up among the countries of western Europe, North America, and Japan over the past few decades.[1]

In the United States within the overall upward swing of the Sun Belt, Houston, Dallas, and Atlanta have done much better in income terms than Phoenix and Las Vegas, such that the former are now in a different development club from where they began. Or take the case of resurgence that was discussed in the previous chapter. Many northern and midwestern cities such as Detroit, Boston, New York, and Chicago underwent serious economic downshifting in the 1970s and 1980s. But it has been uneven, with New York, Boston, and certain others coming back in income terms, along with the London region in the United Kingdom, and reversing their earlier population declines, while many other metro areas continue to move down in the income ranks and lose population. Examples abound elsewhere. In Brazil, why did São Paulo surge ahead of Rio de Janeiro in the 1960s, and Belo Horizonte leap ahead of both in the

1980s? This selectivity of development—between clubs but also within them—is the subject of this chapter. There are four candidates for explanation: specialization, human capital, accidents, and institutions. The four can interact in a variety of ways.

The Where of Specialization

The NEG models examined in chapter 3 provide insights into one reason for specialization: spatial clustering. But they tell us little about the where of such clustering. Comparative advantage approaches to specialization emphasize factor endowments, but do not explain why similarly developed economies can specialize differently. NEG models examined in chapter 3 show why similarly developed economies can differently specialize, because activities build up scale in certain places and not others, or different regions produce different varieties of functionally similar goods and services.

But there are other approaches to explaining development. For example, many economists emphasize the human capacities of a region, or its human capital. Some development economists and economic geographers assign development differences to unique, accidental founding events such as the invention of a key market-changing technology in the region, or a pivotal entrepreneur starting up and thus unleashing the sequence of events that builds a cluster or concentration. This view can be combined with the NEG perspective explored in chapter 3, where once a favorable accident occurs in a place, circular and cumulative causation takes over, expressed in a snowball dynamic of sharing, matching, and learning. This locks in the agglomeration to the region, which in turn increases its positive local wage and price rents along with the local employment multiplier. Regions that miss out on this first-mover effect fall progressively further behind the leaders, thereby contributing to divergence in the urban system as a whole.

One can also combine these two latter views. Thus, the features of a region—such as its historical experience and unusual skills—make it possible for the unique founding events to occur there and take root, and agglomeration processes lock in this initial advantage, but the deep initial advantage is not itself accidental. In practice, the risk is that the researcher thinking along these lines will simply reverse engineer the characteristics of winning regions and call them causes. This is certainly the case with many contemporary accounts of so-called innovative or creative regions, and their ecosystems of success.

A more sophisticated approach is to reverse the causality of the above, and hold that there are lots of places where the "great men and women" (key founding inventors and entrepreneurs) try to get started. The early days of the semiconductor, aircraft, and biotechnology industries bear this out. But only some places have the resources that allow them to turn these initial events into durable success; instead of agglomeration as an automatic lock in after an initial accident, the subsequent success has to be cultivated. Along these lines, Walter Powell, Kelley Packalen, and Kjersten Whittington (2009) show that about ten US regions were early patenters in the biotechnology and life sciences industries, but only three have emerged as agglomerations. In this case, only accidents that sow seeds on fertile ground live to see the future. We have a two-stage causal model.

Moreover, as is suggested in a highly simplified way by product cycle models, success is never permanent or guaranteed (Norton and Rees 1979). There is a moment in the life of most industries when their intermediate trade costs decline to the point that no local measures can suffice to maintain their core agglomerations. Some regional economies will then suffer major job and income loss. In other economies, the loss of routine production activity is compensated for by industries moving up the product ladder or generating new activities through innovative entrepreneurship within the region (Saxenian 1994, 2000; Amsden 2001). Successful adjustment—or "resilience"—essentially comes through sectoral succession or innovation: capturing activities that can become the basis of new regional economic specializations, retaining the retainable parts of existing specializations by reinforcing comparative advantage in a certain part of the activity's value chain, or moving up the product quality ladder within an industry already present in the region (Simmie and Martin 2010; Chapple and Lester 2010). But since there are innumerable concrete ways that this can occur from region to region, we need to know why some places do better at adjustment than others, effectively getting from one successful specialization to another over time, while others fail at this, and decline.

These endogeneity issues with respect to regional specialization can be visualized in the following manner:

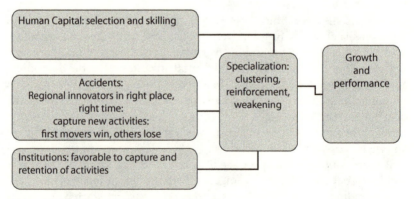

Figure 6.1   Sources of specialization.

The Geography of Skills

Let's first consider the explanation of specialization favored by many development and labor economists. In this account, the supply of skills—or human capital—determines specialization (Rosen 1983). It is the development economics version of the "jobs-to-people" framework considered throughout this book. Along these lines, it has been famously observed by Robert Lucas (1988) that skilled people congregate in expensive cities to be near other skilled people. The specialization of a metropolitan economy is driven by the characteristics of its labor force. It can further be argued that since capital is usually more portable than labor, human capital becomes the factor determining specialization.

For this observation to become a convincing basis for a jobs-to-people assertion, though, the determinants of the location of the labor force have to be identified. To account for intercity income differences, we would want to know why some cities do better at attracting skilled labor than others, and what triggers the divide between more and less skilled cities. This is even more a mystery when we remember that regions within a country are highly open to interregional migration and somewhat open to international flows of people. This means that the stock of knowledge of any given city-region is intimately related to national education and R & D, since people studying or acquiring experience in one region do not have to stay there but instead can take their skills and congregate in other regions of their choice.

For such human capital differences to persist, then, the regional human capital stock at any given point in time must be, in part, *caused by* the regional characteristics that attract, retain, and repel people with different kinds of skills. As noted, the four principal accounts of skilled worker sorting are that they sort according to amenities, creativity, interaction, or consumption opportunities. But we saw in previous chapters that none of these notions do well as explanation of the initial causes of skilled worker concentration.

The other problem with all these explanations is that skills are industry specific, but many amenities tend to be widely distributed; thus, they cannot explain the specific where of development. For example, Los Angeles has high concentrations of skilled movie producers, agents, entertainment industry lawyers, and film scriptwriters. New York has a high concentration of people with skills in moving money around. But both cities have a lot of restaurants, art galleries, museums, and fancy shops. How can these amenities explain why Los Angeles specializes in entertainment and New York focuses on finance?

It is obvious that skilled workers seek interactions with other skilled workers in the sense that if my job depends on having other people around me for certain kinds of specialized needs (e.g., information), I will want to be around them. I may also want to build my career in a place where I can work my way up, and this involves learning as I do so, and learning is a form of interaction. On closer examination, though, does this mean that New York's financial services cluster actually originated from the desire of stock traders to interact with one another, and that the investment banks followed them? Obviously, once the development process is well under way (i.e., there exist specialized clusters of industries requiring skilled people), then individuals will be attracted to existing pools of people—or at least to jobs. It is more difficult to see how the desire for interaction could be an original cause, since without there having been previous rounds of development that led to the concentration of skilled workers in a place, why would additional people with specialized skills want to go there in order to interact?

As discussed in chapter 3, one of the three main forces behind agglomeration is the matching of workers to employment opportunities. In this model, workers are said to concentrate together when they work in a high-turnover industry because they want to be near a large pool of potential employers, as this raises the probability of securing a new post following layoffs, and layoffs are frequent in highly innovative or "young" industries. Likewise, employers cluster together in order to tap into a large pool of available labor, enabling them to avoid hoarding labor during during downturns (Jayet 1983; Combes and Duranton 2006). Such a model is analytically persuasive, but once again the questions are where such dynamics get started and what mechanism kicks off these two dynamics in a particular place. The clustering together of many such firms with unstable labor demands might generate the regional labor pool through in-migration or regional learning-by-doing, and then the two

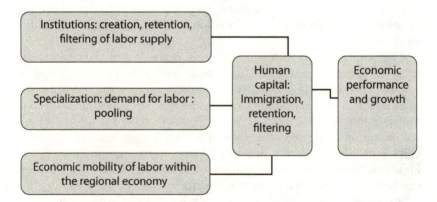

Figure 6.2 Sources of regional human capital.

become mutually reinforcing causes (Scott and Storper 1987). But then the explanation no longer takes the following form: "this city developed as a consequence of workers' quest for interaction"; rather, it is: "this city developed because of the clustering of firms together."

A picture of these endogeneity issues with respect to labor supply is shown in figure 6.2.

Do Institutions Cause Urban Specialization?

A third major branch of development theory argues that institutions shape long-run economic growth (Rodrik, Subramanian, and Trebbi 2004; cf. Glaeser et al. 2004; Acemoglu, Johnson, and Robinson 2004; Acemoglu and Robinson 2012). The term institutions can mean many things. Institutions can be formal organizations, or informal though repetitive practices and interactions. Formal de jure rules of political institutions have a wide range of effects on how markets function as well as on levels of investment, innovation, and effort. Informal institutions shape de facto *governance*, and involve the real, on-the-ground ways that public sector agencies and private sector groups and individuals shape the rules along with their application, how they affect transactions among people, how they select or exclude people from activities, and how they mobilize beliefs and norms in so doing (North 2005). In the overall puzzle of explaining regional economic development, the area of institutions is perhaps the most complex and least well-explored space. Let's now compare the idea that specialization could originate from the region's institutions.

FORMAL INSTITUTIONS IN REGIONS

As noted in chapter 5, when it comes to metropolitan regions, formal government institutions are intricate assemblages of local, semilocal, and regional government agencies. Moreover, their powers are limited when compared to those of states—so a lot of what formal institutions do to affect city-regional development is actually within the formal institutions at other geographical scales where most economic policy matters are settled.

Most metropolitan regions do not have unitary or federal structures for the limited powers that they do possess.[2] The reasons for this are complex. Urban planners like to complain about them as a historical legacy, where smaller units are swallowed up into increasingly large metropolitan regions, but without consolidating authority, so that these regions then become, according to them, "ungovernable." There is a compelling reason for this "integration with fragmentation." The reason is, of course, that people want a say in affairs at the scales of their daily interactions, and these scales do not change all that much. The same planners who often rail about ungovernability are also frequently the advocates of local mobilization and participation as a way to match spatially heterogeneous preferences with responsive government. In democratic countries, we are therefore stuck with the patchwork.

Though local authorities are fragmented, they have considerable power. The most obvious formal power that localities and (in many places) regional authorities have to affect economic development is in the regulation of land use along with major public investments like infrastructure. As we saw in chapter 2, some economists believe that greater restrictions on land use will drive up housing prices and in turn have a selection effect on the labor force (selecting for high-skill, high-wage labor), which then would price in certain specializations and exclude others (Saks 2007). But it seems more probable that regulation principally affects the intraregional distribution of changes in the housing stock (since in reality regulation is almost all municipal) rather than whole interregional capacities to add housing (this is because all metro areas have extensive local margins: their suburbs). In the evidence presented in chapter 2, real wages differ among US urban areas; housing prices are thus not high enough in the high-wage areas to eliminate real wage differences. Additional econometric tests, furthermore, suggest that it is the job composition of regional economies that drives housing price differences, precisely because factor proportions in industries are not elastic among regions (van Niewerburgh and Weil 2009). So land use regulation is not a fundamental determinant of the overall regional level of growth or income.

We can now think about another dimension of these fragmented institutional structures. If they are so fragmented, is there some way that they might shape the regional political process more generally, and determine how political attention is shaped and policy agendas established (Jones and Baumgartner 2005)? Political economists theorize that there are trade-offs between the efficiencies that can be gained from the greater size of jurisdictions and the losses generated (Alesina and Spolaore 2006). The bigger the unit (e.g., a city, region, or nation), the more likelihood there is that there are more heterogeneous preferences of the people within it, and hence the likelihood that many of those preferences will get "washed out" in the conflicts and compromises that must take place in big jurisdictions, or at least will involve higher transaction costs for decision making. In international growth studies, the performance of countries can be partially attributed to how successfully they combine the advantages of scale without creating such contradictory preferences that clear decisions become impossible (Alesina and Spolaore 2006).[3] A large and homogeneous country, for example, would have both high scale and low conflict over what to do; a small but heterogeneous jurisdiction would be handicapped by a lack of both scale and internal agreement. Yet

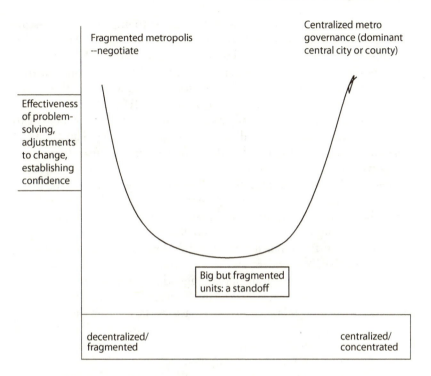

Figure 6.3 The formal structure of regional institutions.

a large and heterogeneous jurisdiction might lie somewhere in the middle, as would a small and homogeneous one.

This reasoning can be applied to the patchwork of formal metropolitan institutions: the size structure of jurisdictions might influence voice, preference aggregation, coalition formation, and decision making (or the definition of policy agendas) in different metropolitan areas (Carruthers 2002; Kenyon and Kincaid 1991; Kenyon 1997; Peterson 1981). In a region with many small jurisdictions, localities have more homogeneous preferences and lower costs of debate as well as compromise, allowing more initiatives to see the light of day. Those initiatives that require scale, however, will only be capable of implementation through cross-jurisdictional coalition building, which has high transaction costs and a high probability of imposing unsatisfactory compromises. Regions with less fragmentation (bigger, more internally heterogeneous jurisdictions) may have problems in reaching decisions and hence generating novelty, but once decisions are made, these regions can more easily implement large-scale projects. This reasoning leads to the hypothesis that the "worst of all worlds" in terms of the de jure structure of decision making would be to have neither what promotes consensus nor sufficient centralization to implement large-scale regional projects (cf. Rose-Ackerman 1983; Stiglitz 1982). This type of formal structure can be expected to generate a standoff or blockage.

In addition to the above, most large cities and city-regions—world-wide—have complex *internal* jurisdictional structures. As shown by Philippe Aghion, Alberto Alesina, and Francesco Trebbi (2002), as cities become both larger and internally more heterogeneous, the propensity to divide political authority into districts or wards increases. The ability of a big city or country (or *Länder*, *département*, or province) to exercise the "power" of its size in a region will depend in part on how it organizes its internal decision making. This in turn depends in part on its forms of local government (such as a strong versus weak mayor), how well the district boundaries group together inhabitants who share similar prefer-ences, and the organization of voting coalitions between districts.

The formal institutional structure of a city-region is thus intimidating to the researcher. Yet understanding it better offers promising insights into the formation of regional policy agendas, the pattern of decision making, and the long-term effects of these on specialization and incomes. Unfortunately, as of this writing, there are no large-scale detailed data sets on the formal structure of institutions at the metropolitan level that would enable a systematic evaluation of the impacts on agenda setting and hence regional economic development.

INFORMAL INSTITUTIONS AND REGIONAL ECONOMIC DEVELOPMENT

City-regions often manifest strong differences in their de facto informal political cultures and forms of political mobilization. Some city-regions have longer traditions of intense community action and established pat-terns of government-business-community cooperation there, while others have much more top-down political cultures, for example (Logan and Molotch 1987). Social capital indexes, which measure such patterns of participation, show that there is much more participation in some city-regions than in others, though the meaning of this for political outcomes has not been firmly established (Putnam 2000). On virtually every mea-sure of social capital, for instance, the San Francisco Bay Area was higher than the Los Angeles metropolitan area in the period between 1980 and 2005. Did this have anything to do with the superior economic perfor-mance of the former region, and if so, what were the precise mechanisms by which it affected performance?

A different view is that the regional politics that affect economic de-velopment are structured less by the broad outlines of civic participation than by narrower sectoral interests. Specific business or civic elites may

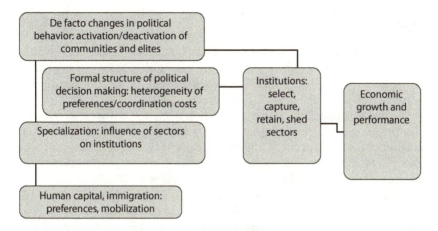

Figure 6.4   The sources of regional institutions.

shape political markets for ideas as well as the policy formation process in a region (Dahl [1961] 2005; Cox 1993). Powerful landed interests may also shape the choices made about urban development, especially in land use, through the place-based politics of landowner and developer groups (urban growth regimes) (Molotch 1976). In this way, sectional preferences can find broad expression through lobbying, interest peddling, and other means of dominating the resource-allocation and policy-setting processes. These two concerns come together in the interesting question of how the broad institutional structure and political process of a region interact with its sector-specific interest groups and institutions, such as business associations (Jaher 1984; Persson and Tabellini 2006).

Figure 6.4 depicts the possible role of institutions in shaping regional human capital, specialization, and performance.

INFORMAL INSTITUTIONS: ACTOR-NETWORKS AND THE REGIONAL "SOCIETY"

The elite networks that influence agenda setting are, in essence, informal institutions. Informal institutions involve complex, dispersed collective action processes that are largely hidden to the naked eye. Moreover, they concern much more than elite processes directed to the deliberate use of public power to extract rents and influence land development, involving action from many domains, both elite and nonelite.

Informal regional institutions can be conceptualized most effectively as actor-networks. Such actor-networks have many impacts on the economic development and performance of metropolitan regions. Key among them is mobilizing knowledge and causing it to circulate; bringing together entrepreneurs, knowledge, capital, and human capital; organizing political attention in local and regional government as well as securing resources from other scales of the public sector (notably national governments); and creating the symbolic and political legitimacy of economic activities that smoothes political transaction costs for specific needs. Such actor-networks might be those of specific groups or "communities," or crosscutting structures, involving informal bridges between communities or formal coalitions among them. A key to understanding regional economic performance and change is to know how the actor-networks that affect economic development are formed, maintained, reshaped, or eliminated (Padgett and McLean 2006; Powell et al. 2005).

Economic sociologists such as John Padgett and Walter Powell (2012) argue that informal actor-networks have a particular role in the adaptation of regional economies to change through what they label "transposition." In response to technological or market challenges, the key tradable activities of a region must evolve. Within a broad cognate area of activity (e.g., finance, high tech, mechanical engineering, and health care), such evolution depends on whether skills can be transposed from existing activity and applied to new ones (Owen-Smith and Powell 2004, 2008a, 2009b). Past examples of it abound, as when the agricultural machinery and bicycle industries of the US Midwest in the late nineteenth century were transposed into the emerging car industry. Transposition is not automatic, though; it requires actor-networks to do it, because precisely the kind of skills and knowledge that go into such adaptation are not codifiable and transferable through anonymous market mechanisms. They are "embedded," to use the language of Mark Granovetter (1985).

Both the normal functioning of networks and transposition seem to depend on particular kinds of agents, who carry out the work of going back and forth between networks, or between critical agents within networks. They are the human bridges between the specific actor-networks that underlie the regional economic system. There is a wide and narrow sense of these bridges. To the extent that individuals are members of different networks, sociologists believe that the probability of one network being able to influence the other's agenda or mobilize it for its projects will be greater (Safford 2009). Thus, regional actor-networks have two principal components: the core communities that exist and the interests they represent, and the degree of overlap or interconnection among them. Another way to phrase this is that interconnections among them are the bridges.

The deep informal structure of regional networks should have a major effect on which regions win and lose in the process of capturing, sustaining, and changing the activities—dynamic specialization—that generate regional income levels and population changes. In concentrating on these largely invisible and in many cases informal sets of actor-networks as well as bridges among them, what place does this leave for deliberate, formal, or organized institutional action for regional economic development? Organized action reflects the power of deeper informal networks; it is the tip of the iceberg in this sense. To take an example, the metropolitan transportation commissions of many city-regions in the United States are similar in formal structure. But their performance varies widely, with some actively pushing a regionalist agenda, and others just serving as a cover to receive state and federal funds (Woeffray 2012). In reverse, such deeper networks can block the successful functioning of organized projects; when Los Angeles went through an economic crisis in the early 1990s involving civil unrest and the loss of its aerospace industry, the formal organizations (Rebuild LA) that were put together to rebuild the economy never got anywhere. In Paris, the complexity of local government frequently bogs down regional-scale projects, leading to regional-level councils (*Conseil régional*), themselves imposed by the central state, creating contractual structures for regional coordination (e.g., the *Syndicat de transports de l'Ile de France*). Sometimes the central state gets directly involved in imposing metropolitan-scale projects considered to be of national significance. An example of the latter is the "grand Paris" project involving the construction of a suburban "super-metro" to ring the entire metropolitan area, sixty-five new stations, and massive development projects around the stations. This type of project comes about less because the formal state authority exists to impose it—since it is in fact highly contested at the formal level—than because there are solid, consensual elite networks in favor of it that span all the major political parties and segments of the national and regional elite.

Where the Networks Are

We thus come full circle in considering how to explain the where of city-region development. The three main elements of explanation are those used by development studies: specialization, human capital, and institutions. There may well be accidental factors that initiate specialization, and there are certainly circular and cumulative agglomeration processes. But in the long run, capturing, creating, and regenerating specialization successfully requires existing networks of actors, as they are the basis of the functioning of the formal institutions of metropolitan government and governance, and they themselves amount to informal institutions that carry out the mobilization and transposition of skills and capacities across different domains of the economy as well as time periods. Such informal networks themselves consist of their primary groups and the bridges between them. The following two chapters examine this dual nature of informal institutions—groups or communities, and their bridges to one another—in detail.

Communities and the Economy

Cities and Their Communities

In the early twentieth-century United States, the Progressive movement attempted to reform urban political institutions by combating the "capture" of city governments along with their use for private gain by clans and mafia-like political networks. Such groups did not disappear, but limited checks and balances on their use of public power are typically now in place in most advanced democracies, although enforcement is highly uneven.

In practice, however, there is little agreement on when groups or informal networks are beneficial, and when they are bad for the economic life of a city. When the African American elite of Los Angeles managed to create and sustain the Baldwin Hills Estates Homeowners Association, it was viewed as a positive image of citizenship and civic improvement. Is it the same for the wealthy white homeowners around the university where I teach (the University of California at Los Angeles) who have blocked additional high-rises in nearby Westwood Village? Do such groups express wider societal preferences, thereby balancing out the narrow interests of developers, insensitive bureaucrats, and the politicians in their pay? In economic matters, do an urban labor union, a campaign for living wages, an apartment owner's association, and a building industry association contribute in the same way to economic governance? Does a disorganized civil society facilitate change by narrowing the power of interest groups, or does an organized one promote and shape it in a positive direction by giving voice to a wider set of interests?

In this chapter, I take the first step in deepening the analysis of the informal institutions that underlie economic development. The basic compositional element of such institutions is groups or actor-networks. In what follows, I will use the terms groups and actor-networks interchangeably with the sociological term communities to refer to informal institutions.

Should Community Have a Bad Name?

Community has a bad reputation in economics and institutional theory. It has a bad name because there is ongoing pessimism about the relationship between groups and individuals, and groups and the society as a whole. In economics, public choice theory, the economics of information, and contract theory all emphasize the ways that group membership frustrates individuals' attempts to satisfy their preferences. According to them, once we join a group, the group has positions that are often far away from our individual preferences. Leaders can never represent each of us perfectly, and instead tend to try to find some unsatisfactory compromise (this is known as the principal-agent problem). Groups, by their very nature, exclude some persons and hence create insider-outsider dynamics. If the economy is organized into groups, which defend their narrow interests, then it becomes harder to reorganize markets and firms in response to competition, new technologies, and changing demand, and therefore harder to sustain growth. Communities, in other words, create sclerosis (Olson 1965).

In contrast to the negative view of communities as structures that block efficiency, much of economics and political economy is favorable to formal institutions that enforce broad rules of the game, providing order and stability in which markets can function. Such institutions limit the damage that informal or interest-based groups can do through things like property rights, the rule of law, constraints on the executive, individual rights, and limits on monopoly power. Good formal institutions protect markets and individuals from the ravages of the informal or interest-based networks of communities.

But community has a better name in other academic quarters. The "blocking" view of community has been countered by arguments that communities can sometimes make exchange more efficient, and that they can do so because they "empower" individuals to identify and act on their preferences. When we know our preferences, we mobilize our efforts to satisfy them, and this enhances growth and efficiency.

In spite of these two recognized sides of informal institutions, we remain locked into an unfruitful debate about whether we should have more or less group life. A better way to frame the issue is what kinds of tasks we expect informal institutions—communities of actors—to carry out.

Interaction: Interpersonal Relations and Impersonal Exchange

In the eleventh century, the Maghribi traders around the Mediterranean faced a problem. These descendants of Jews who had fled the Baghdad region in the tenth century had a close-knit community, but they needed distant agents for their commercial transactions—agents who they could not monitor directly. Avner Greif (1993) shows that this community functioned according to the *lex mercatoria* ("merchant law"), such that any agent who cheated others would not be rehired by any member of the community for a long time, and the options available to such an agent were substantially reduced by such potential exclusion.

From the vantage point of economics, anything that minimizes transaction costs per unit of output is going to raise the potential output. Such costs can be associated with information gathering as well as an evaluation and determination of the reliability of information along with the possible moral hazards of relationships. Group membership can assist in all these dimensions of transacting, through reputation effects, signaling, and the gatekeeping/filtering of participants.

Along these lines, Francis Fukuyama (1996) argues that economies with greater generalized or impersonal trust will more easily build large firms, extending the circle of exchange beyond what it could achieve through personalized (boss) control. Nonrepressive states are the ultimate "wide circle of trust" we have with people we do not know personally. But impersonal trust can also be enhanced by communities such as the Maghribi traders in the sense that we agree to transact with people we don't know, because enough of the people we do know have admitted them to the network of the trusted. A more recent example is the way in which the world high-tech economy emanating from Silicon Valley has been extended to China, India, Taiwan, and Israel through the ethnic communities that AnnaLee Saxenian (2006) calls the "new argonauts"—extensions of impersonal exchange that would not be able to take place without underlying interpersonal networks that define admission into communities.

Greif (1993) asks whether the merchants law was a second-best solution in a world where stable, spatially extended institutions that could guarantee exchange were effectively absent.[1] But in economic life on the ground, it seems often that larger-scale institutions begin as community-based interactions. Technological and organizational innovations almost invariably require small-scale and trust-based interactions to start with, because of their high levels of uncertainty and lack of formality. These activities then sometimes ultimately institutionalize themselves; they "scale up" their successful practices or reorganize them as scale increases. As they do so, they use the language and draw on the judicial power of formal rules.

Take the example of high-tech start-ups in Israel. A high proportion of them involve former members of the Israeli Defense Force's Unit 8200, a part of the signals intelligence branch of the Israeli military:

> Yair Cohen, another former commander of the Unit, argues that "it is almost impossible to find a technology company in Israel without people from 8200, and in many cases the entrepreneur, the manager or the person who had the idea for the project will be someone from 8200. (*Financial Times*, December 1, 2011, 14)

The ubiquity of Unit 8200 alumni in the high-tech sector is largely due to their personal connections. When hiring new engineers and programmers, many Israeli start-ups turn to their former unit, safe in the knowledge that the military has invested heavily in selecting and training its recruits. The unit is an impersonal filter for talent, but membership is interpersonal. By contrast, where scaling up and widening of impersonal relations does not occur, there will be blockage of economic development, as happened in the 1990s in the textile-producing districts of the Third Italy or the jewelry producers of downtown Los Angeles.

Discovery: Knowing What We Want

Does belonging to groups help or hinder an individual in achieving their preferences? There are several parts to this question: knowing what we want (the formulation or discovery of preferences), acting on what we want, and aggregate choice of what we want (making choices).

Until recently, economics eschewed any interest in knowing what we or others want. Social choice theory claims that we cannot know the preferences of others and hence we cannot expect in any meaningful way to align our actions to achieve common goals (Robbins 1938; Arrow 1951). Public choice theory holds that merely being interested in what others want (except in a self-interested way) is likely to involve us in stifling our preferences, because it requires deference to others and to reducing our ambitions to the limited goals we perceive as being jointly achievable.

Yet this idea of a fundamental conflict between discovering our individual preferences and belonging to social networks is misplaced when preferences are intrinsically interrelated.[2] Behavioral economics shows that individual decisions are based on local influences, which we experience in the form of *situations*. Membership in communities (groups or networks) can be thought of as a strategy for supplying ourselves with situations. If groups give us access to situations that help us to know what we want, and in a noncoercive way, then group membership can clarify our desires to us (cf. Bowles 1998).[3]

For instance, the supply of situations might simply be a parameter for individual maximizing behavior. If my neighbors are all members of a racist community, then my payoffs to being racist will rise. If, on the other hand, there is an antiracism group in the area, the existence of this situation changes my payoffs to being not racist. It could well be that joining the antiracism group changes my perceptions of race by giving me information I would otherwise not have. A more subtle distinction, however, is that interaction within and between groups doesn't just provide me more information, it also supplies me with experiences and examples that intersect with my own view of myself, and hence exercise an impact on how I define my preferences (Young and Durlauf 2001). This process of self-discovery is not considered in standard approaches to situations. It is difficult to have a full explanation for the persistent German success in high-quality engineering without bringing in the formation of the identity of the artisan and engineer.

This identity has certain national dimensions in Germany, but is also strongly regionalized and localized, with specific additional dimensions of the Bavarians or those from Stuttgart (Storper and Salais 1997).

Another aspect of the supply of situations is the way we define our welfare goals (Akerlof and Kranton 2000). Amartya Sen (2002) distinguishes between self-centered welfare (which involves no sympathy or antipathy toward others), self-welfare goals (in which maximizing may or may not involve attaching importance to the welfare of others), and self-goal choices (not restrained by the recognition of other people's pursuit of their goals). These three requirements—generally imposed jointly in economic models of choice—are in reality independent of one another. For example, one can violate self-centered welfare (someone else's misfortune affects our welfare), but this does not tell us whether or not their self-welfare goal will contain this criterion or not. People have subjective differences (how they process information) as well as differences in their situations (the information they encounter). When combined, the two generate widely varying propensities for self-welfare goals to take into account the reality of others' lives.

Membership is not a simple sympathy device—sensitizing us to others' welfare and integrating it into our own welfare goals. It can also be an instrument of learning and understanding ourselves, and hence of defining our preferences, whether those preferences turn out to be strictly selfish or more generous. Sen (2002, 215) argues that "we all have many identities that are . . . depending on the context, crucial to our view of ourselves, and thus to the way we view our welfare, goals or behavioral obligations." Ronald Dworkin (2002, 227) contends that a liberal community—one that allows individuals the autonomy to engage in self-discovery and helps them to do so—is not a "superperson, [which] embodies all the features and dimensions of a human life." In the liberal view, community is an important source of resources for self-discovery, but it is not a crushing, all-encompassing machine of total socialization. It can facilitate self-discovery when it is partial, because we can then be members of many communities, and we can have the possibility of exit.

If membership in groups helps actors to know what they want, then larger-scale patterns of institutional development will differ according to the basic tissue of group life. There will be different opportunities for "principals" to learn what they want. Innovation, for example, can be "pulled" by the demand of consumers for design, performance, and quality, which they only learn and sustain through communities (information acquisition, communication, and identity), and then sustained economically through network externalities. Innovation can also be "pushed" through producers' communities of practice; there are norms, capacities, and routines, gatekeeping among, for instance, fashion designers or engineering groups. These communities of practice can help in the work of discovery, and thus give a strong imprint to the cities and regions where they are concentrated. I will discuss this as a source of the genius of cities in chapter 10.

A key question for urban and regional development is to distinguish between those communities of practice that enhance discovery and those that tend to block it. In other words, in examining the group life of a city-region, we want to know not just about groups as defenders of their interests—the typical approach taken in political economy—but also about how they may allow or promote self-discovery for their members, what kind of discovery, and how this relates to the evolution of the capacities of local individuals, firms, and governments.

Getting What We Want: Agency and Voice

Any possible contribution to economic efficiency that could come from helping individuals to discover their preferences must be weighed against the costs of group membership in making choices. The best-explored source of costs is principal-agent dynamics, where principals are constrained to combine (aggregate) their preferences with others, whose preferences may be different, and find an agent to represent them. Even in the ideal case where no such "agency problem" exists, there are costs in defining the "good" collectively, and this would be true even where some kind of collective action or decision is needed for any individual to get what they want. This covers an important set of real-world cases, especially at high levels of social aggregation (big groups and big institutions).

But as we move down in scale toward smaller groups, there is less probability that they describe real welfare losses and more that there are real gains. A key issue is how any economy affects the supply of such situations, notably through the way it structures the transaction costs of group membership. Different such supplies could generate huge variations from one economy to another in the aggregation of preferences and hence in their satisfaction. What types of preferences are these?

First, some outputs are indivisible and lumpy. They cannot be produced without an aggregation of supply. Public goods like public transport fall into this category, as do virtually all consumption goods with strong network externalities. Preferences can be detected through proxies (public opinion polls or elections) or organizations (lobbies). But the organizations only emerge in some cases, so an agent to aggregate and express them is needed, and if transaction costs are high this will not happen.

Second, some preferences are obscure, even to those who hold them, until they get clarified through group membership and agency—as in "discovery," discussed above. Vague desires become realities through group process as well as access to others with similar desires and agents who assist them. Demands for public services or certain kinds of culturally specific goods don't emerge spontaneously from private preferences; nor do certain work methods, ethics, or standards of quality.

Third, some preferences are shameful or stigmatized when they remain strictly private. Many minority rights or tastes fall into this category. In the 1960s, when Black Power emerged as a cultural theme in the United States, it was shameful to affirm one's blackness in looks or behavior, or for black and white individuals to form couples. Until recently, a taste for pornography was shameful, as were many lifestyles now considered legitimate. Such preferences are only initially voiced if they are transformed from fragmented individual desires to aggregates, and often it is the agents who first break the public taboo.

Fourth, some preferences are geographically or socially fragmented, so that those who hold them do not communicate. The preferences become too rare within the boundaries of any effective market area to be satisfied. But if such preferences create strong bonds, then their groups may rank them high enough to bridge time and space, thereby overcoming barriers to aggregation and giving public existence to these preferences. In social organization terms, this is the equivalent of creating a "central place" for rare preferences.

One additional aspect of aggregation in these cases refers back to my analysis of discovery. Some preferences are likely to be found in smaller groups where preferences are strong and homogeneous, and risks are lower. If such preferences are widely but thinly distributed in society, there is a double aggregation problem of first getting to small-group discovery and then aggregation to the larger scale. This has happened many times when minority movements start out small and local, and become big coalitions and ultimately big social identity categories; one clear recent example of this is gay rights.

Membership may also facilitate preference expression through the intrinsic value of being able to have a voice. Sen (2002, 159) argues for the fundamental relevance of the choice act itself. People are acutely sensitive to whether they have choice, and will often opt to make choices that affirm their rights to make choice as opposed to those that maximize their pecuniary interests, because of people's inherent attraction to criteria such as fairness, honor, and responsibility (Appiah 2010). If choice means total independence from social constraint, then groups have no role in it; but if it means being able to express things that cannot be achieved individually, then group membership will have an intrinsic value for individuals.

These agency and voice dimensions of community are directly relevant to the complex daily life of metropolitan regions with their jostling of elite, community, labor, ethnic, professional, neighborhood, and cultural groups. We need to know more about which kinds of preferences get expressed because they reach a minimum necessary aggregation threshold.

How does this affect the overall expression of preferences in different regions and what each region collectively "prefers to prefer?" While data on the politics and preferences of regions have improved a great deal in recent years, we are still generally quite far away from being able to shed much light on this question.

The Emergence of Choice

James Surowiecki (2004) contends that good, large-scale choices come about when certain conditions are satisfied, including diversity, independence, decentralization, and aggregation. He draws this from the economist's notion of the "the wisdom of crowds." This wisdom emerges because even when many actors are situationally irrational or not fully informed (in the ways discussed in the previous section), their preferences will be randomly distributed. As long as the four conditions hold, the crowd will make better choices than individuals, because the randomly distributed individual errors will be canceled out by large numbers.

There are two major objections to this view of things. First, as I pointed out in describing the discovery of preferences, mere independence is unlikely to resolve all problems of situational behavior. The wisdom of crowds theory rests on the notion that diversity, decentralization, and aggregation cancel out the effects of a situation. Yet once we admit that discovery can be improved by being in a situation, it follows that we know little about the effects of diversity and decentralization. Moreover, the standard definition of crowds seems to refer uniquely to helping offset the irrationality of the sovereign individual chooser, because then, so it goes, there will not be intractable principal-agent problems, group think, social pressure, and impacted information. But in choices involving economies of scale and sunk costs, then the interaction of many sovereign individuals may be myopic; they don't know what they would prefer to prefer. Communities of practice have an advantage in these cases because they involve what Granovetter (1973) calls "the strength of weak ties."

One of the strong points of highly decentralized, market-based decision making is that it allows for trial and error. The mechanisms of trial are initiative, mimicry, and imitation. Information cascades provide for sequential imitation. But they also are fraught with many problems—notably hysteresis, herding, and overshooting. In many markets this is not a long-term problem, because the failures that result are resolved ex post, although when they are macroeconomic or financial they can have hugely undesirable outcomes as well as become more difficult to absorb than we would like.

There are two urban situations in which group membership can be helpful in avoiding the ex post "fix-it" solution with its huge costs. One is that it can speed up the feedbacks, and hence enable corrections that weed out emerging bad information cascades to be set into place before the system goes down the wrong path. Trust, norms and conventions, meta-information, and generally anything that facilitates the rapid and transparent exchange of information are all consequences of weak ties. In cases where technological change involves high sunk costs or high costs of reversibility, then such feedbacks can raise the probability of good choices. Another situation where membership helps is that sometimes, bad choices are actually not observable until it is too late and their consequences are magnified beyond repair. We don't have enough access to the results of the choices, because the costs of obtaining or access to observing them are too high. In this case, ties to the others who have made them and the possibility hence of observing the consequences makes the feedback work better. So many of the errors of urban renewal in the United States in the second half of the twentieth century would actually have been avoided if the communities protesting them had been well organized enough to make themselves heard to developers and urban planners. And the same can be said of the construction of freeways deep into downtown areas during that period.

Note that both these features can be combined in diversified expert communities—as, for example, in the health care field. Allowing these communities of practice to carry out aggregation fulfills both these conditions, but ideally the communities should be weakly tied internally and there should be a diversity of such communities, so that a range of opinion and competition of ideas is assured within the process of getting to a decision. This is directly relevant to the elite networks that are often set up to consider questions of economic development and adjustment in metropolitan areas. The good ones, such as the Bay Area Council in San Francisco, have this quality of broad structure and weak ties; the less effective ones are typically captured by narrow sectoral or professional categories, and thus become unable to carry out the work of transposition of skills and capacities.

Club Goods and the Problem of Bundling

Groups are by nature providers of club goods and services, and this is true whether the group is interest based (Olson groups), associational (Putnam groups), or an actor-network, including geographically bounded communities. In order to get the benefits of being in the club, members must accept the interactions that underpin them.[4] All such interactions may have intended goals and impose costs that we accept to reach them; but they may also have unintended costs and consequences for members. In other words, one of the main reasons that people may engage in group blocking behavior is not because they want to do so but instead because it is the price to pay for what they perceive to be the benefits of group membership. I did not join the community of university professors in order to block change in the university; nevertheless, such a community may in fact block some positive change, which is bundled in with potentially bad changes. This is just as true of noninterest-based (non-Olson) groups as of lobbies and other sorts of rent seekers. Moreover, the outcomes of such bundling may make these consequences unclear to the chooser, or so difficult to calculate that decisions about group membership and the rules of group membership for others will be clouded in obscurity.

Actor-networks provide connections to individuals (hence empower them), but they also exclude those who are not members of the network and may have "competences" to join. The door is then open to the construction of institutionalized power by central actors in the network. If the network occupies a strategic position in some economic process (for example, making large-scale choices of infrastructures with huge sunk costs), then its role in making choices may fall short of the optimal weak ties process alluded to earlier. Such actor-networks may come to display serious principal-agent problems and Olson-type characteristics. The same may be said of the routines of a community of practice such as a professional group. It may also apply to neighborhood groups, which might impose bundles of choices that would better be disaggregated, setting up a tension between the need to aggregate in order to define preferences and exercise voice, and the neighborhood as a "Leviathan."

We can now see that the problem of bundling, explored in chapter 5, is one not merely of bricks and mortar but rather people. People bundle together based in part on their physical location (for instance, my neighborhood), but also in part on other interests, which have varying transaction costs across space and hence spatial scales. And the different bundles may not line up that well. Group membership, even in the expanded view of it outlined here, is not an unalloyed good under all circumstances.

The Welfare Effects of Community

A simple way to summarize the case made above is as follows:

$$
\begin{aligned}
&\text{Welfare effects of community} = \\
&\Sigma \,\{\text{interaction/preferences/choice enhancement}\} + \\
&\{\text{empowerment/exchange enhancement}\}-\{\text{blockage effects}\}
\end{aligned}
$$

where:

Interaction/preferences/choice = increased impersonal exchange/ productivity + discovery/incentive + increased agency/incentive + emergent choice/productivity

Empowerment/exchange = social capital + trust + lower transaction costs + better verification of qualities of partners + low-cost sanctions

Blockage = higher transaction costs, coordination difficulties + principal-agent costs + parochialism + rent extraction + bundling

This is a wide palette of possible effects. Unfortunately we lack ready-made tools to measure them accurately at the present time. But if we began to think in this way, we would be taking a first step toward understanding how well (or poorly) the associational or actor-network tissue of a city-region is adapted to improving individual utility and collective effort, which are the two principal components of welfare.

The standard literatures in political economy and institutional economics do not do this because they are concentrated almost exclusively on blocking: interests, rent seeking, and the impossibility of reaching social choice. Recent efforts in economic sociology and behavioral economics give us some ways into how informal institutions can shape preferences along with their discovery, and not always necessarily in bad ways. Recent advances in institutionalist approaches to economic development show that institutions do matter for economic development outcomes, but are mostly concerned with formal institutions and thus have limited lessons for the city-regional scale of economic development. It follows from this analysis that the field of urban and regional studies needs a way to map the informal institutions of city-regions, and measure how they empower actors to discover preferences and make good choices as well as how they may block them.

Robust Action: Society, Community, and Development

Society or Community?

Some analysts describe California's Silicon Valley, the heart of the world's microelectronics and Internet industries, as a tightly woven community whose economic performance depends on informal networks of entrepreneurs and technonerds, much in the way I analyzed in the previous chapter (Saxenian 1994; Piore and Sabel 1984). But others portray it as a set of overlapping markets, with research universities, government financing, venture capitalists, law firms, stock options, high labor mobility, brutal competition, and "accountability" (reputation) underlying its business networks (Cohen and Fields 1999). In the latter version, Silicon Valley takes US commercial culture to its limits; in the former, it is a high-tech version of informally networked communities.

Failure stories in the economic development literature share these different ways of characterizing things. We frequently find accounts (in the Western press, at least) of "crony capitalism" in Asia. Family-based production networks—certainly a form of cronyism—seem to work well in Taiwan, but they are deplored when they become clannish, as in the Mezzogiorno (Gambetta 1988; Leonardi 1995). In the garment, toy, and jewelry industries in Los Angeles, by contrast, ethnic and family networks of small firms do not seem to lead to long-term development; rather, they lock into a vicious circle of cheap products, low wages, and instability (Scott 1993). France has been viewed by some economic historians as owing its successes in economic modernization to a strong state that had the strength to "tame" staunchly localist, family-oriented capitalism (Grémion 1976; Kuisel 1981). But others complain that this same state has left an institutional void, with weak spontaneous associational capacities, making it difficult for France to have a vibrant entrepreneurial economy (Algan and Cahuc 2007; Reynolds et al. 2001; Levy 1999; Rosenvallon 2004).

Starting with Max Weber ([1921] 1968), community was increasingly seen as a hindrance to the expansion of formal, distanced, rule-bound, transparent social linkages (markets and states), held to be preconditions for constructing a successful market economy and industrial society. From Émile Durkheim onward, there have also been fears that too much society and too little community could be problematic to individuals, or even for societal development itself. European conservatism and romanticism were skeptical about modern society, which they considered excessively individualistic and hence unsustainable.[1] From the 1940s through the 1960s, there were regular warnings to social science about the importance of community, and not merely its dysfunctional progress-blocking nature (Polanyi 1944). Daniel Bell (1976), among the most prominent of these voices, warned about alienation and excessive anonymity. As a result, today there is a debate as to whether large-scale, rational, bureaucratic principles—along with the individualization, ephemerality, and mobility they seem to call forth—have not gone too far, weakening forms of community necessary to the social order (Putnam 2000; Sandel 1996; Etzioni 1996; Bellah et al. 1985; Coleman 1990; Douglass and Friedmann 1997; Giddens 1990; Fogel 2000).

A century later, most theories of the "social foundations of development" still rely on the fundamental concepts of sociology—gemeinschaft (community) and gesellschaft (society)—derived from the classical formulations of Weber and Ferdinand Tönnies, or from Durkheim's cognate notion that there are two different kinds of bonds between people—*solidarité mécanique* and *solidarité organique* (Durkheim [1893] 1984). From the late nineteenth to mid-twentieth centuries, sociologists used community to refer to forms of collective life in which people are tied together through tradition, interpersonal contacts, informal relationships, and particularistic affinities. Since then, economics and political economics have concentrated on the society side of the question. For the most part, society is formal institutions that do not depend on interpersonal acquaintance such as states, and the quintessential societal institution is the market, as a place where nonaffinity-based exchanges take place, premised on formal rules of the game, property rights, and self-interest.

In chapter 6, I argued that informal institutions are essential, along with accidents, to which regions capture specializations, and whether they are resilient in the face of external challenges. In chapter 7, we saw that informal institutions are basically communities, which can both efficiently empower or block actors in carrying out the tasks that go into economic development. In this chapter, I add another layer to the analysis of institutions: communities empower actors and enhance economic development when they are balanced out by the forces of society—the broad rules and processes that bridge groups, and bring individuals together into an overarching social order. Thus, instead of the way the debates about economic development are formulated, between partisans of society or community as key to development, such as the examples given above, I will assert that both society and community institutions are essential, and it is their interactions that matter the most.

Society and Community: Bonding and Bridging

Putnam (2000), drawing on a long line of thinking in social theory, argues that there are two types of link between persons: "bonding" among similar types of persons (class, ethnicity, background, and interests), and "bridging" between different such groups or what he terms "people unlike ourselves." Bonding thus corresponds to community as I defined it in the previous chapter, and bridging relates to the informal networks that comprise a social structure.

Virtually the entire literature that considers bonding/community and bridging/society, however, sees them in opposition or contradiction to one another. Thus, voluntary participation and civic engagement rise where there is a lot of bonding or group membership; but such group membership is strongest in more homogeneous societies, according to Putnam. So bonding is negatively correlated with bridging, and high social capital places are really just places with a lot of one component— bonding. Much of the attention to groups has taken the form of studies of civic associationalism, and most students of association have been concerned with issues of social integration rather than economics. Yet there is a long-standing concern with the role of voluntary association in social and economic development, with Fukuyama and Putnam as the most recent major entrants. For example, Alexis de Tocqueville ([1830] 1986) thought that Americans' capacity for association was one reason not only for their vibrant democracy but also for the strength of US entrepreneurship.[2] The literature is nonetheless inconclusive about the relationship between associational life and economic development. For one thing, there are many cases of weakly associational societies that have done well as developers, including France, Singapore, the United Kingdom, Canada, and Australia. By the same token, certain forms of association may hinder economic development; clans and mafias, for instance, raise overall transactions costs by creating insider-outsider structures as well as hindering the development of generalized trust and confidence. These observations suggest two points: that under some circumstances, weak groups can be compensated for by other kinds of strong institutions for organizing the economic process, and strong groups can be bad for development if they are not embedded in appropriate wider institutional structures. Stated differently, it is both the density of ties between groups that matters and the structure of such bridges (Granovetter 2001; Lin

2000). The relationship between society and community is better thought of as a dynamic, uncertain tension between bonds and bridges.

Moreover, Putnam's concept of bonding is too narrow. In their study of the Third Italy, Putnam, Robert Leonardi, and Raffaella Nanetti (1993) argue that social capital, embodied in the group life of local, family networks and civic associations, emerges through long historical processes. Actors trust each other because of their common cultural background, shared values, and strong reputation effects stemming from dense interpersonal networks. This notion can also be found in many other empirical studies of regional economic development (Becattini and Sforzi 2002).

Nonetheless, these definitions seem overly restrictive, because groups can exist in many other forms. Professional associations are based on shared norms of professional performance, not on shared history or interpersonal trust, for example. Along these lines, Neslihan Aydogan (2002) has shown that even in the presence of shallow corporate cultures in Silicon Valley, due to a high level of labor turnover, professional culture makes possible a high level of industry- and region-specific social capital. There is considerable bonding in Silicon Valley, but its networks of venture capitalists, technologists, and others have little to do with the trust- and tradition-based communities of the Third Italy. The bonds between members of a community can be activated through many different kinds of signaling and screening mechanisms. It follows that communities should not be equated with the classical notion of mechanical solidarity or gemeinschaft. In addition, groups or communities do not necessarily express themselves as organizations, deliberate associations, or Tocquevillean civic engagement.

James Coleman (1990) attempted to deal with this issue by distinguishing "primordial" from organized social capital. But he considered the former to be necessarily more powerful than the latter.[3] In my view, there is no persuasive reason to believe that an acquired professional identity, for instance, cannot be as strong as, say, a regional or ethnic identity.[4] Furthermore, a strong professional identity does not necessary take the form of organized civic associationalism or group membership. It can be the result of strong organized processes such as schooling, and subsequently be expressed in a wide variety of ways other than formal organizations. The term community will therefore be used henceforth to refer to a wide variety of actor-networks, including persons with whom we share some part of our identity, expectations, and interests.

The value of these two key modifications by Putnam and Coleman—that bonding and bridging are separate forces, and that bonding has wide as well as complex origins and takes many different forms—emerges most clearly when we consider the relationship between groups and metropolitan economic development.

Developmental Coalitions as Bridges between Groups

The political equivalent of bridging is the notion that coalitions are helpful to economic development (Lipset 1963; Przeworski et al. 2000; Rodrik 1999; Lindert 2004; Easterly 2001). A wide body of detailed, close-to-the-ground research shows that the long-term upward spirals of the East Asian, Irish and Israeli (until recently), and even Mauritian economies—to name just a few—have been made possible by intelligent developmental strategies (Wade 1990; Evans 1995; Amsden 1992, 2001; O'Malley 1998). There are many detailed differences in strategies according to local conditions and starting points, but what they share is their reliance on inclusive political coalitions.

Coalitions are said to be essential to development because they provide a context in which good ideas and policies can be implemented, allow for problem solving and conflict resolution, and counteract the tendency for special interest politics to extract rents and drag down efficiency (Easterly 2001; Grossman and Helpman 2001; Acemoglu and Robinson 2012). Much recent effort has gone into theorizing the emergence of good "developmentalist" coalitions, centering on the architecture of bridging—the different types of underlying informal actor-networks that encourage the formal actors to play the coalition game.[5]

A number of authors emphasize that underlying bonding patterns set the basic parameters for the problem of societal bridging. These patterns include the degree of racial, ethnic, language, economic, and geographical homogeneity, or the diversity of the society in question. Easterly (2001) shows that the more ethnic or racial divisions there are in a society, the greater tendency there is for rent-seeking behavior to undermine development policy and the efficient use of foreign aid. Alice Amsden (2001) maintains that societies with less income inequality have done better in implementing strategies for becoming major manufacturing powers. This is because equality between individuals cuts across groups, and makes it more difficult to disenfranchise other groups and/or subject them to rent-earning behavior by the dominant groups. It also, as Aghion (1998) points out, eliminates the disincentive to effort that extreme inequality can generate, a notion echoed by Sen (1999). In another vein, sociologists such as Alessandro Pizzorno (1980) stress that becoming a "middle-class" society was both a result of the acquiring of common values—echoing the claim made in the previous section about democracy as a form of community—and because the habits of the middle class are bridges between people with different primordial bonds, a set of practices they share, and a common language.[6] Thus, the potential for bridging depends in part on the underlying patterns of bonding. Bonding and bridging are interactive, mutually transformative processes.

In the previous chapter, we saw that groups can empower action, but they can also block intergroup cooperation. In light of the discussion above, these blocking effects are conditioned by the nature and type of bridges between groups, whose absence will strengthen blocking, but whose presence can make coalitions possible, and hence potentiate collective action or social choice.

Bridging between Networks

Jason Owen-Smith and Walter Powell (2008a, 2008b) argue that the background conditions for business deals between two agents are structured by both their social relations and the broader institutional context of their business relationship. For them, "relationships are multiply embedded and the social entanglements that make economic exchange possible are the joint outcome of both networks and institutions" (2008b, 8). What they mean by institutions are organizational fields consisting of routine and recognized practices, which themselves are embedded in networks of agents that "engage in common activities and are subject to similar reputational and regulatory pressures" (ibid., 6). Networks are essential to fields both as "a circulatory system and a mechanism for sense-making" (ibid., 23). But each particular field of activity also shapes the rationalities and strategies of agents. Therefore, institutional logics shape network formation within a field, and consequently shapes individual action within the field. The implication of this is that each region's existing institutional logics (for example, industries and dominant skill groups) will powerfully shape, although not entirely determine, the capacities of their agents to shape new networks or reshape old ones.

Most relevant to our problem of regional economic development is how bridges assist in the transposition of skills, capacities, and relationships from an existing set of activities to another, or what Powell, Packalen, and Whittington (2012) call "cross realm transposition." Bridges, as noted earlier, could potentially take many forms, including systematic interties between formal networks as well as the existence of critical deal makers, brokers, and entrepreneurs who are capable of moving between different worlds in the economic system, and offer incentives for new configurations of cooperation, entrepreneurship, and combination (Feldman and Zoller 2011).

Bonding, Bridging, and Economic Performance

This framework can now be explored by considering certain preconditions for economic development along with the ways that bonding and bridging contribute to them. The first column of table 8.1 lists three main institutional areas in which certain first-order conditions for economic growth must be satisfied: those that assure microeconomic efficiency, those that define the social policy underpinnings of such efficiency, and those that encourage effective problem solving (see also Rodrik 2003).[7] The second and third columns show, respectively, the microeconomic importance of each condition and its institutional forms; the fourth and fifth columns depict how bonding generates the autonomous capacities that contribute to each feature of development, while bridging enforces the responsibility that checks the potentially negative effects of groups.

To take the first such feature, any set of forces that systematically reduces transaction costs and moral hazards creates a microeconomic environment that signals to individual actors that they can have confidence in the economic process. This environment is reflected in their discount rates, risk perceptions, and increased confidence, and hence leads to higher expectations and effort levels.[8] These in turn encourage actors to participate in the routines that are favorable to economic development, as displayed in column three. These routines include encouraging the kind of entrepreneurship that involves innovation and leads to the growth of firms along with the variety of outputs of the economy (Casson 1995; Kirzner 1973; Schumpeter 1991), and improving the coordination of interfirm transactions. Both of these contribute to the development of a more complex and interlocking economic structure—the economy-wide division of labor—which is the sign of long-term development (Young 1928; Stigler 1951).

Confidence is directly related to the central mechanism of contemporary growth theory, which is the accumulation and application of knowledge (Romer 1986). Communities facilitate the selective affinities underlying knowledge spillovers and thus promote snowball effects in the application of knowledge. At the same time, if knowledge stays too much inside such communities—when communities mistrust each other—then such knowledge will have a limited and uneven spread. So there need to be ways of providing more knowledgeable communities with confidence that their knowledge will be well used by members of other communities.

Confidence can be strengthened in deliberate ways. The Silicon Valley Leadership Group, for example, came together at a moment of grave crisis for Silicon Valley and its main function was less to implement any direct policies than to show key actors in the valley that together they had a mass force that was likely to enable them to overcome the initial wave of deagglomeration from the valley in the 1980s. In Jalisco, Mexico, an effective coalition of local leaders in the 1990s was able to overcome pessimism about the region's ability to sustain its attractiveness to inward investors in the electronics industry through a renewed commitment to improving infrastructure, worker training, and especially ongoing good governance (Pike, Rodríguez-Pose, and Tomaney 2006).

TABLE 8.1
Bonding, Bridging, and Development

Foundations of long-term development	Principal micro-economic effects of each foundation	Institutional and routine forms of each foundation	Role of bonding in creating autonomy and capacities	Role of bridging in enforcing responsible behavior
Microeconomic: confidence ↓	Reduces transactions costs Reduces moral hazards Raises expectations and efforts ↓	Encourages Schumpeterian entrepreneur Improves coordination of firm-firm transactions Raises investment levels ↓ →	Reputation effects, shared conventions, identities: (depends on process of group formation): overcome certain information problems in low-cost way (but can encourage rent-seeking) ↑	Overarching rules promote transparency and limit rent-seeking, help to complete markets ↓
Social policy: Effective and acceptable distributional tradeoffs ↓↓	precedent encourages ongoing 'sacrifices' in face of shocks (Rodrik) Overcomes disincentive to participate and make effort (Aghion) ↓↓	Raises investments in skills Raises work and entrepreneurial participation rates Improves willingness to pay taxes (investment) ↓↓ ↑	Voice and loyalty Being in the same boat enhances acceptability Membership may involve real forms of intra-group redistribution ↑	Counteracts corporatism and distributional hold-ups Standards of fairness and efficiency constrain group demands Inter-group mobility (exit), disciplines groups ↓

Problem-solving: Ongoing conflict resolution	Participation of groups is enhanced	Better adjustment of rules governing entrepreneurship and labor markets.	Secure groups encourage coalition formation: voice that gets heard (but risk of P-A problems)	Limits to group power encourage compromise
	minimize rent-seeking from corporatism	Intelligent ideas more likely to receive support as public policy	→	Exit options, defection, make other coalitions possible, hence dynamically limit P-A problems
		Coalitions can form, avoiding chaotic instability		↓
		→		

→↓ : cumulative and/or one-way causal effect
→←: two-way interactions and feedbacks

The second feature of development is an effective social policy environment, as reflected in the distribution of the benefits and costs of growth. When there are social forces that generate acceptable distributional arrangements, such arrangements will encourage necessary sacrifices to be made when economies undergo the inevitable shocks and setbacks of any development process (Rodrik 1999).[9] Alesina and Rodrik (1994) along with Torsten Persson and Guido Tabellini (2002) argue theoretically that high levels of inequality tend to depress growth, which is consistent with the empirical evidence that shows that the highly performing Asian economies have all been characterized by limited inequality. Moderation in inequality improves the overall investments in skill creation, raises the incentives to participate fully in the formal economy and become an entrepreneur (thereby increasing participation rates and levels), and improves the willingness to pay taxes and invest. Manuel Pastor, William Lester, and Justin Scoggins (2009) have made this argument empirically for US city-regions.

No institutional arrangements resolve all problems for good. The ongoing adjustment of the rules governing investment, entrepreneurship, and the regulation of labor markets is necessary as an economy undergoes structural change in the course of development (good institutional forms at one stage are no longer appropriate at others), and as the external circumstances change (Bremer and Kasarda 2002). Thus, the third dimension of my model is problem solving.

In the fourth and fifth columns of table 8.1, I show how bonding and bridging each contributes to these fundamentals of economic development: confidence, distribution, and problem solving. Generalized confidence emerges when the pervasive information problems, attendant moral hazards, and market failures of all modern economies are attenuated, especially in their most creative and innovative activities and sectors. Groups are a low-cost way of resolving these problems by creating trust, reputation effects, and shared conventions, as occurs in the industrial districts of Europe that produce high-quality consumer goods, from Italian fashion and design products to German engineering. But communities can be prejudicial to economic development if they lead to rent seeking; as such, they must be in a delicate and dynamic relationship with the forces that promote transparency along with entry and exit as well as limit rent seeking, helping to complete markets where communities might stifle them. Generalized confidence, in other words, requires both bonding and bridging.

The same can be said of the achievement of effective and acceptable distributional trade-offs. A societal overseer cannot create these alone, nor will they come about from the spontaneous interaction of different communities with each other (and certainly will not come about from the spontaneous interaction of individual agents). Groups are based on loyalty, and they can give voice to agents whose claims would otherwise go unheard by markets.[10] Moreover, group membership has the virtue of diffusing a sense of "being in the same boat," and those who are in the boat can contribute to a mutual sense that fairness has been achieved (as well as injustice and anger). In the former case, the acceptability of any distributional trade-off is enhanced. The difficulties that northeastern Brazilian firms experience in delivering quality improvements to export markets were attributed, in interviews, to the lack of confidence that entrepreneurs have in their workers, who in turn have little confidence that it is "worth it" to improve their skills (Storper, Lavinas, and Mercado 2006).

Ongoing conflict resolution involves, at the very least, an adjustment of the rules governing entrepreneurship, labor markets, and investment. Effective problem solving and institutional adaptation come about when it is difficult for groups to practice excessive corporatism and rent seeking, and when problem-solving bridges are built between the relevant groups. The community-based social bonds referred to above provide groups a certain degree of security, allowing them to be "at the table" so that their voices can be heard, whether formally or in a more diffused manner. Societal forces, however, create limits to group power, so that the position of groups is not so secure that other coalitions are impossible. The participation of many different groups prevents the existing stakeholders from practicing negative forms of exit (resignation or winner take all) from the problem-solving process. This helps avoid the twin dangers of "bad" stability in the form of nondevelopmentalist (rent-seeking) coalitions, on the one hand, or extreme instability, on the other (Alesina et al. 1996). There is less danger that intelligent ideas will be blocked out, because the principal interest groups have less ability and incentive to bind themselves to rigid, exclusively self-serving positions. In contrast to the positive example of the Silicon Valley Leadership Group cited earlier, in Los Angeles, the Southern California Association of Governments and Los Angeles Chamber of Commerce both have been unable to engage key economic actors in learning and problem solving. Major challenges, such as the downsizing of the aerospace industry in the 1990s, followed by the out-migration of six hundred thousand engineers from the region, were met with essentially no vision for reconverting the knowledge base of those people, other than vague calls for entrepreneurship (Engel 2007). Instead of learning about the competitive challenges to a region with high production and factor costs, traditional strategies such as building bigger port infrastructure—which attracts jobs, but at low wages—were preferred, because such projects can be implemented by narrow coalitions that do not require wide and deep bridging between groups.

Checks and Balances between Society and Community

What exactly is the effect of interaction between bonding and bridging? Notice that in each area, the positive outcomes described above are based on a sort of balance, where bonding and bridging allow the positive effects of each to emerge, while each also acts as a check on the potentially negative effects of the other when taken alone. I expect that bonding without bridging or bridging without bonding lead to the less desirable outcomes described in the upper-left and lower-right cases in figure 8.1, and where neither is strongly present, development will be blocked by a combination of insufficient autonomy and widespread irresponsibility. Most of my examples here will be national, because there are extremely few good studies of institutions at the scale of metropolitan regions.

Consider the two polar opposite ideal types shown in figure 8.1. Where both bonding and bridging are extremely weak, the foundations of economic development cannot be secured: confidence will be low, distributional relations will be unacceptable due to winner-take-all behavior on the part of those who are temporarily powerful, and there will be no basis in bridging for ongoing problem solving, but merely for winning and taking from one's neighbors. Societies with weak or almost nonexistent states, beset by unstable relations between clans and tribes, figure in this category. A common error is to think of them as organized by overly strong groups, but without stable rules for bringing the groups together; if they were really strong, or at least if a sufficient number of them were strong, they would come to some kind of inclusive standoff, however imperfect, which would avoid the chaos that reigns when no group is strong enough to impose any real order on things.

In the upper right of figure 8.1 can be found most of the developed economies. All the developed economies have mixes of bonding and bridging that satisfy the basic conditions for successful long-term development, yet these "varieties of capitalism" can be found in different locations within the upper-right-hand box (Hall and Soskice 2001). France has long been considered the exemplar of a strong state that over a period of two centuries, has tried to limit the power of groups (*les corps intérmediaires*) through a legal and administrative structure that is not only quite centralized but also uses the "principle of universality" to erode local and subsidiary versions of social and economic organization.[11] Civil society has never been eliminated in France, of course, and its relationship to this strong "societal" mode of social and economic regulation can be likened to a kind of cat-and-mouse game (Rosenvallon 2004). Nonetheless, much of the work of bonding in other societies has been done, sometimes well and sometimes with a heavy price, by a bureaucratic, rationalist, and universalistic administrative machine in France. In this sense, France is situ-

BRIDGING	BONDING	
	LOW	HIGH
HIGH	Responsibility without autonomy: individual agency but insufficient collective and individual voice § Insufficient public goods § Lower confidence, higher transactions costs § Long-term, unacceptable distributional tradeoffs; § Costly conflict resolution, confrontational society	Autonomy with responsibility: good balance of voice and agency § Facilitates confidence § Facilitates sustainable distributional trade offs § Facilitates conflict resolution; § Strong society modernizes community; § Strong bonding reduces costs assoc. with anonymity;
LOW	Neither autonomy nor responsibility Chaos Law of the Jungle	Autonomy without responsibility: collective voice, but with agency problems Prevalence of "primitive" forms of community; Hierarchical relations between groups Rent-seeking groups Low-trust, lack of confidence; Unacceptable distributional effects due to rents and hierarchy; Permanent conflicts

Figure 8.1   Society-community outcomes.

ated toward the upper-left border of the upper-right cell of figure 8.1. The tendency toward high transaction costs and a lack of interpersonal confidence between agents, and toward a confrontational yet bureaucratic approach to solving problems, are the "borderline" qualities of the French mix of bonding and bridging (Crozier 1964). Some analysts believe that this has led to a vicious circle of expensive distrust that is cumulative (Algan and Cahuc 2007).

France's next-door neighbor, Italy, is the frequently cited case of a weak state and strong groups, at least in the northern two-thirds of the country. Italy is situated at the lower border of the upper-right quadrant of figure 8.1, because there is a tense relationship between groups (including families and local communities), which are sources of strength and coordination in the Italian economy, and tendencies for rent seeking and closure, which can emerge when there is insufficient competition and mobility. This system works best when it corresponds to certain kinds of industries and activities (notably those that are compatible with small-scale enterprises as well as a relatively interpersonal mode of governance of firms and their interrelations) (Storper and Salais 1997). It is much less successful when it involves large firms that require more transparent and anonymous modes of governance, and has long been a source of weakness in building "big capitalism, Italian style." Interestingly, the problem of strong bonding without sufficiently strong offsetting bridging can involve very different roles for the strongly bonded groups. Sometimes, these groups are winners, such as the financial industry today; but sometimes, political losers with strong bonds can block effective action of a weak majority in the political system (Acemoglu and Robinson 2000).

Where the system works even less well is in the Italian south, where strong groups are less subject to the tempering influence of bridging in imposing responsible behavior on them. In the lower-right-hand quadrant of figure 8.1 we find the classical cases of rent-seeking behavior and institutional sclerosis. There are other cases of autonomy without responsibility, in southern Europe and Latin America, as well as regional or sectoral examples in the developed countries. But these are cases among others, rather than a universal condition, as is held by public choice theory (Acemoglu and Johnson 2012).

Finally, strong bridging without much bonding is the dream of suppressing group life while maintaining a responsible social order; this is the notion behind certain forms of modern administrative rationality or authoritarian states. It has turned out to have few, if any, examples in reality. This is also the dream of market fundamentalists, where only individuals and the social order would exist, in a direct relationship mediated only by mobility and competition. Where the suppression of groups has been attempted in a radical way, it has usually led to the paradoxical outcome of domination by powerful clans and groups, much like the lower-right-hand case described above. It can be asked whether in certain respects, economic governance in the United States has been moving in the direction of weakening the offsetting power of groups to provide voice in the face of competition and responsibility. The disempowering of labor unions, the much-cited decline of voluntary associations, or the declining capacity of local governments to negotiate economic development faced with mobile investments might be evidence of the weakening of bonding. At the same time, the growth of income inequality and rise of rent-seeking behavior on the part of business groups that dominate policymaking through lobbying as well as political campaign contributions is weakening the basis for bridging. Thus, the increasing political power of certain industry groups might fit with a movement toward the lower-right-hand quadrant.

Transposition, Communities, and Society

How can this framework be used to consider the institutions of economic development in city-regions? In a regional economy, change necessarily centers on the ongoing adjustment and evolution of existing industries in response to the forces of technology and trade as well as the establishment or attraction of new activities—sectoral succession—as former ones die out or leave. A key part of establishing new activities that are high up the economy's wage and price ladder—innovative activities—is to lock in their agglomeration processes.

In describing the early stages of the formation of biotech clusters, Powell, Packalen, and Whittington (2009, 4; 2012) observe that three regions in the United States exhibited seemingly equal potential to develop successful biotech clusters: San Francisco, San Diego, and Boston. Each had different origins and founding models, but what all three had in common, and what differentiated them from other US regions with nascent clusters, was "similar patterns of organizational diversity and network relationship that supports sustained regional activity." Central to the success of those thriving biotech clusters was transposition, whereby "the initial participants brought the status and experience they garnered in one realm and converted these assets into energy in another domain" (ibid., 6–7). The core factors were the diversity of organizational forms, the presence of an "anchor tenant" (i.e., initial successful firms) operating under norms of openness, and cross-domain network connections.

Los Angeles, for example, was home to Amgen, one of the earliest commercially successful biotech companies in the world. The early industry had plenty of regional scientific resources to tap into, including CalTech and the University of California. Yet these research organizations failed to link themselves durably to companies in the region. In the three successful regions, the initial anchor tenants stimulated wider networks of firms and other actors, and they themselves lost their centrality to those networks, while remaining in them. In Los Angeles, Amgen did not end up playing such a catalytic role but instead developed most of its R & D partnership and supplier connections with firms in other regions. Today, Los Angeles biotech firms are not strongly connected to one another, and the regional interfirm networks have become thinner over time with the departure of the supply companies. In the successful clusters, however, local ties were formed before external ties. Once a turning point was reached for the three successful regions, such

> decisions to locate in particular regions, invest resources, and build a technical community generated increasing returns as a wider number of participants followed them, developed local norms that guided interaction, and subsequently elaborated upon these practices. Identities were learned and interests were forged through interaction, producing feedback dynamics that increased interdependence and consensus among the varied participants. (ibid.)

Long-Run Changes in Society and Community

Most studies of institutions and social capital hold that their effects on development are the outcome of long-run processes with deep structural roots.[12] This is, for example, the case of Putnam, Leonardi, and Nanetti's (1993) *Making Democracy Work*, in which the civic involvement said to be at the root of the economic dynamism of northern Italian regions is traced back to the Middle Ages. A glacial pace of change thus leaves little room for maneuver (or for that matter, hope) in those areas of the country that have been unable to develop the "right" mix of communitarian and societal institutions over the last few centuries, as is the case in the Mezzogiorno. Although the speed of change of communitarian values takes place at a faster rate in Putnam's (2000) subsequent study of US society, the pace is still rather slow, extending over several decades.

Changes in the forces of community and society can have external or internal origins. External change is the outcome of events that are independent of the internal dynamics of the groups involved. Factors such as war, natural disasters, globalization, technological change, or the insertion of new groups into preexisting contexts are likely to upset previous problem-solving arrangements. Their effects can be favorable (new civic contributions) or unfavorable (e.g., new moral hazards or power imbalances). Internal change, in contrast, stems from developments within and between the groups that inhabit a certain territory. The internal evolution of groups often leads to the alteration of or a break with previous configurations of networks, power, and compromise. Revolutions, the seizing of power by a certain group or party with a new political agenda, the implementation of major changes in societal rules (such as the major

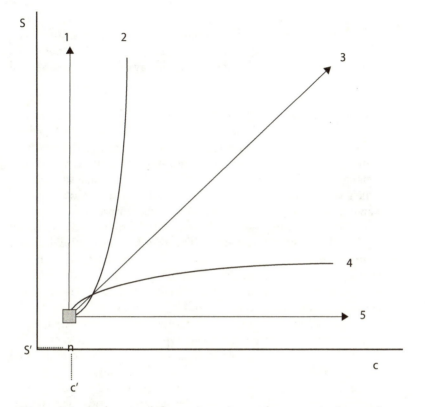

Figure 8.2   Pathways of change in society and community interactions.

devolution of powers), or the emergence of internal conflicts (ethnic, religious, or political) may significantly alter the balance of community and society forces.

The alteration in the relative strength of the forces of community and society generates what can be termed a process of "institutional migration," whose dimensions, scope, and outcome will depend on factors such as the starting point (whether the existing situation was optimal, suboptimal, or worst-case scenario), the relative weight of change in each of the forces, and the conflict-solving capacities of the preexisting situation. I will now inventory the major possible pathways of change.

Suppose that a territory n has a starting point of community and society forces represented by point (c', s') in figure 8.2. The x-axis represents the strength of communitarian forces, and the y-axis portrays that of societal forces. In this case, both bridging and bonding are weak—an example of the worst-case scenario depicted in Table 8.1 and Figure 8.1.

Suppose in addition that some exogenous or endogenous event or process alters the relative strength of these societal and communitarian forces, resulting in a change of position of point n. The direction of change in the starting point n will be determined by the interplay of both forces. Several scenarios can be envisaged:

1. If society but not community is strengthened, the displacement will follow vector 1, possibly leading to an oversupply of society, where weak interests will have insufficient voice because of the frailty of communities. Territory n would then migrate from a worst-case-scenario to a better though suboptimal institutional situation in which the stronger societal order would reduce certain kinds of transaction costs, raise confidence and the enforceability of contracts, and generate powerful incentives for certain kinds of human and physical capital investments. This is in fact the classic dilemma of many rich countries and regions: managing the tensions generated by the long-term strengthening of the societal order with respect to the weaker agents in the system. It is such a powerful tendency that most such countries and regions now deliberately assist groups of all sorts in organizing themselves and participating in "governance" processes of various types, hoping that these "civil society" groups will be able to help smooth economic and social processes in ways that official bureaucracies cannot.

2. If the outcome is an increase in both the forces of society and community, but with the former strengthening more than the latter, institutional arrangements n will migrate to a new point along vector 2. Under this scenario, societal and communitarian forces may initially develop in parallel, but in the medium run, societal forces come to prevail. This may be as a result of inherent or ensuing weaknesses in the buildup of communities, or because of the greater development of the institutions of the state after a certain point. In this case, communities may nonetheless be able to exert some checks on the potentially negative externalities generated by societal forces taken alone, resulting in better economic outcomes than under the first scenario above. Many successful metropolitan regions have done so by the creation of societal "super agencies." For instance, the Port Authority in the New York region did so in the 1930s, and the various infrastructure and New Town plans that were imposed on the Paris region directly from the central state (and that overrode local and regional authorities in many ways) were certainly key to overcoming potential development obstacles at crucial moments in their growth.

3. If change in both forces is of equal strength, the institutional arrangements in territory n will move along vector 3, eventually resulting in something close to an "optimal" institutional arrangement characterized by autonomy with responsibility along with a good balance between voice and agency. Such underlying strengths can take many different concrete institutional forms. Regionalist forces in the San Francisco Bay Area, exemplified by the Bay Area Council, and the intense involvement of environmental groups in regional governance represent an interesting case of parallel growth of the two types of forces.

4. If the increase in communitarian forces is greater than those of society, the trajectory of change will follow vector 4, leading to a situation under which community prevails, but moderate reinforcement of societal arrangements succeeds in instilling some checks on the potentially negative aspects of communities. Along these lines, Southern California was a highly successful region from the early twentieth century until the 1970s, as reflected in its ability to simultaneously add millions of people to its population while raising per capita income toward a convergence with the wealthiest metropolitan areas in the United States (most of which grew more slowly than Los Angeles during that period). Los Angeles based its dynamism during much of the post–World War II era on the pillar of a strong society with relatively weakly organized social and ethnic groups. Up until the 1990s, Los Angeles behaved much like a city-state where powerful, semiautonomous development bureaucracies and a cohesive business class provided farsighted strategic planning. But community and environmental resistance have grown significantly in recent years. As these community-based organizations have become better organized, political institutions have not kept up with them, leaving what is widely thought to be an increasingly conflictual situation in place, with growing problems of governance and negative externalities (Erie 2004). Since the 1980s, Los Angeles has fallen behind its former peer group in per capita income, opening up significant gaps in the latter with such metropolitan areas as New York, Washington, DC, and San Francisco.

5. Finally, an increase in community but not society is described by vector 5. Stronger community will generate greater autonomy for actors to exercise a collective voice and facilitate their joint action. There is likely as well to be a serious increase in the agency problems, however, such as high transaction costs, widespread rent seeking, inequality, and a lack of trust. The example of post–Soviet Russia is the poster child of this unfortunate trajectory.

Robust Action: Events, Accidents, or Structural Determinants?

In "Robust Action and the Rise of the Medici, 1400–1434," John Padgett and Christopher Ansell (1993) argue that the formation of new institutions—in their case, the state in renaissance Florence—can be understood only by penetrating beneath the veneer of formal institutions, groups, and goals "to the relational substrata of peoples' actual lives." With extremely detailed archival evidence, they show that Cosimo de Medici built the new Florentine state by finding ways to provide preexisting groups—some of whom were in competition, and many of whom were facing difficult external conditions—with new rules for interaction. These preexisting crosscutting networks were buffeted by external events (wars or fiscal crises), but they were also slowly eaten away at by their exclusion of various kinds of new actors (the "new men"). The resulting holes in the structure allowed Cosimo to knit some of the old elements together with some of the new ones and generate a dynastic state that lasted for three centuries. Padgett and Ansell maintain that Cosimo did not know exactly what he was doing when he did it—state construction was a by-product of his personal goals. In this sense, his action can be thought of as robust, because while certainly informed by his interests and those of other participants, it was not not part of a big plan, nor a calculus of optimization.

The development of Silicon Valley provides a spectacular illustration of these issues. In the late 1950s, it was not clear that an area south of San Francisco would ultimately become the world center of information technology, thereby propelling the entire metropolitan area up the US income ladder. The initial pattern of semiconductor production in the United States was quite dispersed, and if there was any nascent geographical center of gravity for the sector, it was the Northeast coast, from Boston to New Jersey; the principal forerunners of the information technology industry—that is, the radio, telephone, and television equipment industry—were all located in that region. Yet because the semiconductor industry was extremely new, it lacked a clear production process and commodity chain and therefore did not have clearly defined factor demands or even linkage patterns. There were a number of areas in the United States with abundant engineers working on what would become the new technology, from northern to southern California to the East Coast, and even in the Southwest. This is what we previously labeled a "window of locational opportunity" (Scott and Storper 1987). Such moments of openness existed in the 1900s in the film industry or the late 1920s in the US aircraft industry. In the life sciences industries, such a window appears to just now be closing around the centers of Boston, San Francisco, and San Diego (Powell, Packalen, and Whittington 2009).

There are often many places that can satisfy the initial factor requirements of an industry. Perhaps in the Silicon Valley case, there *were* many regions that were—more or less—equally well prepared to become the future world center of the information technology industries. But only one of these "candidate regions" happened to get ahead just a little earlier than the others. Is this because some actor in that place happened to be the first to come up with a breakthrough "killer application" that tipped the agglomeration economies toward that place by taking market share, causing suppliers to stream into the valley to fulfill new needs and network efficiencies to grow while other places found themselves outdistanced, even though they were about equally good as one another prior to this tipping point? The extreme version of this story of accidents or idiosyncratic causes holds that William Shockley, the inventor of the chip, moved to Silicon Valley because he wanted to be closer to his mother, who lived in Menlo Park. Agglomeration dynamics then locked in the locational structure of the industry. This kind of accidents-of-history explanation is now incorporated in NEG's basic core-periphery model (Fuchs and Shapira 2005). It fits well with the case of the aircraft industry in the 1930s, where many localities in the United States or elsewhere were equally well placed to become major centers of aircraft production, but Los Angeles got ahead because of a single event: Donald Douglass invented the DC-3 in Santa Monica, and the aircraft subsequently captured a high market share of commercial aviation. Douglass' production system in Southern California expanded as a consequence, and this tipped the geography of aircraft production there by attracting other producers that wanted access to its supply structures and rich community of knowledgeable experimenters (Scott 1993). The idea that unique events powerfully influence why some cities grow and develop one way versus another in the medium run of thirty to fifty years is a difficult pill to swallow for those who formulate urban policy, and want to predict the outcomes of their efforts and expenditures, because it implies that there is a chance element in economic development (Boschma and Kloosterman 2005; Rigby and Essletzbichler 1997).[13] In this vein, evolutionary approaches to economic development are stronger on the preconditions for subsequent evolution than they are on the possibilities for revolution—that is, changes in developmental pathways (cf. Boschma and Martin 2007).

Do these events or shocks deserve the analytic status of *fully* exogenous accidents (Sewell 1996)? It may be that certain preconditions must be satisfied even to have the possibility of the right breakthrough occurring, in order to then lock in the geography of the sector. Such necessary preconditions can be identified as statistical regularities. For high technology, there is a long laundry list of such preconditions argued to have been necessary, such as the presence of universities or certain pools of engineers. A different laundry list is used for financial centers, another for creative cities, and so on, just as in the past such lists were developed for manufacturing centers in the developed countries. But it is a regularity more akin to "climate" than to "today's weather": if preconditions exist in many places, but only some develop, then there is a wedge between broad and deep structural conditions and outcomes (Hodgson 1993), or between the necessary and sufficient conditions for such development. It subsequently becomes difficult to estimate the structural parameter linking such necessary preconditions to precise outcomes.

Such regularities might be more related to institutional context than to a precise list of factors. There are many examples in the history of innovation where superior ideas do not get implemented because they do not find such a favorable environment (Mokyr 1991; North 2005). Thus, if potential seeds of agglomeration emerge in different city-regions, they may flourish in some, but wither on the vine in others. Some noted analysts of the Silicon Valley case (e.g., Saxenian 1994) contend that it was Silicon Valley's institutions—the actor-networks of the merchant semiconductor producers and their culture of open competition—that caused it to capture the industry, and that this generated the specialization it still enjoys today as the county with the highest per capita income in the world's wealthiest economy. But once again, we fall into the endogeneity hole: Boston and Phoenix were early centers of semiconductor production, and only later on did Silicon Valley pull ahead of them. These actor-networks cannot be said to have initially caused the industry to emerge in Silicon Valley, since they emerged contemporaneously with it as a part of the growth of the industry itself. Two of the critical elements of the Silicon Valley de facto institutional context today—the venture capital industry and the legal firms that specialize in technology law—are obvious products of the valley's development; they were not there prior to the existence of the information technology cluster. The alternative institutionalist explanation holds that key actors at Stanford University (especially the dean of the Stanford Business School) established the Stanford Business Park, and through this institutional entrepreneurship allowed Silicon Valley to do better than Boston or Phoenix (Saxenian 2000; Kenney 2000). In this version of things, Motorola's massive early investments in Phoenix did not find a favorable institutional environment there, or Motorola simply made the wrong strategic choices, and hence the Phoenix agglomeration folded. Yet this wouldn't seem to be the case for Boston, which had multiple and diverse actors who saw what was happening, and tried to capture the information technology industries at the same time that Silicon Valley was also doing so. Saxenian's (1994) contention that they did not do so well in Boston because the institutionalized corporate culture there was not well adapted to the merchant semiconductor sector is convincing, but it does not answer the question of whether the institutions in Silicon Valley were the chicken or egg.

As noted above, existing networks of actors and practices can generate capacities that are useful in the creation, capture, and sustenance of new industries, new products, or branches of existing industries through transposition. In all the above examples, though, there was not only structure but also robust action. Thus Fred Turner (2006) suggests that Silicon Valley benefited from the Bay Area's antiestablishment counterculture in distinctive and important ways, mixing it with engineering and business elites to produce a new amalgam in a cutting-edge city. Richard Walker (2008) makes an analogous point in analyzing the extensive networks of tech-savvy environmentalists in the Bay Area whose networks overlapped to some extent with the new engineering and entrepreneurial groups that went into Silicon Valley. In his commencement address at Stanford University in 2005, Steve Jobs explicitly referred to the influence of the regional counterculture and especially the *Whole Earth Catalog* in inspiring him. These actor-networks—a tissue of different communities of counterculture, business, and engineering—needed to have their bridges driven across by robust actors—and these robust actors were William Shockley, Fred Terman, Stewart Brand, Alf Heller, Steve Jobs, the people at Xerox Parc, and a host of others (Brown and Duguid 2000). We can also think of the example offered in chapter 7 of the importance of Unit 8200 to Israel's high-tech economy. Robust actors created Unit 8200 to achieve one set of goals: the rapid, cost-effective development of signal detection and analysis. The effects of their actions were also felt in a powerful entrepreneurial-technology machine that was not part of their initial intentions.

Long-term processes of economic development are not, thankfully, entirely dominated by first-mover advantages. The economy also affords abundant second-mover opportunities. As sectors mature, they develop more complex internal divisions of labor, and the trade costs internal to the sector tend to decline. This leads to the possibility of the geographical fragmentation of the sector and deagglomeration of some of its activities. Perhaps more important, as an industry matures, it develops a wide variety of product outputs as well as many complex intermediate stages of production. Product differentiation and quality ladders are a basis for interplace differentiation and competition, serving as a formidable opportunity-creating device (Grossman and Helpman 1991). This leads typically to the establishment of secondary clusters. Austin, Texas, developed as a crucial, secondary cluster in the US information technology industry once the personal computer was already developed in Silicon Valley. But Michael Dell made the Austin cluster viable by mastering consumer product differentiation and improvement. He was sufficiently successful to create economies of scale in his firm and its supply structure, and hence could serve as an anchor tenant for a secondary cluster. Subsequently, the cluster has continued to move up the quality ladder.

Conclusion: Specialization in Relation to Events and Structures

Throughout the past several chapters, I have explored the forces that can affect the development of regions in general, and those that select particular places into roles within those broader systems. As noted, most economic research prefers to focus on structure and broad pattern, eschewing interest in specific places. Their formal models as well as inductively empirical approaches are structural in the sense that they seek the parameters associated with growth across a wide panel of cities. But even those models ultimately refer to decisive events when the medium-run fates of particular economies are cited. For example, Detroit declines "because" of the restructuring and decline of the US car industry; Los Angeles per capita income grows slowly "because" of a massive wave of low-skilled immigrants in the 1980s and the downsizing of the Cold War military-industrial complex in the 1990s; and Washington, DC, becomes richer "because" of rapid growth in the high-wage lobbying industry.

This ambiguity is especially potent with respect to agglomeration-generated specialization. Theories of agglomeration show that localization economies have a structural character in that once started, they can be strongly self-reinforcing, but as noted, explaining their origins may require recourse to one-off events as well as structural factors. In the framework I have developed in this chapter, therefore, human capital and institutions can be situated clearly as structures, yet specialization may be both structural and event driven. Events include the nonintentional robust action of critical agents, whose actions take hold in the context of the interaction of bonding and bridging networks, and the region's society and community.

PART III

Social Interaction
and Urban Economies

Technology, Globalization, and Local Interaction

Innovation and Local Interaction

Globalization and local interaction are complementary. This is nowhere more true than in the critical activity of innovation. Information, technology, and skills circulate in a global space more easily, more completely, and at speeds never before seen. Yet the evidence on the importance of city-regions to innovation is abundant. Rates of patenting and invention are higher in dense and—for the most part—big city-regions than elsewhere. The technological profiles of city-regions are also highly varied; city-regions specialize in different areas of innovation. Science and engineering are global, and they speak the global Esperanto of math and statistics. Yet the talented scientists who speak these languages cluster unevenly on the landscape, and their commercial ventures are highly focused in a small number of prominent places. We need to know why interactions remain local in such a borderless world of knowledge flows.

Technology can be thought of in two senses here. It is an output of the economy. But in its form as transport and communications, it is also the basic enabler of all trade and production. The cost of shipping goods from one place to another has declined relentlessly over at least the last hundred years. Edward Glaeser and Janet Kohlhase (2003) document that the share of US GDP in transportation industries has been halved over the twentieth century. They also show that the real dollar cost per ton mile for US railroad shipping has decreased nearly tenfold over a century. French data exhibit a similar trend. Pierre-Philippe Combes and Miren Lafourcade (2005) document a decline of nearly 40 percent in the cost of road freight over the period from 1978 to 1998. There is thus little doubt that unit domestic transport costs have declined significantly. The evidence on international transport costs is arguably more difficult to assess (Anderson and van Wincoop 2004). David Hummels (2007) documents a dramatic fall in air transport costs since at least the early 1970s and a significant decline in sea transport costs since 1985 (where containerization, which improved shipping quality and efficiency, led to higher prices between 1970 and 1985).

This steep decline in transport costs has led many analysts to predict the "death of distance" (e.g., Cairncross 2001). But distance is not dead; it is not even sick. Evidence abounds. More systematic proof provided by Russell Hillberry and Hummels (2008) shows that in the United States, shipments within six kilometers are three times larger than shipments beyond this radius. How can such local interactions remain so important, and possibly become even more so, when transport costs decrease? Anecdotes also abound on the living force of distance. After an initial wave of offshoring service centers and data processing in the early 2000s to places such as India, many firms had to re-onshore at least parts of their consumer service chain; there were too many breakdowns in quality. And Boeing's ambitious—or some would say hubristic—notion of producing its 787 Dreamliner through an outsourced and offshored global production chain cost it four years of delay between 2008 and 2011, and will have cost it billions of dollars in lost markets. Earlier on, and at a smaller geographical scale, Airbus had a major breakdown in the production of its A380 superjumbo, because the wiring harnesses fabricated in Germany didn't fit together properly with fuselages fabricated in France. Both of these major problems were attributed to the breakdown of coordination at a distance—in this case within a single firm.

Some firms such as Walmart or IKEA source from global supplier chains. But other globally successful firms, such as Zara, have maintained strong local clusters in design and some production (Ghemawat and Nueno 2003). In Germany, Munich is the core of a cluster of big car firms and their input suppliers—the famous *mittelstand* firms. Is this an anachronism of Bavarian conservatism, or a model for successful production and innovation? The possibility of communicating in raw terms—cheapness and access—doesn't mean that actual communication is easy across long geographical distances and cultural borders. Thus, London has a much higher rate of placing phone calls to Norwich than it does to New York, the other major financial center across the pond, and New Yorkers call Miami and the Dominican Republic much more than they call London (Reades 2010).

Innovation and Trade Costs: The Paradox

The persistence of local interaction is not surprising; historically, every previous transport revolution has increased urbanization and urban density (Pred 1973).[1] The main reason for this seeming paradox is that reduced transport costs can generate rising trade costs. They do so by making local and distant activities able to interact more. This in turn increases the ability of the economy to combine and recombine things, and this then opens up possibilities for making more varieties of products as well as more complex ones, and to change them more frequently by recombining inputs and equipment. All these latter features of the economy, because they involve more interaction, tend to have high trade costs. This feedback relationship is the one that generates new waves of urbanization of highly skilled people and innovative firms while at the same time allowing certain (more routinized and generally large-scale) activities to be peeled away and spread out. In this chapter, I will examine the different facets of this fascinating dynamic of the local and global in the production and use of technology.

A STYLIZED CASE AND A MODEL

As a way into this problem, let us consider a stylized example, drawing from Meric Gertler's (2004) study of distance and trade costs in the machinery industry. In this industry, the design, development, customization, installation, start-up, servicing, and updating of complex pieces of equipment require frequent interactions between producers and end users.

A machine has to be bought from a machine producer. The higher the quality of the machine is, the higher the marginal productivity of labor for final goods that are produced by the user of this machine. Machine-making firms can produce higher-quality machines at an increasing (labor) cost to themselves. Each machine is specific to its final user, and requires a lot of servicing and adjustment to obtain the quality as well as productivity desired. This leads to a risk for the consumer of the machine that the quality will not be as expected, but that they will not be able to get out of the deal afterward, having sunk a lot of cost and time into it. In the absence of trade in machines between countries, final producers buy their machines locally.

But when we allow for international trade in machines, better machines can be obtained abroad. To obtain them, however, there are higher total trade costs. These trade costs are high because they consist of user-producer relations. Machine producers must customize the machines for their customers, install them, and train their workers to use them. When machines are exported, all these operations involve a large amount of traveling back and forth between the two countries. Thus, lower transport costs lead to better-quality machines for exports and higher wages in the importing country, as they make it possible to import potentially better machines where formerly there was a barrier.

This explains Gertler's (2004) example of the failure of Canadian and US manufacturers to adopt the latest generation of machinery, mostly produced in Germany, in the 1980s and 1990s. Having to modernize their equipment, manufacturing firms in the US and Canada faced a scarcity of competitive local machinery producers. Instead, German producers were perceived to offer superior custom-made products. Nevertheless, buying machinery from German producers turned out to be difficult because of all the transaction costs mentioned above. US and Canadian manufacturers often ended up with machines that were well below what they expected even after they incurred large costs of installation, training, and servicing. German machine producers also ended up dissatisfied because despite their efforts, their machines had much worse performance in North America than at home with German manufacturers. Beneath all this is an indication that the cost of trading machines across the Atlantic has increased—not decreased—over time.[2]

Thus, when a strong distinction is made between *transport costs* (i.e., the physical cost of a shipment) and *trade costs* (i.e., the sum of all the costs incurred to deliver a good to its user, including in this case significant back-and-forth exchanges between the machine producer and its end user), a decline in transport costs need not imply a decrease in trade costs.[3] In this way, trade costs can be seen to be endogenous and may not monotonically increase with transport costs. Lower transport costs may, in particular, act as an incentive to produce goods for which overall transaction costs are higher and therefore more costly to trade.[4] This means that one form of technological innovation—transport—can create a feedback effect that raises trade costs.

But this is not all. The dissatisfaction described above ultimately led to the development of a local service sector to maintain the better-quality imported machines. Hence, long- and short-distance interactions are not linear substitutes but instead are frequently complementary.

David Hummels and Alexandre Skiba (2004) look empirically at these issues for a broad cross-section of goods imported in the United States and five Latin American countries. They focus on shipping costs (the part of trade costs that can be measured using customs data). Shipping costs have both a per unit component (e.g., the energy cost of a given shipment) and an ad valorem component (e.g., tariffs or insurance costs). Interestingly, Hummels and Skiba find that higher per unit shipping costs are associated with higher-quality goods—a feature consistent with Armen Alchian and William Allen's (1964) prediction that the "good apples" are shipped away and the lower-quality ones are consumed at home (Hummels and Skiba 2004). In contrast, higher tariffs (i.e., higher ad valorem costs) are associated with a lower-quality mix.

Another instance of this paradox can be found in the wine industry. The bulk of wine consumption in Europe used to be low-quality wine transported directly in containers. The trade costs for low-quality wines were probably quite low. Today, wine quality is much higher, and bottles rather than containers need to be shipped. This makes the shipping of wine much more difficult—all the more so since the temperature and storage conditions must be closely monitored. On the consumer front, the number of varieties has also considerably increased, making the choice of wine much more difficult, and the same is likely true of many other goods and services. As in the machine industry, trade costs for wine are also likely to have increased following an increase in product quality. Still another example may be found in the clothing industry. The Spanish firm Zara now has stores in many cities around the world. Its policy is to turn over about one-third of the product mix every ten days, and to do so differently from one store to another, depending on the local market. As a result, Zara's trade costs to market outlets are relatively high. Moreover, in order to innovate in product mix so rapidly and continuously, the firm has agglomerated much of its supply chain in the Basque region of Spain. This clustering facilitates rapid decisions on new clothing items, because Zara can use face-to-face contact with designers and suppliers, and the firm relies on reputation to select suppliers and cooperative relations with them to roll out the test versions of new clothing items quickly.

Anne-Célia Disdier and Keith Head (2005) along with Combes and Lafourcade (2005) also documented an increase in the sensitivity of trade to distance, and Matias Berthelon and Caroline Freund (2004) find that this evolution is not the outcome of the composition of international trade having shifted toward more distance-sensitive industries but rather one within industries.[5] Along these lines, there is some empirical evidence that overall trade costs have indeed increased in the last thirty years; this can be interpreted as proof that the dynamic feedbacks described above apply to many sectors. In his estimation of the trade cost parameter of an NEG model, for instance, Gordon Hanson (2005) finds that internal US trade costs increased between 1980 and 1990. These findings are all consistent with the logic of a feedback relationship between cheaper long-distance transport, higher unit trade costs, more variety and quality in the choice of inputs, and greater sensitivity to distance in certain user-producer relationships.

The Seven C's of Geography and Technology

The role of rising trade costs is nowhere more manifest than in the geography of innovation itself—the where of the generation of new ideas and practices in the economy.[6] Certain regions have become wealthy as technology centers, with the economic effects analyzed in chapter 4. Oddly enough, this comes at a time when we are surrounded by anecdotes and indicators about the globalization of technology. We hear incessantly about the rise of China along with its legions of scientists and R & D collaborations with Western multinationals, the rise in the number of national R & D and science ministries in the world, and the apparent rapid growth in international mobility, collaboration between research scientists and engineering teams, and the rise in scientific publications in East Asian emerging economies (Archibugi and Iammarino 2002; World Intellectual Property Organization 2007). These images correspond to four themes in the academic literature: that technology is now globally accessible; that it is globally sourced or created; that major innovation centers are emerging in new places; and that innovations diffuse globally more rapidly than ever before.

These claims could mean many things for city-regions. The complete globalization of technology sourcing, for example, might be consistent with city-regions being the principal sites of innovation, but they would become less distinctive from one another. For example, San Francisco and Shanghai would both be innovation centers, but they would directly compete with one another rather than being complementary in what they do. If more places are getting into the innovation business, moreover, then they should enter the club of economies receiving the M-A rents I described in chapter 4. The specific city-regions that do so should move up the hierarchy of regional incomes within their countries and in the world urban system as a whole in a catch-up effect that would be reflected as beta convergence in city-region incomes.

A more radical vision of the death of distance in innovation is that the playing field gets leveled among city-regions everywhere. In this case, the geography of incomes I analyzed in chapter 4 undergoes radical change. The local M-A rent-driven benefits of innovation would be driven down across the board, and we would witness broad compression of income differences among city-regions (sigma convergence). This would cut off the ability of high-income regions to outrun imitators, thereby leading to declines in their real incomes. The space-time diffusion process I described in chapter 4 would be radically altered.

There is also no agreed-on way to measure the overall technology levels of different economies. In recent years, the most advanced methodologies have used the unit prices of outputs as a proxy for their quality and embedded technology or knowledge. Tom Kemeny (2011) finds that there is overall stability in the degree of unevenness of technology in the world, as shown in its gini coefficient, the coefficient of variation, and other dimensionless indexes of variance. This stability masks two important dynamics. On the one hand, a club of modestly sophisticated economies has emerged from extreme backwardness, and this has increased the average world absolute technology level. On the other hand, there is a positive skew to the world distribution, with the initial developed world leaders who have outpaced the rest (Castellacci and Archibugi 2008).

One can thus view these facts as either a glass half-empty story of the ongoing global hierarchy or a glass half-full story of the spread of technology that is bringing more capacities to more places. Since we don't know whether technological capacities are linear or not, it is impossible to say whether the spread of the last few decades is building up steam for an eventual takeoff of certain developed areas as well as a shake-up in the global hierarchy of technology creation and use.

A fair guess is that the overall spread of technology contains within it a great deal of uneven development between countries and city-regions. Moretti (2012) argues that a new "great divide" has opened up among North American metropolitan regions—a distinctive pattern of innovation hubs outdistancing other regions. This pattern maps well onto the metropolitan income dynamics I analyzed using a modified NEG framework in chapters 2–4. There are some other differences among major world regions. In the United States, metropolitan regions are highly specialized in both what they produce and innovation, and the rate at which patentors cite one another regionally has actually risen in recent years (Sonn and Storper 2008; Ács 2002; Feldman 1994). In Europe, regional economies are more diversified and less technologically specialized than in the United States (Crescenzi, Rodríguez-Pose, and Storper 2007). China seems to be more like the United States and India appears to be more like Europe as they consolidate their urban systems as well as geographies of innovation (Crescenzi, Rodríguez-Pose, and Storper 2012). The cutting-edge activity of the economy is more and more localized in cities, because of the way it is strengthened by lower long-distance trade costs. Within this general pattern of the continuing urbanization of innovation, there are winner and loser places along with a great variety of different innovation profiles.

There are many forces that shape these geographical patterns of innovation. In what follows, I examine seven of them, or what I label the seven "C's:" codes and communication; channels; clustering; communities; context; coordination; and competition.

CODES AND COMMUNICATION

Technologies depend on different kinds of knowledge, which relate to distance differently. Basic technologies that have been around a long time rely on knowledge that has been boiled down to forms that can easily be copied and used. By contrast, technologies that are basic and new have generally not been subject to investments in rendering their embodied knowledge widely accessible. Thus, in considering the costs of communicating or using technologies, we distinguish between knowledge that is codifiable and explicit, and that which because it cannot be fully codified, has a strong tacit dimension (Polanyi 1966; Balconi 2002; Gertler 2003). Tacit knowledge requires more costly investments of time, cognitive capacity, epistemic closeness, and back-and-forth efforts between inventors and users, or among users, to get the use right and have confidence in what is being communicated (Johnson, Lorenz, and Lundvall 2002). Ikujiro Nonaka and Hirotaka Takeuchi (1995) argue that within a firm, parts that relate to each other through tacit knowledge will tend to be colocated to a greater extent than those that use largely codified knowledge in their intrafirm interactions. Agglomerations also seem to have more activities that rely on tacit knowledge than the economy as a whole, as was suggested in the discussion in chapter 3 of learning as a microfoundation of clustering.

Some contend that actors use tacit knowledge to exchange codified knowledge in global networks; rather than a trade-off, their relationship is complementary (Faulconbridge 2006; Sturgeon 2003; Balconi 2002). Others argue that the process of development inexorably leads to codification, as in the product life cycle (Cowan, David, and Foray 2000), or that long-distance connections can be deliberately developed through additional investments in communication infrastructure, even in the presence of tacit knowledge (Amin and Cohendet 1999; Malmberg and Maskell 2006).

So there is probably not a perfect mapping of formal equals codified equals long distance equals large firms and informal equals tacit equals local equals small firms but rather complex combinations of these along with processes that involve learning and mixing, geographically and organizationally. At the end of the day, though, the relevance of the distinction holds: it is harder and more costly to transmit less codified knowledge over long distances. In some cases, this means that it is a force for colocation; in other cases, it brings about meeting between people as channels of knowledge transmission, and tacit knowledge may be a key tool used to apply codified knowledge over long distances. Cities are not the exclusive location of tacit knowledge; organizations and commodity chains are as well. But cities are a critical geographical scale in the use of tacit knowledge and relationships, as I will show in a detailed analysis of both telepresence and face-to-face contact in chapter 11.

CHANNELS

When we find that knowledge does or does not move over long distances, it likely has something to do with the channels used for moving it. A new highway, for example, is a channel for goods or people to move over distances. What would channels be for moving knowledge? The Internet is a channel for moving information. In moving goods or people over longer distances, we need not just the new channel but also the vehicles for going through it; a better highway ultimately requires better cars or trucks to maximize its potential. Their productivity effects are joint. The Internet is a big, wide, and cheap channel for information. But what are the vehicles or channels for going through it? The channels could be different for weakly coded information, coded but highly complex information, and coded and rather simple information.

Jane Jacobs (1969) made the classic suggestion about the city as a channel in her celebration of unplanned contact and serendipity in dense city neighborhoods. Since then, though, the research focused on knowledge transmission has identified many other possible channels. For David Mowery and Arvids Ziedonis (2001), markets are channels, but specifically localized ones, among firms. Lynne Zucker, Michael Darby, and Jeff Armstrong (1998) identify markets of star scientists and the firms with whom they collaborate, but these are not the fully anonymous, spatially dispersed markets of standard theory. Others identify organized networks as opposed to markets as the principal channels (Almeida and Kogut 1999; Anselin, Varga, and Ács 1997; Cowan 2005). Woven throughout this work on labor and entrepreneurship markets is whether knowledge transmission occurs more through formal or informal contact processes via contracts or networks (Dahl and Pederson 2004; Gordon and McCann 2005), or even through something more subtle, which is relationships among people who are members of shared "epistemic communities" (Håkanson 2005).

Long-distance mobility of persons, temporary or permanent, is also a channel of technology diffusion and knowledge transmission (Edler, Fier, and Grimpe 2011; Saxenian 2006). This can include not just migration but also events such as conventions and trade fairs (Bathelt and Schuldt 2008; Maskell, Bathelt, and Malmberg 2006), the use of foreign experts (Markusen and Trofimenko 2007; Görg and Strohl 2005), temporary long-distance worker mobility (Fosfuri, Motta, and Rønde 2001), or organized collaborative networks (Hoekman, Frenken, and Van Oort 2008). Local mobility may also play a role, as in job hopping within labor markets (Fallick, Fleischman, and Rebitzer 2006; Klepper 2005), job mobility within firms and between them (Lenzi 2006), and another form of human mobility, which is entrepreneurship, in the sense that entrepreneurs "move" within the system, changing roles, and bringing together other people, capital, and ideas, thereby generating knowledge transmission (Ács et al. 2009; Feldman 2005).

Scholars have also asked whether channels are stronger within industries or between them. If there are high geographical costs to transmission, then if costs are higher between certain industries, there will be pressure for innovative cities to be diversified; if costs are higher within innovative sectors, then such cities will be highly specialized (Glaeser et al. 1992; Puga and Duranton 2001; Duranton and Puga 2000, 2005; Feldman and Audretsch 1999).

Underlying much of this is the key question of local versus long distance, or the geographical scales of channels. There are arguments that "global pipelines" are substitutes for local contact, and hence that the geography of knowledge transmission is changing (Bathelt 2007; Bathelt, Malmberg, and Maskell 2004). But we don't know much about the shape of such pipelines, when and how they might substitute for local communication, and in what circumstances. Do global pipelines and local channels contrast in their degrees of formality, markets, networks, and reliance on labor markets versus interfirm relationships? Is each systematically related to different mixes of tacit and codified knowledge, or do global pipelines eliminate the relationship between tacitness and high costs of distance?

Linked to the question of whether channels can create new patterns of transmission and geographies of innovation is whether they also transform innovation in subtle ways. Internet search engines are new vehicles within the Internet channel, but they have selection bias (algorithms for page rankings, principally). They both add and subtract information compared to other vehicles and channels. Thus, instead of pipelining, "stovepiping" (or siloing) information is an unintended consequence of the use of such engines (Lanier 2010). Global channels transform, but they also involve selection bias in what they channel.

One dimension of this is the matching of star scientists to firms. Such scientists have access to worldwide networks of collaborators and sources of information. But the matching is highly regionalized, with most ventures occurring close to home (Zucker et al. 2007), and academic research spillovers in general are highly localized (Adams 2005). The presence of brokers and deal makers is exponentially related to the size of agglomerations and number of firms in them (Feldman and Zoller 2011). So in spite of the presence of global channels, there are circular and cumulative matching processes along with selection biases, and this continues to open up divergence among regions in innovative industries.

CLUSTERING

Technology creation and use are geographically clustered. The seminal texts, based on the localization of patents include Jaffe (1989), Jaffe, Trajtenberg, and Henderson (1993), and Audretsch and Feldman (1996).[7] Significant gaps remain in our understanding of the relationship between technological innovation and clustering, beyond what is noted above about how codes and channels affect it. To use the analogy from urban economics, if such clustering were mostly an urbanization effect, then all cities of equal sizes should be equally innovative. But all city-regions are not equally innovative, even within city-size classes; moreover, cities are innovative in different fields, so they are specialized in innovation in the same way that they are in the production of tradable goods and services. In other words, it's a combination of specialization and urbanization.

Some scholars believe that the big, diversified cities of the world have an edge in certain kinds of innovative activities because of interindustry spillovers (Glaeser et al. 1992). Perhaps big cities just appear to be highly diversified, but this is merely a reflection of the fact that we have a poor understanding of which activities are really "close" or related technologically. If this is the case, then we are overestimating diversity and understating the relatedness of activities in an urban agglomeration (Frenken, van Oort, and Verburg 2007). Perhaps big cities also have superadditive communication processes, or "buzz" (see chapter 11). In all these instances, there is "glue" to the big city economy that is as yet poorly understood. Innovation and clustering are probably causes of one another (Braunerhjelm and Feldman 2006). Furthermore, at least under certain conditions, they are mutually reinforcing, and can be cumulative and increasing.

COMMUNITIES

Having noted that there is evidence of the geographical clustering of innovation, however, we still do not know whether innovation is enhanced by being in a diversified economy (consisting of several clusters), a specialized one centered on a single industry, or a domain of activity. The benefits of a narrower economic base might include concentrating agents, firms, and labor market processes in narrower domains of activity that might give them a more communitarian mode of functioning, thus enhancing both the knowledge flow as well as social capital and trust among the agents.

The communities of people that carry out innovation can range from credentialed nonaffinity networks to those based on kinship, origin, or even ethnicity. The most formalized professional communities have credentials; but many are semicredentialed, partially open "communities of practice," based on knowledge and involving screening to get in (Brown and Duguid 1991, 2000; Amin and Cohendet 2005). The channels they create will be somewhat different in the two cases. There is debate about whether "strong ties" within these networks, involving interpersonal knowledge, or "weak ties," involving more distant and thin forms of knowledge about others, are better at facilitating innovation (Granovetter 1973; Rost 2011). Even credentialed communities ultimately require some measure of interpersonal, nonanonymous network in order to screen for the "real" skills of those with credentials and smooth the hard work of creating innovations (Bunnell and Coe 2001; Cooke 2006). There are many organizational settings, moreover, where such networks are formed, including firms and academia (Balconi, Breschi, and Lissoni 2004).

None of this tells us whether such communities are spatially localized or can be spread out over long distances. One key to this question is whether there are differences between "cosmopolitan" innovation communities and traditional affinity-based networks, or whether they are substitutes for one another. International scientific networks are increasingly common (Edler, Fier, and Grimpe 2011; Hoekman, Frenken, and Van Oort 2008; Lorentzen 2008). But as previously discussed, Zucker and Darby (2006) show that even star academics with worldwide scientific reputations overwhelmingly collaborate close to home. International scientific communities do not map directly onto innovation communities. Furthermore, localized social capital seems to enhance the ability of certain kinds of local producer R & D relations at acquiring both local and long-distance knowledge (Laursen, Masciarelli, and Prencipe 2011), although movement away from communities seems to carry some of the relationship bonds established locally over long distances (Breschi and Lissoni 2003).

In chapters 6–8, I discussed the transposition of skills and capacities from one major domain of activity to another. Transposition necessarily involves bridging between existing networks, as when venture capitalists who are accustomed to working in the information technology world begin to act as angel investors in biotechnology and the life-sciences-driven parts of the economy. Who does this? Powell, Packalen, and Whittington (2009) argue that it is specific agents who are able to make the connection between the two communities, in what is called "brokering" by Maryann Feldman and Ted Zoller (2011). Subsequently, when deals are successful, a new set of practices and relations diffuses to a wider group of actors, effectively forming another network, in a process of institutionalization (Porter, Whittington, and Powell 2005; Powell, Packalen, and Whittington 2012; Powell and Owen-Smith 2012). Are such connections more likely to be made and be successful at certain geographical scales? Zucker and Darby (2006) along with Feldman and Zoller (2011) suggest that if a regional scale is more likely at the beginning, with time and the institutionalization of networks and practices, perhaps transposition subsequently can be scaled up (Powell, Packalen, and Whittington 2012).

Mobile scientists and entrepreneurs have roots in more localized nodes or networks (Filatchov et al. 2011), and these bridging agents might involve diasporas or even complex forms of circular and return migration

(Saxenian 2006; Mayr and Peri 2008; Saxenian and Hsu 2005). This would effectively make it possible to combine the benefits of long distance and localization in innovation, possibly enhancing the benefits of localization (Saxenian 2006).

CONTEXT OR "LOCAL GENIUS"

Much decision making and action is situational. Actors receive, perceive, and interpret information as well as rank alternatives in highly variable ways; they discount the future in relation to their specific present; and they often proceed by emulating others with whom they are in contact. These are the "animal spirits" of the economy (Akerlof and Schiller 2009). Context is not the same as epistemic communities or communities of practice. Context is the integrated, behavioral "experience" factor that has mostly been relegated to the black box of cultural differences.[8] I will explore context in detail in chapter 10 and so will only make a few remarks about it here.

Contexts have geographically bounded elements insofar as access to information, persons, and roles to emulate along with visions of the future are informed by what we know. Some of the forces I have examined in relation to innovation—codes, channels, and communities—might also create opportunities for the geographical stretching of contexts or even decontextualizing action by substituting standardized protocols for real experience. Search engines, for example, might decontextualize at the same time that they open up sources of information, redefining the search pathway as they do so, and thus stovepiping certain kinds of information and views of the world (Lanier 2010). It seems unlikely that all the behaviors relevant to innovation could be decontextualized, or that all could be made remote. But in considering the evolution of the effects of distance on innovation, we need to understand not just the communication costs of different kinds of information in relation to codes and channels but also the extent to which innovation is embedded in context, and the degree to which the elements of context can be reproduced in different places.

COORDINATION

Innovation involves actors in different organizations (firms, universities, laboratories, and so on) as well as the use of knowledge and different material objects and artifacts. The communication among all these fields and actors from different specialized areas of the economy is shaped by codes, channels, clustering, and communities, which are all forms of institutions.

Much of the literature on the coordination of innovation has asked how organizations can coordinate more open, interactive, and rapidly changing interactions. This problem has a geographical aspect: coordinating innovation actors and organizations over significant geographical distances. High levels of coordination are required when there are high fixed system costs or dedicated parts that have to fit together, but in principle coengineering and production planning can reduce its costs while increasing its feasibility. The early attempt at this was Ford's "world car" in the 1970s—an experiment that resulted in failure. As noted earlier, the world's two big civilian aircraft producers have each recently tried to create a major new airliner via a global coengineering and production chain, and suffered major setbacks. These examples suggest that there are coordination barriers over distance, even in sectors where top-down and centralized engineering is inherent to the nature of the output boundaries (Hart and Moore 2005).

In sectors where such engineering requirements and high fixed costs are not present, however, the global coordination of fast design and production has been more successful. Starting with Benetton in the 1970s, firms began using newly available information technologies to generate more rapid feedback between points of sale and productin (Camuffo, Romano, and Vinelli 2001; Belussi 1987). Zara, H&M, and other fast-fashion companies, by contrast, seem to have a regional core cluster, which they use to design products, generate prototypes, and roll out production in limited quantities in the cluster before globalizing the supply for successful, large-volume items, so that the global and local are mutually enhancing (Ghemawat and Nueno 2003; Saliola and Zanfei 2009; Oxley and Sampson 2004).

In the first part of this chapter, however, I argued that the relationship between lower trade costs (essentially a type of coordination costs) and the geography of innovation is a two-way one. Thus, even as coordination capacities over distance continue to grow, they will generate their own recursive effects on localization, in the manner I described earlier. For each spreading out due to enhanced coordination, there probably will be invention, product differentiation, and product quality changes that will generate production relationships that cannot be coordinated fully at long distances.[9]

COMPETITION

Theory instructs us to look for the improvements in human welfare that come from the globalization (or more generally, geographical integration at any scale) of innovation. Thus, for example, countries could eliminate overlaps and redundancies in the expensive activities of R & D and experimentation. They could increase spillovers, and hence increase the recombination of knowledge and create greater Romer effects (see chapter 4). In this way, they could create greater economies of scale and efficiency, and increase returns to innovative assets and labor.

This can also lead to spectacular winner-take-all development processes—cities and countries that earn visible innovative rents, and attract a great deal of attention. The globalization of innovation also seems to involve more interfirm, intergovernmental, and interregional competition to become the winner in each innovation game (Boldrin and Levine 2006). This raises the prospect of redundant competition in the form of the innovation equivalent of "smokestack chasing" (Grossman and Lai 2011; Gilbert 2011; Lerner 2009; Jaffe and Lerner 2004; cf. Donahue 1997). Most trade rules prohibit direct subsidies of production costs, but are not empowered to prevent the support of innovation.

We do not know, though, if such competition leads to faster, more, or better innovation in a dynamic sense—such as learning or spin-offs that cannot be seen in the present—or whether it impedes getting the economic benefits from geographical specialization (described in chapters 3 and 4), or even whether it leads to geographical distributions that are good. Innovation can also have a crowding-out effect on less glamorous tasks for public and private action, such as simply improving productivity or old products. This may be the price to pay for improved overall innovation output, but how they impact regional economies has not been established.

Innovation and Local Interaction

The reality of the globalization of innovation is thus rather far from that suggested by images of a "flat world" or the death of distance. Not only are there many reasons for the highest-level innovative activities to be highly localized, but many innovations in global transport and communication technologies have the paradoxical, roundabout effect of increasing comples and time-dependent interactions in the economy, which themselves have high trade costs and require localization. Globalization and local interactions are joined at the hip in these respects. None of this tells us much about the where of innovation.

This analysis allows me to frame an important question about interaction and city-region development: Are there some cities that are more interactive than others? There is no hard evidence with which to respond. Yet the preceding analysis suggests that highly interactive cities are those that are either first movers in innovation, or are capable "recombiners" and refiners of products and services, as in my machinery industry example. Highly interactive cities will have a higher percentage of nonroutine tasks than less interactive city-regions along with higher incomes, as in the data that I presented in chapter 1. And over time, the more interactive cities will be more resilient in income terms (though will not necessarily grow more in population terms) than those that are specialized in carrying out routine, less interactive tasks in the interregional division of labor.

Local Context

THE GENIUS OF CITIES

The "Dark Matter" Problem: Difference in the Economy

German and US cars are systematically different in quality, feel, and performance. Yet they share a great deal of technology and embodied engineering knowledge, and their designs incorporate elements obtained through imitation and mutual observation. Economics has long struggled with how to explain differences in the quality of outputs of economies with similar income levels and similar average factor productivity.[1] When goods and services are tradable, and the factors used to make them are mobile, there is no clear reason why such differences should exist. Perhaps Germany and the United States have subtle—unobservable—differences in factor endowments for producing cars. These in turn give rise to subtle differences in productivity that then are reflected in the quality of each country's cars and varieties (models) each can successfully market. Trade reinforces this self-selection; when trade costs decline, economies of scale in each quality or variety niche can be reinforced, thus augmenting the number of different models that are available. But then we need to explain different factor endowments, if these are not due to natural endowments. One approach is to assign them to history—for example, German shop-floor efficiency versus the US penchant for de-skilling production jobs (Hall and Soskice 2001). Another is to emphasize demand, such that, in this case, each country has different factors because Americans have different preferences for cars from those of Germans. Notice that our models are better at describing the what and how of differences than the why.

Institutions could create the differences in factor endowments mentioned above; education, the organization of firms, industrial policies, and the organization of R & D could generate different ways of doing things from place to place. But this causality can also be reversed: institutions could reflect initial differences in endowments; in each economy, the scarce factors are the ones likely to require collective action to improve either their supply or allocation. In labor-scarce countries, for example, this is said to encourage education, thus maximizing the output of the scarce factor, or it could encourage immigration-friendly policies (Acemoglu, Johnson, and Robinson 2004). Anthropologists have long considered the latter point of view, arguing that differences in economic organization between societies reflect initial resource endowments, which then lead to different power structures (Sahlins 1995).

These accounts, however, are too general to help explain the detailed quality differences referred to above. Along these lines, it is hard to account for why certain cities, regions, and countries do certain things so well, and why this imitation is so difficult, even in a world of benchmarking and information exchange as well as courses and delegations from one place to another. There are excellent restaurants in London, New York, Paris, Tokyo, Hong Kong, Mexico, and Lima. But even within ethnic categories—say, French cuisine—they are not perfect substitutes. We often associate the highest end of certain kinds of products with certain city-regions, such as Munich and Stuttgart for those German cars. In many other subtle ways, from fashion to finance, even in our highly globalized world, cities have a particular genius, which is different from that of other cities. Institutions and factor endowments undoubtedly contribute to such differences. Yet something is missing; there is dark matter in explaining difference.

In what follows, I argue that local interaction structure is a source of difference; I will call this interaction structure the local context.

A Story of Context

Let's consider a lighthearted but analytically serious example of the dark matter problem. My Franco-American godson has been passionate about food and cooking since he was about ten years old (he is now in his mid-twenties). In the early 2000s, he worked in high-level restaurants in Los Angeles, Chicago, and New York, and made good friends with an excellent restaurateur in Paris and some food critics. We had an ongoing conversation about food quality, cooking, and the food system, like many upper-middle-class urban people. He kept returning to the conclusion that although in the best US kitchens there is a great deal of innovation and excellence, it is nonetheless more difficult to get a reasonably priced excellent meal in even the most gastronomic cities in the United States than it is in France. In order to get such a meal in the United States, you generally have to go rather high up the quality ladder to the "big-deal" restaurants. There are many such restaurants in the United States. The difference is that there is a higher proportion of excellent but unassuming restaurants in France at more modest prices than in the United States.[2] In other words, we are not comparing the best restaurants in different places; rather, just below this top level, there remains a huge difference in the French and US supply curves for good cooking. A fair guess is that the same would be said of Japan versus the United States (in addition, Tokyo has more than double the number of starred restaurants in relation to Paris).

My godson long thought about trying to open a simple, excellent restaurant in the United States, but he concluded that it would be much more difficult than in France, and perhaps impossible to make it economically viable. What are the differences? First, there is the supply chain for ingredients. This begins with the massive market at Rungis near Orly Airport, for which there is no equivalent in the United States. Perhaps more important, that market is complemented by numerous alternative ways to get high-quality ingredients, many of them just by going to the right vendors at the Paris food markets. Though in some North American regions such markets have been developing in recent years (as in Seattle/Vancouver and the Hudson River Valley), the best ingredients are available only to the high-end US restaurants, because relative prices for such ingredients are much higher in the United States than in France. This leads to the second difference. Because nonstar chefs get hold of such ingredients relatively easily in France, there is an inherently lower barrier to entry to excellent cooking than in the United States. Thus, and this is the third difference, to use these ingredients profitably, US restaurants generally compensate by operating at a higher scale than their French counterparts.[3] They are also pushed to a higher scale by the different "granularity" of urban structures in the United States, where location and bigger size are essential to capturing a sufficiently big market to offset the higher fixed-cost structure they face. Fourth, there tends to be a different production process in the US kitchen. In the generally larger US restaurant, a greater proportion of the staff will be carrying out orders in a steeper hierarchy than in the excellent but not-big-deal restaurant in France.[4]

The point is that a relatively simple restaurant, which operates at a modest scale and offers excellent food, in turn relies on easy access to external inputs, a moderate scale of operations, and a moderate hierarchy in the kitchen. These features enable it to keep its offerings focused and simple, and hence control costs. In the United States, the incentives work in the opposite direction, so this type of restaurant is rare, pushing producers and consumers toward the big, "star-quality" restaurant model.

The fifth consequence is that the restaurant production system has a feedback effect on the talent pool in both countries. In France, there is a proportionately bigger, more open, and competitive milieu for cooking talent, and this is an ongoing "nursery" of talent for both the "normally good" and higher-end restaurants. In the United States, this type of training milieu is much thinner and more elitist.

Italians in the United States have perfected the exception to this US pattern, and it is a telling exception. The average size of their successful restaurants is still higher than their versions at home in Italy, but they are not huge affairs like the multistarred restaurants. The Italian success comes from relying on the clan method: bringing in virtually the entire staff (often with the family at its core, plus investors from their hometown) from Italy, sometimes (but more rarely) down to the waiters, but often including the architects and business managers.[5] In essence, rather than drawing from a local context in the United States, they import it, which the French generally don't do.

The sixth consequence has to do with the type of innovation carried out in the two places. According to my godson, the top US restaurants innovate in the creation of new dishes—new combinations of flavors or ingredients. Innovations in technique as well as fundamental sauces and flavors still mostly come from France, Italy, and Spain. The division of labor between conception and execution found in most US restaurants is a disadvantage in innovating fundamental sources and flavors, but quite good at creating spectacular new dishes. Both systems innovate, yet they do so in different ways.

That such differences should persist is curious, given strong international knowledge spillovers in cooking and the restaurant industry. In recent years, a worldwide milieu of gastronomic restaurants has come into being, involving the mobility of labor (celebrity chefs), flows of knowledge (cooking schools, books, and magazines), and flows of capital (investors and owners). A sophisticated clientele travels, eats, and compares. There are long-distance networks and collaboration as well as a few truly multinational chefs/restaurateurs. In other words, the story does not seem to be one of knowledge that is so uncodified that it cannot travel. Increasingly, the knowledge does travel via more and more institutionalized channels that connect far-flung areas. That knowledge is then used differently when it arrives in different places. The causes of such differences cannot be reduced to history, culture, and ways of life, either. Ways of doing things can be altered by learning, information exchange, and factor mobility. In this sense, the experiences of a certain population of discriminating cooks and diners in both France and the United States have already been mutually influential to a high degree. Factor endowments, basic preferences, and the organization of production systems have converged to a much lesser extent.

This is a quaint story, but the same type of account could apply far and wide across the contemporary economy. Even in markets where products aim to be substitutable, German cars remain resolutely different from their US counterparts, and French service firms deliver mass-produced consumer and infrastructure services systematically differently from the way that US firms do so. In other markets, there is a deep and recursive relationship between product qualities and production systems, as in my restaurant example—such as Hollywood and Bollywood, Milan fashion versus New York fashion, or Danish food processing versus French or US food processing.

The Regional Context: The Actor's Situation

Psychologists who work on the economy suggest that difference is not a simple aggregation phenomenon, where regions add up different mixes of endowments or preferences, and the different combinations then make them seem culturally different. Instead, they drill down to the level of individual actors' experiences as the source of such aggregate differences. They start by challenging the notion that actors have universally similar and rational cognition (Ariely 2008). Choices are typically made with imperfect information and on the basis of a set of limited criteria, notably local points of reference, or anchors. The unifying theme in behavioral economics is *situationalism*—where we are matters to what we know and what we choose (Ross and Nisbet 1991; Haselton, Nettle, and Andrews 2005). Five dimensions of the situation of the actor can be highlighted.

First, valuable specialized information is not uniformly available. There are costs to obtaining it, and there are also barriers to access—one's social and economic position defines whether as well as under what conditions, and sometimes at what cost, one can obtain information. In productive activity, our needs for information and access to it are defined by our place in the economy's division of labor. Divisions of labor are dizzyingly complex in the twenty-first century. Few people have anything close to comprehensive knowledge of the productive chain in which they work, not to mention the millions of other specialized systems that affect their lives as workers, consumers, and citizens. This may be the beauty of the division of labor—that is, that we don't need to know these things in order to benefit from the productive power unleashed by such complex structures.[6] But this also means that what we know is partial. Hence, the situation that we define for ourselves is a local—in the sense of partial—one.[7]

Second, people engage in limited search behavior, and put enormous weight on limited reference points, even when these are quite arbitrary and ephemeral (Kahneman and Tversky 1979). Third, social and economic networks underpin access to information along with knowing what information to look for (Granovetter 2005; Powell 1990). Since networks structure our string of opportunities and roles, our membership in them affects who we *become*, and therefore how we *frame* preferences and choices.

A fourth dimension of situationalism is how actors form their goals. In the place of fully subjective preferences, on the one hand, or rationally constructed ones, on the other, an enormous body of evidence shows that goals are strongly influenced by comparison and emulation. Status comparison affects virtually every dimension of preference formation. The borders between shame and honor, and thus what we want to emulate, are different over time and space (Appiah 2010). What we compare to and emulate is not an exercise in global maximizing but instead depends on our social and geographical positions in networks, our role in the division of labor, and what is honorable (Frank 2001; Fine 2006). Detailed studies show that even well-traveled economic elites have different sensibilities and preferences (Lamont 1992).

Fifth, the information we do access is generally processed in a relatively narrow way. Mental accounting shows that people mostly make decisions by ignoring events and consequences outside a particular narrow domain (Thaler 1985), and most decisions are made using rules of thumb that are far removed from the processes that would be necessary to maximize their payoffs (Ariely 2008).[8] People tend to be conservative in their decisions, as shown by the endowment effect; they want to keep what they have over almost any other goal (Thaler 1994). They are also averse to small-value risky gambles, and are frequently vengeful (Fehr and Gachter 2000). None of this means that decisions are merely the unleashing of emotions, because economic actors may be able to learn to manage, interpret, and manipulate their own emotions (Gul and Pesendorfer 2001). But they cannot cut around them and construct a nonsituational world for themselves (Gilovich, Griffin, and Kahneman 2002).

I can now propose a definition of the term context. The division of labor and the networks in which actors find themselves defines the structural component of a context. This is the informational environment for individuals, and hence their "input" structure of cues and reference points. In turn, individual actors engage in their search behavior (prospecting) and goal formation (emulation/aspirations), leading to choice and evaluation behaviors (strongly influenced by rules of thumb and framing that unfold in both network as well as geographical environments).[9]

Certain kinds of goods and services are characterized by high variety, low codifiability, and imperfect substitutability; these are the innovative areas of the economy. The context encompasses the behaviors or animal spirits of mobilizing the inputs to these activities. Contexts involve firms that transact a great deal with one another and local labor markets, and contexts cannot be fully internalized within organizations such as firms. As a result, contexts have a strong local social multiplier. They are akin to the "neighborhood effect" of the deep talents and mentalities that underlie the genius of particular city-regions (Durlauf 2004).

Context and Tweaking

Context has a specific role to play in certain kinds of innovation processes. Ralf Meisenzahl and Joel Mokyr (2010, 5) define three levels of innovative activity:

> One were the macroinventions and other major breakthroughs that solved a major bottleneck and opened a new door. We will refer to these inventors as major inventors, and they are, by and large, the ones that made it into economic history textbooks. Another was the myriad of small and medium cumulative microinventions that improved and debugged existing inventions, adapted them to new uses, and combined them in new applications. The people engaged in those will be referred to as *tweakers* in the sense that they improved and debugged an existing invention. Some of the more important advances among those may have been worth patenting, but clearly this was not uniformly the case. A third group, and perhaps the least recognized of Britain's advantages, was the existence of a substantial number of skilled workmen capable of building, installing, operating, and maintaining new and complex equipment. The skills needed for pure implementers were substantial, but they did not have to be creative themselves. We will refer to these as *implementers*. It goes without saying that the line between tweakers and implementers is blurry, but at the very least a patent or some prize for innovation would be a clear signal of creativity.

In my restaurant example, the key form of behavior that differentiates one restaurant city from another is tweaking. Local genius gets expressed in this way. Context is the environment that shapes tweaking and potentiates it.

Tweaking skills resist being reproduced or transmitted through long-distance pipelines. As Meisenzahl and Mokyr (2010, 41) argue:

> The story (of the industrial revolution), however, was not a national but by and large a local one: innovations in textiles, iron, mining, hardware, and instruments, to pick a few examples, were all local phenomena, relying largely on local resources including talent.

The reason that context and the genius that is expressed through tweaking are highly localized is that they cannot be codified:

> We should focus neither on the mean properties of the population at large nor on the experiences of the "superstars" but on the group in between. Those who had the dexterity and competence to tweak, adapt, combine, improve, and debug existing ideas, build them according to specifications, but with the knowledge to add in what the blueprints left out were critical to the story. (ibid.)

The past few chapters now offer some tools for understanding the pattern of innovation among city-regions: the economic geography of agglomerations and their technological spillovers (learning); the complex feedback between the globalization of technology as well as local interactions of invention and recombination; local context and tweaking behavior; and of course, how local networks of deal makers and other robust actors allow tweakers to implement what they come up with.

Time, Space, and Contexts

The economy's intricate organizational and geographical structure shapes the actor's relation to the external world. Some resulting environments are specialized and relatively homogeneous, while others are diverse, with more irregular and heterogeneous contacts. These relationships have a geographical dimension as well: they are shaped by geographical location, which is in turn strongly related to productive organization—that is, the division of labor and the trade linkages between its different parts. An engineer working in the automobile industry in Detroit is likely (nowadays) to have strong connections to Tokyo, Stuttgart, or Munich; an agent in Hollywood probably has links to New York; and a vintner in Mendoza likely has ties to Bordeaux or Chianti.

In a local context such as a city, we can find firms involved in high levels of internal communication, using algorithms and rules, and highly organized long-distance professional supply-chain relationships as well as local, spontaneous, diverse interactions. The architecture of the actor's context, in this case, is some mixture of the two, which is as yet rather poorly understood. Likewise, in the geographically fragmented, highly organized supply-chain environment, there is still likely to be some leakage of unplanned information from the local or long-distance environment. The core issue is how the information and signals, which are the key inputs into the actor's situation, are defined and channeled, and then how such channels influence how actors frame things, whom and what they emulate, how they choose, and what they learn.

Let us now think about some examples of this phenomenon. The apparel industry has a high level of product differentiation. Market structures and geography are correspondingly diverse within this industry, which exhibits everything from geographically fragmented chains of mass production within large firms to highly localized, specialized clothing clusters or districts. The processes of emulation, learning, and innovation differ according to these contexts. Skills do not transfer readily between them. There is some spillover from one to another in that mass production tries generally to knock off and copy what comes from fast or high fashion, which in turn learns from an alternative circuit of cities, the arts, and the "street." German, Japanese, and US carmakers have significant differences in the organization and geography of their core activities; so do companies that make consumer electronics (Sabel and Zeitlin 1985; Hall and Soskice 2001; Scranton 1991). Thirty years of competition between Detroit and Tokyo has left them with distinctively different products, and Detroit has failed to imitate Tokyo successfully even when it has announced its intention to do so. Even in a world of enormous technology sharing and information circulation, the actors in each system appear to be keyed into differences in information, different emulation dynamics, possibly discounting (time horizons), and choice behaviors. They frame problems differently (Whitley 2004).

A third type of case is that of winner-take-all systems in the world, such as the City of London, Silicon Valley, or Hollywood, or industrial districts built around a combination of distinctive products and locally constructed techniques rooted in the local system as a whole (Bathelt, Malmberg, and Maskell 2004). These systems are not only at the technological frontier in their respective activities, but that frontier is occupied by a small number of systems. Such highly successful clusters serve the global market, and are caught up in all sorts of long-distance, formal organizational procedures, professional and regulatory norms, and so on. Each core region has a context whose individual dimensions can be imitated to some extent. But copying whole contexts is an almost-impossible collective action problem because the incentives for actors to frame and emulate are interdependent, and hence these aspects of their behavior are strongly interactive and cumulative; this is the local multiplier effect. There are offshoots of Silicon Valley around the globe, but there is only one Silicon Valley.

Distributed Context: Another "Great Transformation"?

As we saw in the seven C's of geography and technology in chapter 9, major changes are occurring in the possibilities for fragmenting production, organizationally and geographically. In light of the existence of a local context or particular collective local forms of genius, what might a set of radical changes in the relationship of local to global mean for local genius and the geography of genius? Another way of asking this question is to speculate about what a great transformation in local versus long-distance relations would look like (Polanyi 1944).

Such a transformation toward what may be termed geographically distributed contexts would consist of several major dimensions. First, up to now, many complex relationships at long distances have to be internalized within organizations, whereas simpler long-distance exchanges are carried out in open markets, and those with intermediate complexity are contracted. Those that are complex and resistant to codification or routinization are local. New technologies that facilitate coordination and monitoring at a distance, if sufficiently powerful, could help spread out contexts by making open-market relations and complex contracts feasible at longer distances with higher degrees of interaction as well as complexity.

Second, the boundary between formal and informal processes of co-ordination, contracting, and monitoring would be profoundly modified. It would be possible to quasi-formalize, thus combining the ease of deal making that currently occurs locally or in direct contact with long distance and flexibility—the best of both worlds. Third, all types of important information, knowledge, and know-how would be obtained via global pipelines (Bathelt, Malmberg, and Maskell 2004).

Such geographically distributed contexts therefore would have more of an organizational than a geographical nature. Their organizational basis would be radically different from the past, managing fully complex interactions via the radically increased intermediation of information technologies. Geographically distributed contexts would change the genius of cities as we now experience it, if not eliminate it altogether. In chapter 9 I showed that we are probably far from this point, even though there are many experiments in technology and coordination; in chapter 11 I will argue that face-to-face contact is still a powerful instrument of economic coordination, and that telepresence is unlikely to diminish it. In spite of these doubts, there is heuristic value in considering the properties of a great transformation from a local or national context to global one.

Economics of Distributed Contexts: Optimality and Welfare Effects

Trade theory instructs us to think of the possible advent of distributed contexts as a natural and unproblematic dimension of economic development. If geographically distributed contexts replace geographically rooted ones, would the world economy benefit from a rise in the level of "global genius" relative to the existing level of "local genius"? If Hollywood were a global production network with no local core, would it be the same industry as it is with its current organization and geography? A producer of different but better outputs? Viewed in light of a theory of context, we can ask how a change in context is likely to alter the framing, emulation, choice, and learning behavior of actors, and as such, the developmental dynamic of the sector in question. A producer of worse, less welfare-enhancing outputs? Globalization, in this perspective, is not just a matter of choosing alternative techniques but instead has effects on what people know, and what they know how to produce (Martin and Sunley 2006; Boschma and Lambooy 1999; Jaffe, Trajtenberg, and Henderson 1993).

As suggested in my restaurant example, when we go from local to geographically distributed contexts, the resulting products are imperfect substitutes. There is not just a change in production technique but also in the envelope of outputs. In this case, the information used by actors would be stovepiped via the global division of labor. This information would increasingly take precedence over information coming from outside such a network (e.g., from a local or national context of information exchange) in the key processes of emulation, cognition, and learning. Certain formal models of trade with heterogeneous firms predict this reduction in variety (Baldwin and Forslid 2006). In other words, the decision to restructure a production chain involves "roads not taken" (Arthur 1989, 1994; Hodgson 1993; Essletzbichler and Rigby 2004; Dosi 1998). We can compare the road taken to the existing road, but we cannot measure the possible qualities and quantities of future outputs of contexts that are being eliminated or transformed by today's actions. The creation or elimination of contexts is largely an unintended outcome of decisions made about the organization of production and location, with these dynamic effects not figured into the decision-making process or priced in any way. They are developmental externalities of the globalization process in the same way that there is a creation and loss of cultures and languages as the world integrates.

The genius of cities and regions is therefore not just a local affair, any more than innovations emerging in specific places yet widely used are a local affair. Local genius is not automatically preserved or favorably changed by greater integration, any more than all trade can be said to automatically generate positive outcomes for all places. Considering the future of local context or genius does not stem from protectionist or nostalgic motivations; instead, the concept of context and local genius allow us better to consider when such contexts should be nourished and when the economy as a whole would be better off by letting others disappear.

Face-to-Face Contact

Face-to-Face Contact Remains Important

Extremely dense urban centers fascinate us: Why are all those people crowding so closely together?[1] In general, density intrigues economists, because there are so many inconveniences—congestion costs and other negative externalities—associated with it. Dense office districts, clusters of galleries, and nightlife neighborhoods are all expressions of the continuing hold that interaction has on us. It cannot be because of the costs of transport, which have declined so much. Preferences for a dense form of development such as Hong Kong or Manhattan, or old plus dense plus beautiful cities such as Paris or London, do not seem to explain development either, since amenities can be delivered in many different types of built environments and so can beauty, as I showed in chapter 5.

It is true that clustering many galleries enables the art hound to economize on search costs and time, and hit many of them in a single afternoon, and clustering restaurants near Times Square makes sense as a spin-on to the clustering of the theaters. But it is more than the effect of clustering. The economy allocates enormous resources to meeting in spite of the growth of much more effective electronic communications (Leamer and Storper 2001). Over the past quarter century, long-distance business travel has grown faster than trade and output (Hall 1998). There must be powerful reasons for economic agents to congregate and see each other, given the high pecuniary and opportunity cost of travel, whether local or long distance.

The dense clustering of people has additional properties beyond economizing on the cost of information exchange, or searching for the best cinema or restaurant. As was discussed in chapters 2 and 3, three main forces are thought to lie behind the persistence of urbanization and localization: the backward and forward linkages of firms, including access to markets; the clustering of workers; and localized interactions, mostly among skilled people. Underlying all these is deal making, evaluation, and relationship adjustment, all of which—as we will now see—depend strongly on face-to-face contact. An *analysis* of these mechanisms is therefore incomplete unless grounded in face-to-face contact.

TABLE 11.1
Face-to-Face Contact

FUNCTION	ADVANTAGE OF F2F	CONTEXT
Communication technology.	High frequency. Rapid feedback. Visual and body language cues.	Non-codifiable information. R&D. Teaching.
Trust and incentives in relationships.	Detection of lying. Co-presence a commitment of time.	Meetings.
Screening and socializing.	Loss of anonymity. Judging and being judged. Acquisition of shared values.	Professional groups Being "in the loop."
Rush and motivation.	Performance as display.	Presentations.

The Specific Properties of Face-to-Face Contact

Table 11.1 lists four major properties of face-to-face contact: it is an efficient communication technology; it allows actors to align commitments and thereby reduces incentive problems; it allows screening of agents; and it motivates effort.

FACE-TO-FACE CONTACT AS A COMMUNICATION TECHNOLOGY

The first row of Table 11.1 refers to the advantages of face-to-face contact as a communication technology, particularly when much of the information to be transmitted cannot be codified. As noted in chapter 9, codifiable information has a stable meaning that is associated in a determinate way with the symbol system in which it is expressed, whether it be linguistic, mathematical, or visual. Such information is cheap to transfer because its underlying symbol systems can be widely disseminated through information infrastructure, sharply reducing the marginal cost of individual messages. Acquiring the symbol system may be expensive or slow (due to language, mathematical skills, etc.), as may be building the transmission system, but using it to communicate information is cheap. Thus, the transmission of codifiable information has strong network externalities, since once the infrastructure is acquired a new user can plug in and access the whole network.

By contrast, noncodifiable information is only loosely related to the symbol system in which it is expressed. This includes much linguistic, words-based expression (the famous distinction between speech and language), or especially what might be called "complex discourse" (Searle 1969). For example, one can master the grammar and syntax of a language without understanding its metaphors. This is also true for some mathematically expressed information as well as much visual information. If the information is not codifiable, merely acquiring the symbol system or having the physical infrastructure is not enough for the successful transmission of a message. The transmission of uncodifiable information may have limited network externalities, since the successful transmission of the message depends on infrastructure that is largely committed to one specific sender-receiver pair. Gregory Bateson (1973) refers to the analog quality of tacit knowledge: communication between individuals that requires a kind of parallel processing of the complexities of an issue, as different dimensions of a problem are perceived and understood only in relation to one another.

Face-to-face encounters provide an efficient technology of transaction under these circumstances by permitting a depth and speed of feedback that is impossible in other forms of communication. As organizational theorists Nitin Nohria and Robert Eccles (1992, 292) point out,

> Relative to electronically-mediated exchange, the structure of face-to-face interaction offers an unusual capacity for interruption, repair, feedback, and learning. In contrast to interactions that are largely sequential, face-to-face interaction makes it possible for two people to be sending and delivering messages simultaneously. The cycle of interruption, feedback and repair possible in face-to-face interaction is so quick that it is virtually instantaneous.

This echoes the findings of sociologist Erving Goffman (1982) that "a speaker can see how others are responding to her message even before it is done and alter it midstream to elicit a different response."

But it is not just the uncodifiability of much information that makes face-to-face a superior technology. Communication in a face-to-face context occurs on many levels at the same time—verbal, physical, contextual, intentional, and nonintentional. Such multidimensional communication is essential to the transmission of complex, tacit knowledge. Social psychologists argue that creativity results from several different ways of processing information at one time, including not only the standard deductive way but also analogical, metaphoric, and parallel methods as well (Bateson 1973; Csikszentmihalyi 1997). These different means of communication lead to connections being made that cannot be had through strictly linear perception and reasoning. The full benefits of diversity and serendipity, including the urban phenomena of bumping into people that was celebrated by Jacobs (1969), are only realized through these multiple levels of communication. Linguists such as John Searle (1969) and J. L. Austin (1962) strengthen the case for face-to-face, arguing that language is behavior and face-to-face dialogue is a complex, socially creative activity. In a similar vein, sociologists such as Goffman (1959) and Harold Garfinkel (1987) show that the interaction that comes from copresence can be likened to being onstage, playing a role, where the visual and corporeal cues are at least as important to knowing what is being "said" as are the words themselves.

Trust and Incentives in Relationships

The second row of Table 11.1 refers to the ways that copresence reduces risks in economic relationships. With tacit knowledge there is always uncertainty about what the other agent means and intends to do, and hence it is possible for one to free ride or manipulate the other. These moral hazards can sometimes be reduced through improvements in the transparency or clarity of the information itself, or in how well it can be verified. But when this isn't possible, reducing them requires a relationship between the interested parties. Being close enough literally to touch each other allows visual contact and emotional closeness—the basis for building human relationships.

For example, the contemporary knowledge-based economy involves many projects in which individuals come together to acquire and exchange information. Typically the later stages of such a project—writing the report, executing the transaction, or constructing the investment—involve codifiable information. It is the earlier stages where information is more uncertain. Is the project a good idea? Should one approach be followed or another? Answering these questions requires that partners in the project undertake research and share their results. Often neither the inputs nor the outputs of this research are observable. Thus, a partner can conscientiously research the project or simply free ride, hoping that other members of the team will do the work.

It is easiest to observe and interpret a partner's behavior in a face-to-face situation. Knowing the intentions of another actor enables us to decode the practical consequences of what they are expressing to us (Husserl 1968). Humans are effective at sensing nonverbal messages from one another, particularly about emotions, cooperation, and trustworthiness.

Putnam (2000, 175) observes that "it seems that the ability to spot non-verbal signs of mendacity offered a significant survival advantage during the course of human evolution." Psychologist Albert Mehrabian (1981, iii) notes that "our facial and vocal expressions, postures, movements and gestures" are crucial; when our words "contradict the messages contained within them, others mistrust what we say—they rely almost completely on what we do."

Face-to-face may promote the development of trust. Trust depends on reputation effects or multilayered relations between the parties to a transaction that can create low-cost enforcement opportunities (Gambetta 1988; Lorentzen 1992). Trust also comes from the time, money, and effort spent in building a relationship. These costs are sunk, so increasing them signals a willingness to embark on a repeated relationship; absent a second date, the value of the first date disappears. Yet to create a relationship bond, the costs must be substantial and transparent. Email, paradoxically, can be so efficient that it destroys the value of the message. The email medium greatly reduces the cost of sending a message, somewhat reduces the cost of receiving the message, and makes the costs mostly nontransparent. A return receipt only means that the recipient has opened the message, but the sender cannot be sure that enough attention has been devoted to it to absorb the content. In this sense, for complex context-dependent information, the medium *is* the message. And the most powerful such medium for verifying the intentions of another is direct face-to-face contact.

Screening and Socialization

Even if face-to-face contact is an efficient technology of transacting, it is nonetheless costly, not least because it is time consuming. We do not have the luxury of face-to-face encounters with the entire world, so we need to screen out the people with whom we want to interact. How do we identify such people? One way is formal screening procedures—examination and certification. Another is the development of informal networks in which members of the network develop and share a pool of knowledge about members' competence.

Social and professional networks of this type often—although not always—require face-to-face contact. They are necessarily based on individuals losing their anonymity; a member of the group is continually judging other members of the group, being judged, and sharing judgments with members of the group. In some internationalized professions—such as academia—this does not always require colocation, although is certainly reinforced by face-to-face contact in the conference circuit. In other activities, these information networks can only be maintained within a restricted geographical area. In such fields as fashion, public relations, and many of the arts (including cinema, television, and radio) there are international networks "at the top," but in the middle of these professions networks are highly localized, change rapidly, and the information used by members to stay in the loop is highly context dependent. In parts of the financial services and high-tech industries, local networks intersect with long-distance contact systems. In almost anything relating to business-government relations, networks have a strongly national and regional cast.

The screening of network members and potential partners is complex because much of what is most valuable about partners is their tacit knowledge, whose meanings are highly culture and context dependent (Lakoff and Johnson 1980). Karl Polanyi (1966, 4) argued that tacit and metaphoric knowledge is deeply embedded in specific contexts. Thus, potential partners need to know each other, or have a broad common background. They learn to share the "codes" that show that they have certain criteria of judgment, which in turn signal to others that they belong to the same social world (Coleman 1990).[2] This gives them the means to get in the loop. Socialization is inevitably achieved in large measure through face-to-face contact, from family, schooling, and the social environment in one's community and workplaces.

Notice, then, that face-to-face contact performs its screening role at two timescales in the economic process: in the long run, by socializing people; and in the short run, by permitting potential collaborators to evaluate others' performance in professional groups and networks.

"Rush": The Motivation that Comes from Face-to-Face Contact

The final row of Table 11.1 shows another dimension of the incentive effects of face-to-face contact, which goes beyond verbal or visual communication. Face-to-face communication does not derive its richness and power merely from allowing us to see each other's faces, and detect the intended and unintended messages that can be sent by such visual contact. According to Goffman (1959), face-to-face communication is a *performance*—a means to information production and not merely more efficient exchange. In this performance, speech, intentions, role-playing, and a specific context all come together to raise the quantity and quality of information that can be transmitted. Moreover, performance raises effort by stimulating imitation and competition. Psychologists have shown that the search for pleasure is a powerful motivating force, and certain kinds of pleasure are linked to pride of status and position: we imitate others, try to do better than them, and derive pleasure from succeeding at so doing. When we make an effort, and are on the route to success, there is a biophysical rush that pushes us forward. All pleasure, however, quickly recedes as it blends into the preceding "normal" state, and it is only by once again changing this state that pleasure is found again; the search for such pride of status and position must therefore be continuously renewed (Scitovsky 1976). Face-to-face contact provides the strongest, most embodied signals of such desire, and can generate the rush that pushes us to make greater and better efforts. It is thus no surprise that even with the sophisticated computer monitoring that can be carried out on employee performance today, few workplaces—which are essentially centers of face-to-face contact—have disappeared. It is not just that it is easier to monitor employees when they are present; it is also that such presence is motivating (Kahneman, Diener, and Schwartz 1998).

Why People Engage in Face-to-Face Contact: Two Models

With these basic properties of face-to-face contact in mind, we can see how face-to-face improves the coordination of economic agents. I can now describe two models of face-to-face contact, drawn from Storper and Venables (2004). The nontechnical reader may want to skip this subsection. In the first model, face-to-face contact overcomes incentive problems in the formation of working partnerships; in the second, it allows actors to evaluate others' qualities and leads to the formation of in-groups that support more efficient partnering and increased motivation. These models both show that productivity is raised by face-to-face contact.

In the first model, suppose that two people are considering undertaking a joint project, but they are uncertain about its ultimate value or quality. All they know, initially, is that the project is either good, yielding final payoff A, or bad, yielding zero; they both attach the same prior probability, ρ, to the project being good. We can model a game between them with two stages. The first involves the acquisition of information about the quality of the project, and the second involves information sharing, deciding whether or not to undertake the project, and project implementation.

At the first stage, the two individuals undertake research independently, and obtain a signal of whether the project is good or bad. The signal obtained by player I may be favorable, g_i, or unfavorable, b_i. The signals are not accurate, however; a good project can send out a signal that it is bad, and vice versa. By expending effort, e_i, each player ($I = 1, 2$) can improve the quality of the signal received.

At the second stage of the game, players truthfully reveal their signals to each other.[3] Using standard Bayesian techniques, the players utilize their combined information to estimate the probability that the project is

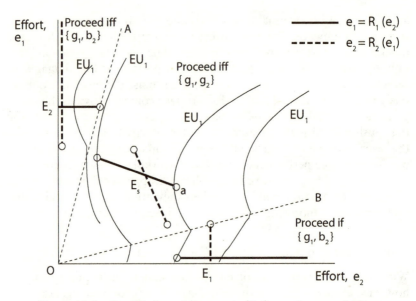

Figure 11.1 Equilibriums in a game of information acquisition and sharing.

good; this probability is higher the more good signals have been received and the more effort has been expended, improving the quality of the signals. The players then decide whether or not to proceed. Proceeding costs C and yields payoff A if the project turns out to be good, and zero otherwise; we assume $A\rho = C$, so (prior to research) the project yields zero expected surplus.

The incentives faced by individuals and the equilibrium outcomes are illustrated in figure 11.1. The axes are the effort levels of the two players, and the lines OA and OB divide the space up into three regions. Between OA and OB the effort levels are such that players will, at the second stage, choose to go ahead with the project only if they have both received good signals, $\{g_1, g_2\}$. Nevertheless, below OB player 1 is putting in so little effort relative to player 2 (and hence 1's signal is so unreliable) that they proceed if 2 has a good signal and 1 has a bad one $\{g_2, b_1\}$. Similarly, above OA they proceed with signals $\{g_1, b_2\}$. The curves labeled EU_1 are expected utility indifference curves for player 1, increasing to the right, and kinked where they cross lines OA and OB. The best response function for player 1 to each effort level e_2 is given by the bold solid lines, $e_1 = R_1(e_2)$. We see that if e_2 is low, then player 1 will ignore 2's signal and put in a constant amount of effort (in the region to the left of OA). Conversely, if e_2 is high enough, player 1 will free ride, putting in zero effort (in the region below OB). At intermediate levels of e_2 player 1 puts in a positive level of effort, decreasing in e_2. Just as the solid bold lines are the best responses of player 1 to 2's effort levels, so the dashed bold lines (their reflection around the 45° line) give the best responses of player 2 to 1's effort levels.

As illustrated in figure 11.1, this game has three Nash equilibriums, labeled E_S, E_1, and E_2, occurring where the best response functions of the two players intersect. E_S is symmetrical and involves both players putting in equal amounts of effort. E_1 and E_2 are equilibriums where player 1 (respectively, 2) exerts no effort; but given this, it is privately optimal for the other player to put in effort to the level illustrated. This free riding means that little information is gathered, and at these equilibriums more projects are undertaken than at E_S, the proportion of failing projects is larger, and the aggregate returns are lower.[4]

The multiplicity of equilibriums reflects the incentives for individuals to free ride in projects of this type. What can face-to-face contact do to select the symmetrical equilibrium where free riding is reduced? Face-to-face contact—a meeting between the players—can play two distinct roles. First, a face-to-face meeting prior to the start of the game may allow players to coordinate on this equilibrium. It is quite difficult to go into a meeting maintaining a commitment to put in no effort. This is partly because of the inherent simultaneity of the meeting: the two players are placed in a situation where neither has a mechanism to commit to making no effort. And it is partly because of the psychological effects of face-to-face contact; participants want to be highly esteemed by others, and this is likely to be fostered by cooperation rather than conflict. With face-to-face contact, it is thus difficult for one player to maintain the position that they will put in no effort and free ride on the other.

A second role that a face-to-face meeting can play derives from the fact that meetings are a relatively costly form of information exchange. Suppose that players can only exchange their information in a meeting. Attending the meeting has a real cost, and crucially, each player makes the decision of whether or not to attend on the basis of her *own* information; it is in the meeting that information is shared and the decision on whether or not to go ahead with the project is taken. How does this change the situation, as compared to costless information sharing? If the meeting cost is high enough, then players who have done no research (as well as those who have received a signal) will not find it worthwhile to attend the meeting. As a consequence, doing nothing is no longer privately profitable; each player has to pay a cost (that of attending the meeting) before obtaining the partner's information, and the cost is not worth paying given the original information.

In terms of figure 11.1, there is a change in the shape of each player's indifference curves. Critically, below OB it is no longer worthwhile for player 1 to turn up to the meeting if their signal is bad. In this event there is no prospect of sharing surplus from the project, reducing EU_1 in the region below OB, compared to above. This change in the shape of the EU_1 indifference curves means that the best response function $R(e_2)$ is extended to the right from point a. Extending it sufficiently far, point E_1 (and similarly E_2) cease to be equilibriums. The best response functions now have a single intersection at E_S where both players have positive effort levels. The meeting therefore reduces the set of equilibriums to the unique one at which both players make an effort.

This analysis, while highly stylized, formalizes two different possible roles that face-to-face meetings may have. One is as a form of preplay communication to coordinate on one of the possible equilibriums. The other is as a way of increasing the cost of free riding; a player who makes no effort will not find it worthwhile to attend the meeting, and so cannot make a positive return from the project.[5]

The Formation of In-Groups: Getting into the Loop

The prior screening or socialization of potential partners can be provided in some contexts by formal certification and institutionalized screening mechanisms such as professional examinations. In other contexts, however—particularly in creative activities, where ability is difficult to evaluate, and where performance criteria cannot be codified and institutionalized—such formal techniques may not be useful. Instead informal networks—being in the loop or the in-group—may take their place as screening mechanisms. We can think, in this regard, of the example given in chapters 7 and 8 of how belonging to Israel's Unit 8200 screens individuals who get access to high-tech entrepreneurship networks in that country.

What is the informational basis of such a group? Where prior screening and certification of individuals' ability or effort is not possible, there has to be open although not necessarily costless membership to all. Yet once in, members cease to be anonymous, knowing who is in the group, observing the performance of members, and in turn being observed by other members. This information is used to maintain the quality of the group. At its simplest, a record of failure is used as the basis for expulsion from the group. Group members are therefore continually judging and being judged, and know exactly who is in and who is out.

The process of in-group formation works in the following manner.

> Insiders work harder than outsiders because they fear ejection from the group.
> This effort effect is greater for more able people because the potential payoff of joining the group is greater, and this has the

effect of further redefining the group—high-ability people work
harder, are more likely to succeed, and hence have a still-higher
probability of staying in the group.

All individuals can enter the group, but there is a cost to entry—
perhaps the cost of working in a more expensive city or the time
invested in building initial contacts with the group through face-
to-face meetings. This is a fixed cost that varies across individuals.

A higher proportion of high- than of low-ability individuals enters
the group initially. Entry costs therefore act as a self-selection
mechanism, further increasing the ability gap between insiders
and outsiders. People in the group work harder than the outsiders do. The effect is to increase both group size as failure prob-
abilities are reduced and the proportion of the in-group that is
high ability.

Thus, by joining, high-ability people have a higher probability of undertaking successful projects so they are more likely to survive as members of the group. Members of the group will (conditional on their ability) have higher earnings than outsiders because they are matching with
(on average) higher-quality people. Members of the group will also work
harder than outsiders; the earnings differential creates an incentive to
stay in the group, and the probability of staying in is increased by hard
work. Finally, although initial access to the group is open to all, there may
be an entry cost, perhaps in the form of time and effort to become known
as deserving of belonging to the group. Even if this is the same for people
of all abilities, it will have a greater deterrent effect for the less able because their income gain from being in the group is less.

Who gains and who loses from this process? If no group existed, all
high-ability individuals would have the same utility, as would all low-
ability individuals. The existence of the group creates a gap between insiders and outsiders, and this gap is larger for high-ability individuals
than low-ability ones, and is greater when the effort is endogenous and
entry costs shape the selection of individuals initially entering the group.
Outsiders are the big losers, as refinement of group membership forces
them to make worse matches. The gainers from the in-group are the high-
ability insiders.

Thus, face-to-face contact removes anonymity, and allows people to
judge and be judged. If you have been observed to fail, then there is some
probability that you are branded an outsider and group members will no
longer seek to match with you. The magnitude of this probability parameter is, in many activities, inherently spatial. In a faceless and anonymous
world, in-groups cannot form. By removing anonymity, face-to-face contact raises the probability of good, step-by-step iterative judgments about
the abilities of others. An in-group that forms to generate and share this

information improves the quality of matches made by workers, also sharpens the incentives for individuals to succeed, and increases the work effort of group members.

Telepresence and the Future of Face-to-Face Contact

There is much speculation today about whether generalized telepresence can somehow replace face-to-face contact.[6] Telepresence will likely substitute for routinized contact in some ways, and prolong the relationships built up via face-to-face contact, over time and space. We cannot entirely predict the future of telepresence, which depends not only on the quality of telepresence technology—likely to improve greatly—but also on social and individual learning to use it. The future of telepresence will be the outcome of a two-way process. It will engender new and complex functions in the economy, which in turn will reinforce the need for face-to-face contact in these areas of the economy, even as it makes it possible to substitute telepresence for others (Charlot and Duranton 2006; Olson and Olson 2000). This is another example of the two-way street between lower unit trade costs, complexity, and trade that I analyzed in chapter 9.

A communication technology such as telepresence can affect the division of labor in three different ways: as a substitute for existing tools, as when telepresence replaces the telephone; as a complement for existing tools, as when telepresence increases the flow of email (since the interactive meetings made possible by telepresence provoke more use of email); and as an enabler of emergence, as when facilitates much more fluid and unplanned social networking.

Information technology in firms has had all these effects: it gradually moved from simple linear substitution for the typewriter and the intraoffice memo to the decline of secretarial services with the advent of email, and then to the rise of the self-contained mobile office. Table 11.2 rates different forms of communication in terms of the qualitative and quantitative dimensions of the typical use to which the tool is put. For the sake of simplicity, it describes only situations where the communication outcome is successfully achieved, and the means used to engage in the interaction is both effective and efficient.

In the first column is the case of a traffic light. This is a low-sophistication, low-bandwidth tool. The message sender programs the traffic light to change from red to green, and when it does, the signal is clear and simple for the receiver. The communication is synchronous, since if there is no one waiting for the light to change at that moment at that intersection, the signal is then simply wasted.

In the second column, a traditional postal letter exemplifies asynchronous communication, since the sender knows that the receiver will get the

TABLE 11.2
Quality and Quantity of Communication Relationships

	Traffic Light	Letter	Lecture	Meeting
Degree of "complexity"	Low	Medium	High	Highest
Extent of "bandwidth"	Low	Medium	High	Highest

message at some later time. A letter can contain a large or small quantity of information that is exactly pertinent to the needs of both the sender and receiver. Yet its nonsynchronous form restricts the quantity and quality of what can be transmitted.

The third column is a "one-to-many" synchronous broadcast. Although there are many forms of asynchronous broadcast communication such as television, a synchronous professor's lecture involves nonverbal cues and trust, as in face-to-face exchange. The lecturer can thus assess the degree of attention and engagement of the participants, and the listeners are witnessing a performance involving a great deal of parallel processing of verbal, physical, and interpersonal cues. The last column is the case of a face-to-face meeting to discuss a project or brainstorm an idea.

Table 11.3 extends this reasoning to offer illustrations of how the four types of communication might interact with changes in the division of labor as well as the nature of tasks on the assumption that telepresence is high quality, inexpensive, ubiquitous, and widely used.

Telepresence opens up the potential to both alter the division of labor and create new tasks through substitution, complementarity, and emergence effects. Substitutions include ways that letters, lectures, and meetings could be in part replaced by telepresence. As for complementarities, one could imagine telepresence inspiring people to write letters after they have "seen" someone via telepresence or for people who attend a lecture via telepresence to then seek out a face-to-face encounter. The emergence effects of telepresence on the division of labor that are still within the logic and functioning of existing systems might include asynchronous video letters (vodcasts), or—for the one-to-many lecture form of communication—some blending of synchronous and asynchronous telepresence that allows for new kinds of multimedia broadcasting. As for "emergent-internal" effects due to telepresence combining with meetings, we can imagine a further unbundling of the different aspects of a face-to-face meeting—the pre- and postmeeting phases, for instance, could allow for a refinement of the use of face-to-face contact in ways that enhance efficiency, but also give the "real face-to-face" moment added significance

TABLE 11.3
The Impact of Telepresence on Communication

| | Substitute | Complement | Emergent | |
			Within-system	External to system
Traffic light	None	Modest: central traffic cop info	Auto-pilot: remote driver	Auto-pilot: new supply networks
Letter	Modest– replaces some letters	Modest– generates some letters	Asynchronous video-letter	New identity formation, communities– letter-video performance art
Lecture	Depends on content of lecture: high for entirely codified, lower for rest	Significant– generates demand for F2F	Vodcasting & TP customized blends alter product & production process	End of mass broadcast?
Meeting	Low for non-routine meetings	Modest for follow-on meetings	Unbundling of meeting functions, significant refinement of division of labor	TP in virtual reality and significant shift in cultures of trust, verification, identity & community formation

and new codes. This analysis, together with that of chapter 9, strongly suggests that telepresence will not eliminate the need for a great deal of face-to-face interaction. As with previous innovations in transport and communications technology, though, it will alter the boundaries of what can be done nearby and what can be done far away (Miller and Storper 2008).

Buzz

Face-to-face contact is an efficient technology of communication; a means of overcoming coordination and incentive problems in uncertain environments; a key element of the socialization that in turn allows people to be candidates for membership of in-groups and to stay in such groups; and a direct source of psychological motivation. The combined and super-additive effects of these features is buzz. These various internetwork, highly dynamic, and unplanned contact systems were alluded to by Jacobs (1969) in her intuition that urban diversity is central to certain kinds of economic creativity, because of the specific advantages of unplanned and haphazard internetwork contact.

The examples of buzz are abundant. The design, entertainment, and advertising industries have strong crossover effects in their development of content, and this is why places such as New York, Los Angeles, London, and Paris concentrate them together (Pratt 2002; Scott 2005). Higher education, finance, and government are a powerful nexus of ideas and contact networks for the socialization of elites along with the coordination of their joint projects. Colocation is especially important to these processes because it provides a low-cost way for new ideas and talent to make their way into existing activities by facilitating access for newcomers as well as lowering the costs of evaluation on the part of those already in the relevant loops. New relationships are hence made easier, cheaper, and more effective than they would be without colocation. Buzz cities continue to have such force today because they are the places where, more than ever, critical problems of coordination in the modern economy are resolved through face-to-face contact.

Paradoxically, buzz cities are often those we most closely associate with globalization because they are important nodes of highly developed international business and culture networks, with high levels of international travel-and-meeting activity, and high concentrations of both high- and low-skilled immigrants. They frequently host many multinational enterprises. The highest levels of international business also require insertion into locally grounded government and political networks in order to function efficiently. The most globalized cities also seem to have the most localized buzz.

How to Develop Buzz

In recent policy thinking about how to make cities successful, city leaders have been enamored of the notion that attracting skilled workers and enhancing their opportunities for creativity will make cities prosper, working backward from observing cities such as Hong Kong or London. I have extensively critiqued these accounts—in chapters 2–4—as having effectively reversed the order of causality: places grow and prosper because they get the firms and jobs that attract these kinds of people. And yet it can be seen that it is quite logical for certain people to have a strong preference for interaction through face-to-face contact, and want to locate themselves where the planned or serendipitous interactions will be more probable. To kick off this dynamic, however, a minimal threshold of colocation of firms must first occur, which in turn generates the critical mass of people that in turn raises the benefits of face-to-face contact. The chicken of the process is the spatially concentrated demand for skilled labor; the eggs are interaction, deal making, and learning-by-interacting.

Along these lines, one question to which scholars have no firm answer is: Why are the world's big cities economically viable (Combes et al. 2009)? Economies of scale in most industries are exhausted at levels that can be satisfied by metropolitan areas that are much smaller than New York or Los Angeles. In still-developing countries, hypermetropolitan development is a residue of uneven and scarce agglomeration economies, skill pools, and transport links; this was the case for the extreme dominance of São Paulo in the Brazil of the 1970s. This is not true of developed economies, though, and yet their biggest metropolitan areas continue to not only be viable but also to grow. Some kind of range of related skills across different but related sectors seems to form the demand structure that sustains buzz. Understanding the role of buzz in tying together the different activities of diversified urban economies may provide the key to explaining why big cities maintain their edge in a world of steadily declining communications costs.

PART IV

The Political Context of City and Regional Development

Exit or Voice?

How Important Are Cities to Human Development?

Are cities really that important? If one thinks about some of the most vital issues for humanity—war and peace, economic development, macroeconomics, social mobility, education, technology, the environment, or art and culture—it's not immediately evident that cities are high on the list of their causes. Most wars do not seem to be the direct result of the existence of cities, nor in the modern era are they between cities. Technology advances largely because of science, engineering, property rights, markets, and culture. Culture and art are produced everywhere, and not necessarily in cities.

And yet at least since the stirrings of social science in the nineteenth century, cities are the subject of extravagant claims about their significance to the main human development processes. The extravagance is both negative and positive. Cities were hellish according to Charles Dickens, Émile Zola, or Karl Marx, but city air was claimed to make men free according to a medieval German expression (*stadtluft macht frei*) that has been picked up in the writings of Georg Simmel, Emile Durkheim, and many other theorists of the link between urbanization and modernity. Contemporary social science has pretty much reproduced this divide. There are abundant literatures on the city as the locus of poverty, segregation, violence, inequality, pollution, mass manipulation, and cultural dumbing down. There are equally abundant claims that cities are where social and economic progress largely takes place, as evidenced by their systematic association with higher than average levels of education, productivity, social mobility, ethnic diversity, income, innovation, and culture.

There are more nuanced positions on how cities relate to the big processes of socioeconomic development. Poverty, culture, productivity, conflict, literacy, and mobility could all be determined by discrete compositional causes; urban poverty, for example, could be caused by sorting individuals with low skills into cities, but without urbanization itself adding to the total incidence of poverty in the population as a whole. In contrast, poverty could be exacerbated if the colocation of unskilled individuals inhibits their skill acquisition and causes them to get bad signals about individual strategies because they only interact with other poor people (Durlauf 2004). In the end, the urban is probably both an expression and a partial cause of many crucial dimensions of human development, but we have difficulty precisely drawing the line between them, defining their relative magnitudes, and understanding the sequences of their development.

Moreover, whether or not cities are causes of these phenomena, they are going to concentrate, cheek by jowl, strong doses of them both. Local policy—urban or regional—is not going to abolish segregation, poverty, and inequality. Nor will it inspire a new era of flourishing cultural achievements, or stunningly change the rate of technological progress and economic growth. But it is in cities that many of the symptoms of these big forces of change show up in people's lives. Hence, it is in cities that we can harvest their bounty, or if things go right, temper their negative effects.

Urbanization as a Source of Economic Development

Let me focus on just one dimension of whether cities are important: economic development. Cities and city-systems do not just express development; they are an essential input into it (Henderson 2010). The basics are argued convincingly by NEG and summarized well in the World Bank's (2009) *World Development Report*. Without the basic processes that enable cities to flourish, all the other dynamics that contribute to economic development will be hampered. Development is strongly inhibited where—as the World Bank puts it—distance is too costly, divisions between places create barriers to trade, and there is not enough density. These are the "three D's" that link urbanization and economic development. In order for certain types of economic growth, cultural achievement, better education, and social inclusion to become possible, urbanization has to be possible.

The *World Development Report* is another in a long line of attempts to establish the link between urbanization and economic as well as social development (Black and Henderson 1999). Beyond establishing that urbanization and development go together, many such works go further, arguing that city-systems should adopt a particular form. They look for universal laws of city sizes, consisting of an optimal number and size of cities. The results of this research are modestly robust in the sense that there are some regularities in the number and size of urban units relative to population. But there are many notable exceptions, such as the many countries that have an "oversized" city. Paris, London, Buenos Aires, Mexico, and Tokyo all account for high proportions of their national population and economic activity, and there is a huge gap between them and the second city-region in each of those countries. This doesn't seem to have stopped those countries from developing. Moreover, all approaches to optimal urban systems have weak theoretical foundations in the sense that we are not told why such statistical regularities should exist or why they would be good for economic development. As noted in chapter 3, NEG dangles the possibility of explaining the size of cities, based on economies of scale in industries, but NEG has not yet succeeded in operationalizing this bottom-up explanation for city sizes, from firms to agglomerations to cities.

The typical response to irregularities and variations in the shape of city-systems of developed countries is to claim that they are "effects of history." Thus, in countries that have been unified for a long time, there are long-established large market areas. This promotes economies of scale for firms and industries, and has allowed relatively big cities to develop. In other countries, more division and late unification, generally reflected in political decentralization, distribute city sizes more evenly and prevent the growth of megacities. These effects of history explain why all urban systems do not neatly have the same shape.

But it is easy for path dependency to become just another black box for explanation. For example, the size and number of urban units should be reshaped by changing economies of scale of firms in each economy along with the agglomerations they generate. As trade costs decline and internal borders are taken down, thus reducing divisions between market areas, markets areas become bigger. This in turn allows firms, agglomerations, and cities to become bigger. History nevertheless seems to get in the way again. In Europe following integration, this has occurred mostly in homogeneous "commodity" industries, and much less in industries with a lot of product differentiation (Midelfahrt-Knarvik and Overman 2002; Midelfahrt-Knarvik et al. 2002; Storper, Chen, and De Paolis 2002). Most urban economics then just returns to the "frictions" argument: that there is a time lag, due to the existence of sunk costs and certain kinds of political barriers between scale changes and the reconfiguration of urban systems.

Moreover, it has not been established how, or if, deviations from these optimal urban systems affect the economic development of a country or its individual city-regions. It would be one thing if only underdeveloped countries had oversized biggest cities. But this just isn't the case. Rich economies have a fairly wide band of mixes of distance, division, and density. For the time being, we do not have the tools to identify precisely the range of city-systems that are compatible with the most effective overall economic development, though scholars and consultants regularly make assertions in this direction when they advocate regional policies.

City-Systems and Spatial Habits

I propose an additional way to explain the wide range of variation of urban systems. They are the consequence of institutionalized spatial behaviors along with the social and political feedbacks of these behaviors. Hirschman (1970) identified three options for behavior in market societies. We can leave (exit); we can stay in order to try to shape things by speaking or expressing preferences (voice); and in some cases, we can combine the latter with the strategy of letting others know we won't go away (loyalty). In geographical behaviors, the mobility of firms and individuals is exit, and the level of exit from places is inversely related to loyalty, and a substitute for voice.

Exit is a key behavior in all market economies, with powerful geographical effects. It shapes factor mobility and the matching of factors to one another in places. Exit is not just the spontaneous calculus of individuals and firms. There are many large-scale political, institutional, and cultural forces that shape how firms and individuals select, filter, and sort themselves among cities (at the interregional scale) as well as within them (at the intraregional scale between neighborhoods or localities). I label these forces "spatial habits." Spatial habits have major effects on geographical patterns of wages, living costs, job opportunities, and income distributions. I will now examine spatial habits in two ways; I will begin with a highly focused and technical example of how they affect innovation differently in the United States and Europe. The spatial habits of Europeans and Americans create different geographies of innovation in the geographical United States and the European Union.[1] The higher level of exit in the United States leads to more long-distance geographical mixing and matching of inputs to innovation in the United States than in Europe, and this impacts their overall innovation levels. Following this, in the second half of this chapter, I will turn to a broad interpretation of the role of exit in the United States—a revisiting of the well-known "frontier thesis." I will examine the geographical process in relationship to a wide variety of political, social, and economic outcomes in the United States, and their differences when compared to Europe.

The Territorial Dynamics of Innovation:
A Europe-US Comparative Analysis

The European Union and the United States are characterized by surprisingly different economic geographies of production and jobs. European city-regions are, on average, more diversified than their US counterparts, which are in turn more specialized (Le Galès 2004). On average, in Europe an industry or output sector will be spread across a greater number of regions in smaller clusters than it will be in the United States. This difference—inherited in Europe from a long past of high trade and factor mobility barriers—has not changed much, even with the opening of European borders and monetary integration (Midelfahrt-Knarvik and Overman 2002; Storper, Chen, and De Paolis 2002). Moreover, and consistent with this pattern, there is more "spatial interaction" between European regions—meaning that there are more short-term flows of people and inputs from one region to another, as a proportion of the total stock of those factors, than there are between US city-regions. This may reflect geographical closeness in Europe, but gravity models show that it is not due only to short distances. In Europe, because of the more fragmented, less specialized geography of jobs and output, more interregional contact is used to match capital, labor, and information than in the United States, where these matching processes occur more at the intraregional scale, and regions are more self-contained.

In spite of their similar levels of structural development, the EU15—the fifteen western European members of the European Union prior to the European Union's admission of several eastern European countries in the early 2000s—manifest much less science-based innovation than the United States. When considering scientific activity, such as the number of scientific publications and citations weighted by population (as reported in Dosi et al. 2006, using Organization for Economic Cooperation and Development [OECD] data), the science output gap between the EU15 and the United States is immediately apparent, with 4.64 publications per 1,000 inhabitants in the United States versus 3.6 in the EU15 in the 1997–2001 period. This gap is even wider when the impact of such scientific production is assessed in terms of article citations (39.75 per 1,000 inhabitants in the United States as opposed to 23.03 in the EU15) or shares in the top 1 percent most cited publications (0.09 top 1 percent publications per 1,000 inhabitants in the United States versus 0.04 in the EU15). When considering technological output, the United States shows the best innovative performance as measured by its share of the total triadic (US-European-Japanese) patent families (36.4 percent in 2003 in contrast to 30.3 percent of the European Union).[2] When the triadic patent families are weighted by population, US patent intensity is 47 percent higher than for the EU15, and almost double that of the EU25 (OECD 2006). Aggregate indicators of the world technology hierarchy, based on detailed measurements of the unit values of products that are exported by countries, continue to indicate that the United States has a higher proportion of products with such high unit prices, which can be considered a proxy for their original technological content (Kemeny 2009).

Existing analyses have mainly addressed the differences between the two continents in terms of the major inputs to innovation. Thus, the total amount of the resources devoted to innovative activities varies significantly. In 2004, 1.9 percent of the GDP was spent on R & D in the EU25 (1.95 percent in the EU15) (Eurostat 2006a) compared to 2.6 percent of the GDP (National Science Foundation 2006) for the United States. Furthermore, the nature of such expenditure differs considerably. A large percentage of this US public expenditure is for R & D carried out by private firms, or about double the corresponding figure in the European Union. US private firms not only benefit from a larger share of public funds than their EU counterparts but they also devote a higher proportion of their internal resources to R & D. Industry-financed R & D expenditure is about 1.9 percent of the GDP in the United States (ibid.), but only around 1 percent of the GDP in the European Union (Eurostat 2006a).

Second, the gap in human resources devoted to R & D is large and significant. "In 2003, the number of researchers (in full-time equivalents) per thousand of the labor force amounted to only 5.4 in the EU against 10.1 in Japan and 9.0 in the US. This EU deficit is mainly located in the business sector" (European Commission 2005, 6). The advantage of the United States in this area is not only quantitative but also qualitative, as the United States attracts and retains a large proportion of high-impact researchers; of the top 1,222 most cited individuals in 14 scientific fields, 66 percent live and work in the United States, while only 20 percent are from the sum of the EU countries (Batty 2003). In 2004, only 34.1 percent of all 20-year-olds were enrolled in higher education in the EU25 (and 33.4 percent in the eurozone), in comparison to 46.2 percent in the United States (European Commission 2005). Moreover, public and private investment in education is significantly higher in the United States than in the European Union; in 2003, the expenditure per student in higher education—adding public and private expenditure—was just 39.3 percent that of the United States in the EU25 and 41.1 percent in the eurozone.[3]

The two continents also show marked differences in the institutions and policies governing the invention, development, and adoption of new technologies. "The foundations of the US national system of innovation were largely put in place during 1945–1950 [when] demobilization for peace was replaced by Cold War rearmament" (Mowery 1998, 640). There is yet no analogous Europe-wide system in place—that is, one that could complement and integrate existing national systems in the way the US institutions do (Gregersen and Johnson 1997; Borrás 2004; Stein 2004). The United States' integrated (though decentralized) system was forged by the large-scale, federally funded projects carried out mostly by private firms and supported by basic research. As a result, the US national innovation system is heavily oriented toward radical innovations (Ergas 1987).

Furthermore, the antitrust and intellectual property regulatory frameworks of the United States seem to offer a fertile environment for the marketing of new technologies (Hart 2001).[4] This business environment allows for a more effective adjustment of the sectoral structure of the economy with the prompt start up of new firms in response to new market opportunities in emerging sectors. The higher degree of specialization in R & D–intensive sectors along with the stronger presence of small- and medium-size R & D–intensive firms in the national market (Smith 2007) are both causes and consequences of the US shifting capacity in a circular process supported by the intrinsically different system of innovation conditions. Conversely, EU firms on average have historically had weaker entrepreneurial culture and greater resistance to organizational change (Delmas 2002). Major constraints also arise from barriers to the access to venture capital (a major source of funds for US innovation) and European labor market rules, which frequently lead to mismatches between staffing patterns and the true demand for skills, since they slow down the recomposition of staff in response to technology and market shifts. All these factors directly influence innovative performance. But in addition to this, they lead to different patterns in the spatial organization of innovation on each continent.

The spatial distribution of innovative output in both Europe and the United States, as proxied by patents, exhibits a strong tendency toward disproportionate concentration in a few locations. "During the 1990s, 92 percent of all patents were granted to residents of metropolitan areas, although these areas account for only about three-quarters of the US population, and for about 20 percent of land area of the continental United States" (Carlino, Chatterjee, and Hunt 2001, 1). The cumulative percentage of the total patents recorded by the hundred most innovative EU15 regions and US MSAs is similar on the two continents, and in both contexts the twenty most innovative regions account for around 70 percent of the total patents.

Agglomeration and density influence a variety of economic processes. Agglomeration increases innovative output even after controlling for differences in human capital, high-tech industry structure, and R & D university infrastructure, both in the United States (Carlino, Chatterjee, and Hunt 2001; Sedgley and Elmslie 2004) and some EU countries (e.g., for the case of Sweden, see Andersson, Quigley, and Wilhelmsson 2005). As Antonio Ciccone (2000, 214) points out, the "agglomeration effects in European countries (France, Germany, Italy, Spain, and the UK) are only slightly lower than in the US and do not vary significantly across countries."

Yet density does not adequately capture the potential complexity of the geography of matching and learning. Matching and learning are logical outcomes of the many ways in which agents move, signal, and match to other agents. This means not just "being" in established patterns of proximity to other agents; it also involves the dynamic process by which such densities and proximities are achieved, and how they adjust over time. Such adjustments refer to the *flow* dimensions of matching and learning. Analyzing how factors move and are matched, as a dynamic process, is a complement to what the literature has to say on the *levels* of density, proximity, and innovation.

In this regard, even similarly dense economic fabrics may be exposed to external knowledge flows to different degrees, with different levels of knowledge spillovers from neighboring areas. Therefore, rather than thinking of agglomerations one by one, it is helpful to consider their interrelations and connections to other places. The use of tacit and highly specialized knowledge is maximized in the "core" of dense agglomerations, but some of that knowledge travels more widely (Anselin, Varga, and Ács 2000; Varga 2000; Ács 2002; Sonn and Storper 2008; Bottazzi and Peri 2003; Greunz 2003; Crescenzi 2005; Moreno, Paci, and Usai 2005b; Rodríguez-Pose and Crescenzi 2008). This means that regions benefit from their relations to other innovative neighborhoods.

Interagglomeration knowledge flows are different on the two continents. The higher-average population density of the European Union, with major metropolitan areas relatively closer together than in the United States (where instead metropolitan areas are farther away from one another), limits the distance decay of useful knowledge. Thus, innovation spillovers average between 200 and 300 kilometers from the point of origin, whereas they drop off between 80 and 110 kilometers in the United States. As such, in the United States, the production of knowledge and innovation are more localized, and generally more concentrated in bigger agglomerations than in Europe. In Europe, then, agglomerations are on average smaller, and this reduces their scale advantages and the importance of matching within the agglomeration, but they partially compensate this by interacting between agglomerations, which are denser and closer to one another than in the United States. In the United States, innovative centers are different from those in Europe in that they depend more on both highly localized matching of innovative resources and very long-distance relations; in Europe, they have less local matching, and depend a lot on interactions to rather-nearby centers, but not so much on continent-wide exchanges of knowledge and people.

In addition, an agglomeration is not merely a stock of resources. Migration flows contribute to the creation of new knowledge at the local level, increasing its intensity or changing its mix (Ottaviano and Peri 2006). In the most innovative places, migration updates the matching of knowledge, skills, and competencies to accompany the evolution of the technological frontier. On the contrary, where agglomerations have restricted in-migration (possibly due to divisions), innovative agents may benefit from traditional proximity relationships, but find it more difficult to discover new skills and ideas. The degree of interregional labor mobility is substantially higher in the United States than in the European Union, as extensively documented by Klaus Zimmermann (1995, 2005), François Vandamme (2000), Patrick Puhani (2001), and Peri (2005), in a comparative perspective, and there are considerable differences in foreign in-migration as well.[5]

Where the broader historical, institutional, and political forces inhibit mobility, they could prevent the cluster from adjusting in such a way that the most efficient combination of the two types of external economies is maintained, thereby hampering innovative productivity. This could be the case of Europe, where incomplete economic integration, redundant technological competencies among countries, and overall duplications in economic structures have acted as brakes on specialization.

While the United States has shown a tendency for interregional convergence in innovation levels, this was mostly a result of the initial development of the South. It was a onetime event, based on initial catch-up processes. In the long run, the innovation geography of the United States is based on more geographical concentration in a smaller number of highly innovative regions, and these regions are more specialized than in their European city-region counterparts. The long-run tendency in Europe is to share more of a given type of industry in more cities in the urban system, for urban systems tend to be less turbulent than in the United States in their economic and demographic performance, and for midsize metropolitan regions to play a bigger role in Europe than in the United States.

Whether one system or another is truly better for long-term innovation and economic growth cannot yet be known with any certainty. As noted earlier, Ciccone (2000) shows that the level of agglomeration economies is not substantially different on the two continents. My results indicate that the contribution of agglomeration to the production of new knowledge cannot be reduced to the level of agglomeration but also must be understood in process terms. Seeing geography as a process opens up fresh questions about how different regions capture or develop new technologies. For example, will Europe flunk out in capturing biotechnology if it can't build a single big cluster in the critical first-mover innovation stage, because its factor matching is too slow and limited? By contrast, is China's ability to build huge clusters going to enable China to move up the ladder of innovation faster than smaller developing countries (or even the developed countries)? Can cluster size limits be compensated in smaller countries if they concentrate on a smaller number of products and doing each one at the scale required by the world economy?

Spatial Habits and Sociopolitical Development: The US Case

Let's now take a broader look at the effects of spatial habits. Exit, mobility, and matching over geographical space have many consequences, some of which are the urban and regional pattern itself, and others of which are in other areas of social and political development. To see this, we can examine four principal dimensions of the US geographical process: the ability to create new city and regional authorities and governments; the rate of migration of firms and people from region to region; the role of land and land development in the economy; and the degree of differences in labor regulation and wages among regions. These four aspects of the geographical process in the United States in turn shape a variety of economic, social, and political outcomes. In what follows, I explore three such outcomes: technological dynamism, the formation of political coalitions and alliances, and the distribution of income.

THE INNOVATIVE AMERICANS:
A GEOGRAPHICAL INTERPRETATION

Historians of US economic growth have long debated the sources of the US industrial revolution in the mid-nineteenth century and the country's process of becoming the world's richest large economy. All agree, however, that technological progress is a central part of the story (Mokyr 1991; Rosenberg 1982). A key feature of such progress is that the United States began as an underdeveloped agricultural economy, but ultimately followed a more capital-intensive pathway to industrialization than its nineteenth-century competitor, Britain. And Britain was already more capital intensive in most industries than other European economies (Allen 2009).

Proponents of the "Habbakuk (1962) thesis" argue that US capital intensity was stimulated by unusually high wages due to a labor scarcity in the United States. But Carville Earle (1992) counters this from a geographical perspective to hold that US industrial centers had access to abundant low-wage labor during the takeoff to capital-intensive innovation due to the availability of surplus labor from rural regions and foreign immigration. The capital-intensive pathway was made possible because low wages compensated the unusually high cost of capital. Capital-intensive techniques, in turn, were diffused quickly throughout the territory through the land grant colleges, which applied federal funding to local economies while stimulating interplace competition.

Mass production was invented and perfected in the United States following the breakthrough to interchangeable parts—the "American system" (Hounshell 1984). US geography was the fundamental stimulus to mass production. The outputs of manufacturing were redesigned by Americans to respond to their needs for faster, lighter, and cheaper versions of outputs than Europe. US locomotives had to cover great distances; US firearms were destined toward markets of frontier settlers, not just rich aristocrats going hunting for leisure. A corollary to this is that when such products broke down, they were often geographically far from skilled labor that could repair them. Interchangeable parts that could be shipped to distant places and installed by less skilled labor were a solution to this problem. First-nature geography (natural features) along with a vast and distant frontier shaped US technological dynamism.

NEG theories also suggest that second-nature geography—the spatial distribution of resources and people created by the society—shaped US innovation. Geographically extensive markets can be a disadvantage for attaining economies of scale if internal transport costs are extremely high. But if those costs trend downward dynamically enough, then the reverse happens: extensive markets become big ones. And the initial big markets were in infrastructure technologies that provided the means to overcome the distance (railroads) and agricultural machinery needed to efficiently use vast, relatively homogeneous spaces with relatively scarce labor. As such innovations took hold, mobility was reinforced, and it strengthened the homogenization of tastes and practices, creating a virtuous circle of bigness. This, in turn, reinforced innovations oriented toward standardization and scale economies. In the mid-nineteenth to early twentieth centuries, these conditions were unique to the United States, replicated nowhere else in the industrial world.

In the twentieth century, the United States not only came up with many fundamental technological breakthroughs; it also led them rapidly through a growth process to standardization and mass marketing (Rosenberg 1982). The appeal of mass production and distribution was natural to the relatively homogeneous US economic and social environment, with its low transport costs, high levels of mobility, and weak role of highly differentiated tastes and practices from one place to another. These advantages are less and less unique to the United States in the twenty-first century, although recent examples in distribution (Walmart) and the transformation of high-tech objects into mass consumer products testify to the ongoing strength of the US ability to link innovation to mass production. The geographical scale of the United States as well as the geographical processes developed to cope with and exploit it are arguably central to US technological dynamism for better than a century and a half.

SPACE, CLASS POWER, AND SOCIAL MOBILITY

Compared to most other countries, in the United States, it is relatively easy to create new communities and endow them with local government authorities. Sukkoo Kim and Marc Law (2012) show that in the New World, the countries with less centralized political institutions, especially the United States, allow for the creation of new cities and jurisdictions more than do countries with centralized institutions, even when controlling for population dynamics and natural geographical features. We do not know whether this ease of city creation and community building is a cause of the US geographical process or an outcome of US spatial habits, but in either case, it has important further political and social consequences.

In any country, the geographical origin of powerful groups in the economy and how they change over time affects the construction of a national politics along with informal networks of political power. Regionally based industrial groups, for example, were strong actors in European industrialization, but often impeded the integration of national economies (Perroux 1950). In some cases, such as France, political power was used to consolidate these groups at a national level (by nationalizing them) or restructure them. In still other countries, such as Italy, regional elites predominated over national economic social networks, and do so even today.

Regionally based economic elites based in powerful regional families are less important in the US industrialization process than in these other countries. As in other countries, US industries have arisen in particular regions. But in the United States, they frequently have come about through the in-migration of new elites. Moreover, even though the United States long ago became a mature industrial economy, this greenfield effect has continued to dominate, as with the rise of the West Coast as the center of many new industries in the 1940s to 1980s, and now with the rise of certain metropolitan regions in the South and Southwest as potential centers of major new innovation clusters. "Windows of locational opportunity"—the possibility of establishing major new industries in new places—are used much more in the United States than elsewhere (Storper and Walker 1989; Scott and Storper 1987). Major corporations actually move headquarters between cities in the United States; it would be unheard of, for example, for the equivalent of Boeing in another country to pick up and move its headquarters to another city (as Boeing did from Seattle to Chicago a few years ago), except in the case of a merger and acquisition. The geographical process in the United States thus adds new elites in new places more fluidly than it does in other countries, and their loyalty is shorter lived, though not necessarily shallower (Jaher 1984).

Labor rules and work practices in the United States are an outlier among industrial countries in that they are more legally and functionally decentralized as well as fragmented than elsewhere. The United States has a national labor relations law, but it allows high levels of variation among the states in how the law can be applied. The primary division is between closed shop states (compulsory union membership for all workers in any firm where a majority accept the union), and right-to-work states where even if a majority votes to be unionized, individuals are not required to join the union or even accept the union contract terms in order to work in the firm. No other advanced country has such a wide regional variation in labor law, including wide variation in the detailed regulation of work contracts, occupational safety, minimum wages, and work rules.

The United States has wider intraoccupational wage gaps from region to region than in other wealthy countries. Some of this may be due to the size of the United States, and reflects interregional cost-of-living variations, but cost-of-living differences are not great enough to account for the gap (OECD 2005). Nor is wage equalization within skill levels and occupations achieved by the high level of worker mobility between regions, even after correcting for cost-of-living differences (see chapter 2). Thus, the United States presents the paradox of a large-scale national labor market that is more integrated from a process point of view than most other countries—through exit and mobility—but more fragmented institutionally, with great gaps in outcomes in wages and work practices. These are ways that the internal frontier is durably institutionalized. In turn, this frontier is expressed through geographically based political sectionalism—political competition according to the interests of the major industries of a region—in contrast to other developed countries, where competition is principally among national parties.

The US geographical process is also an opportunity creator. Throughout the US expansion into the North American continent, a geographically spreading economy has provided extraordinary opportunities related to community building through land development, building, trade, local commerce, and the reconstruction of a relatively nondurable built environment. These opportunities exist in all economies, but not in the same way as in the United States. Part of this is simply because the level of regulation of much community-building activity in the United States is either lower on average than in other wealthy economies or is more decentralized, and hence it has greater variation across regions. Part of it is that because of greater spatial mobility, new groups of actors get in on the action more easily than in more settled economies. Land development and its related activities have reached far down the class ladder. Geographical mobility has generated one of the sources of economic independence of nonelites, providing opportunities to individuals who are not members of economic elites, and through local politics, a base for countervailing power to the old elites.

THE BIG SORT: WAYS OF LIFE

The creation of new communities is to consumption what the mobility of production is to process technology: it facilitates the introduction of new habits in daily life. Such new habits ultimately are grafted onto old cities and communities, as anyone who lives in Rome can attest. But not in the way, or at the speed, that this has occurred in places like Los Angeles in 1940 or Las Vegas in 2000.

Spatial habits—mobility, location, sorting, filtering, joining, and separation—shape the biographies of individuals, with each generation experiencing such habits in distinctive ways. I called attention in chapter 10 to this as the situation of the actor, which influences the information they take in, the symbols they encounter, the worldviews they form, and the roles and people they emulate. The United States was for a long time an outlier, even among wealthy developed countries, in the organization of daily life in territorial space. Spatial fragmentation along functional (activity type) and social (race, class, and even age and lifestyle) is more finely tuned in the United States than it is elsewhere in the developed world. Indeed, the United States has recently once again distinguished itself from European countries. In western Europe, intermetropolitan incomes continue to converge, as do indicators of schooling, divorce, infant mortality, and such. In the United States since 2000, intermetropolitan incomes are diverging, but so are social indicators and political attitudes (Bishop 2008). This reflects the effects of intensified spatial sorting in the New Economy, according to skills, education levels, and income (Moretti 2012).

Moreover, individuals in the United States face a more rapidly shifting set of spatial requirements for their daily lives than in other developed places. Claude Fischer (2010, 97) quotes Samuel Ferrell, a contemporary of Tocqueville, as observing that

> perhaps there is nothing more remarkable in the character of the Americans than the indifference with which they leave their old habitations, friends and relations. Each individual is taught to depend mainly on his own exertions, and therefore seldom expects or requires

extraordinary assistance from any man. Attachments seldom exist here beyond that of ordinary acquaintances—these are easily found wherever one may go.

Individuals are reconstituted into new types of local and regional community more rapidly as well as radically than in other similarly developed countries. This happens everywhere that there is development, but the lower level of exit in many countries and higher level of tradition in daily life generate profound international differences in the use of space as the material basis for social and economic change. Thus, though there are replicas of US suburbs almost everywhere in the world today, those replicas are inserted into daily life and geographical process in different ways from the central role they play in the US development process and daily life.

MEMORY, INEQUALITY, AND THE POLITICS OF REDISTRIBUTION

The experiences of places—their "social memories"—are shaped through the mobility of their constituent individuals. They are not limited to them, since all places incorporate and integrate new arrivals. But the rate of mobility in the United States and the thinner layer of collective institutions that function as guardians of the collective memory—official or unofficial, accurate or inaccurate—mean that the denominators of recent experience must serve as the basis for the collectivity.

One of the motivating questions for the "American exceptionalism" historians is: Why was the United States never socialist (Laslett and Lipset 1984)? Earle (1992) contends that geographical differentiation in the nineteenth century was key to the internal divisions within unions at that time—North versus South—thereby preventing the emergence of a unified national union structure, or the basis for any national-scale socialist political movement or party. To this perspective could be added the role of geographical mobility in the twentieth century: by reconstituting individuals into communities, it effectively erases some of the basis for the collective memory of shared experiences of economic and political processes. Individuals are, of course, capable of making sense of out such processes in other ways. But moving around and having thin relationships to place effectively requires that people construct narratives of change—winning and losing, justice and injustice—without much direct experience of concrete places over long periods of time.

This geographical process is likely linked to another way in which the United States is an outlier among advanced countries. Peter Lindert (2004) explains differences in redistributive social welfare policies between the United States and other advanced countries by using social affinity theory. On average, citizens of other countries have a higher propensity to believe that they could fall down the class ladder and need assistance than they do in the United States, and hence on average, have greater affinity for those in other income categories than do Americans, who share more affinities with those in similar income classes. And yet there is no single objective reason for this difference in subjective affinity, since individual Americans are just as likely to have periods of downward social mobility as Europeans, and are about at par when it comes to long-term average upward intergenerational mobility.

Spatial sorting and filtering of winners and losers, however, is exceptional in the United States, as I have argued above, because of the way it combines higher rates of mobility along with both interregional and intraregional sorting, leading to greater turbulence and change. This reinforces the perception that fates are created largely by choice and strategy, rather than by accident or structure.

The other side of this phenomenon is the tendency of Americans to engage in voluntary associative life, creating their own sources of membership and memory. Americans develop extraordinary integration skills, given their high levels of mobility. But the places with greater stability have persistently higher levels of social capital, as one might expect, than rapidly growing communities with high levels of population turnover or outcommuting (Putnam 2000), and lower levels of various social ills. Fischer (2010, 99) writes that "'contractualism' or 'covenantalism' is central to American voluntarism. Individuals make this implicit contract by joining the group: I am free to stay or leave, but while belonging I owe fealty to the group." High levels of exit and entry, and the option of future exit, shape this intersubjective process.

Political scientists have begun to consider the geographical basis of the changing politics of the United States in recent years (Bartels 2008). When Lyndon Baines Johnson as president signed the civil rights legislation of 1963, he remarked to his aides that he had lost the South to the Democratic Party for fifty years. At the time, that would not have been a fatal blow to that party; since 1963, it has become lethal because the South has grown immensely in demographic importance. One might have thought that the arrival of millions of nonsoutherners would dilute the effect of traditional southern social and economic conservatism. And yet this has not been the case.

Southern conservatism is, in political terms, an outlier among rich nations. It might be an effect of self-selection or spatial filtering, where individuals who are more conservative than the US average are more likely to go to the South (Texas Politics 2011; Mayer 1993). Spatial sorting could reinforce southern conservatism; it could also help create pockets of extreme conservatism in regions that are otherwise closer to the political center in selected suburbs and exurban communities around the country (Bishop 2008). This phenomenon is not found to anywhere near the same extent in other developed countries. Spatial self-selection also seems partly responsible for the growing social liberalism of coastal California as well as certain parts of the Mid-Atlantic coast and New England (Bartels 2008). Whether this spatial self-sorting is due to the search for jobs or "political amenities" is not at issue here (but see my discussion of this in chapter 2); in the United States, the geographical process allows this type of sorting to have a particularly crucial role in rapidly reshaping the political landscape.

A second possible reason for political polarization may be the way that the newly arrived are integrated into communities. Their landscape of socializing institutions is highly uneven in the United States; to take extreme examples, there are more progressive community groups in San Francisco and more evangelical churches in Tulsa. This may make it easier for the newly arrived in San Francisco to turn to the Left and the immigrant to Tulsa to turn conservative in another geographical shaping of the social multiplier. Demographers have remarked that political and sociological polarization seems to be operating at multiple spatial scales in the contemporary United States—a paradox in a country with such high levels of mobility, exchange of populations, and secure national identity. Overall, Fischer (2010, 149) asserts, the balance of changes in the American way of life work against neighborhood solidarity. The possibility of choosing the kind of daily situations ("lifestyle") in which we live, and hence of not only living separately but also differently, may be rising through sorting (as well as through other dimensions of experience, such as the use of the Internet to stovepipe our information and cultural contacts). Fischer (ibid., 181) concludes that "Americans' preference for the private and the parochial, for the small voluntary community, has become easier for Americans to attain." The exception to this may be when demographic processes involve the replacement of one population by another, separate one. Thus, for instance, when northern Orange County, California (a suburb of Los Angeles), once one of the most politically conservative counties in the United States, turned majority Latino, its politics changed by replacement rather than incorporation. But this is merely another example of separatism at work.

At the national scale, the rise of a vigorous set of conservative institutions in the South, combined with that region's demographic growth, has of course had a major impact on national politics, tilting it to the Right while strongly offsetting the more liberal tendencies in the Northeast and coastal West as well as in the biggest metropolitan areas in general. The existence of a huge and complex hinterland, combined with strong administrative federalism, makes the objective economic and social conditions different across the US territory. In comparably developed countries, no such role for the hinterland as a political and administrative phenomenon, and not even in terms of ways of life, is in evidence. Why is there no socialism in the United States? In this light, it is conceivable that if the United States did not have the South, its politics would look a great deal more like those of European countries today.

The frontier lives on in the form of many objective practices and subjective processes. It is both extensive and intensive, and continuously redefined and reinvented—as an institutional field—at many detailed spatial scales of interaction. It permeates many different kinds of spatial choice and sorting behavior. It underlies the formation of communities, individual meaning, and social memory. These geographical habits along with the geographical processes they animate influence large-scale politics, society, and economics in the United States.

THE US URBAN FABRIC AS A PRODUCT OF EXIT

Urban economists and regional scientists have emphasized the ways in which the basic behaviors that shape US urban and spatial organization are not exceptional (as a locational choice by utility-maximizing agents). They account for the specific pattern that US urbanization principally takes as a result of exceptionally low transport costs, low preexisting population densities, cheap land, and first-nature geography. For these scholars, the US urban system is just a somewhat less dense yet similar distribution of cities and activities that is found in every country at a similar level of income and development.

But this is a static, cross-sectional view of cities and urban systems, and it does not account for geography as a process. Such standard "outcome" snapshots of urban systems do not detect the exceptionalism of the US process. There is greater turbulence in the ranks of US cities than in other developed countries, even where the overall rank-size distributions are similar. Moreover, within US cities there are lower levels of public goods than in the cities of similarly developed countries. Fiscal decentralization is high in the United States compared to these countries, setting up stronger competition for development than in other countries and more powerfully magnifying gaps in local economic success between places. The growing or wealthy places have the means to outpace the others in local expenditures, thus reproducing rather than countering the effects of shifting comparative advantage.

The lower public good levels in the United States do not spring entirely from a national or society-wide preference; they emerge in part from the competition between winning and losing places, as the former enjoy enhanced total revenue and can obtain it at lower tax rates than in declining places, requiring other places to engage in fiscal competition with them.

Interregional coalitions for public goods are restricted to those that can unite both growing and declining places—something that occurs mostly for nationally financed infrastructure. Such coalitions are rare when it comes to context-specific urban improvements that involve declining places, or social services or economic adjustment assistance.

These features of the geographical process institutionalize other practices and policies. In most other developed countries, city-regions with declining populations are propped up through redistribution from outside. In the United States, they are largely responsible for managing their own decline, taking dramatic forms such as the physical emptying out of places like downtown Detroit and the destruction of its buildings. In other countries, the economic effects of geographical redistribution and propping up (place or regional policies) are often highly questionable, since they frequently serve merely to lock local economic actors into increasingly unattractive places (Glaeser 2008). Indeed, exit from places, as noted above, has probably been an essential element in US economic dynamism, but it has a particular set of distributional effects—political and sociological in nature—on both people and places.

One paradoxical outcome—which is difficult to grasp for non-Americans looking at the United States from outside the US experience—is that social integration in the country—the basis for the US "community"—is of a sort not known anywhere else in the developed world. The process that makes it tick is exit and mobility—as was first theorized in the Frederick Jackson Turner's (1921, 1925, 1932) "frontier hypothesis." The resulting pattern of population, social groups, and economic activities has a high level of functional integration as well as a unique combination of unified national identity, but with local communities in unusually intense states of flux and rivalry. US geographical processes can be considered exceptional in the way they function, and in their outcomes for distributional politics, politics in general, and national "tropes" that relate individuals to society.

Cities Are More Important Than They Might Appear to Be

The geographical process emerges from spatial habits that are expressed subjectively through belief, have observable consequences for spatial organization (urban systems along with urban fabrics and ways of life), and are also institutionalized objectively in the form of political choices. In this light, I can respond to the question I asked at the beginning of this chapter: Are cities really that important?

Cities may not be as extravagantly significant to human economic and social development as has sometimes been claimed. Much of what happens in them is just the outcome of wider processes of sorting, matching, and exit behaviors. But their importance should not be underestimated; spatial habits, of which cities are the medium and expression, are indeed important to a wide variety of social, economic, and political processes. Cities are thus central to human social and economic development in ways that conventional approaches to the urban tend to underestimate.

Justice, Efficiency, and Cities

Justice and Efficiency in Economics

Economics is inherently concerned with justice, and all economics has normative foundations, whether these are implicit or explicit. Justice concerns both the economic process ("fair" interactions) and economic outcomes ("good" consequences). Economics is also centrally concerned with efficiency. Efficiency can be conceived of as principally static and allocational (how to get the most out of resources), or dynamic (how to make productivity increase as well as generate growth and development). Modern economics formulates the relations between these two concerns in the first fundamental theorem of welfare economics, wherein an optimal allocation of resources comes about because we use the right procedure for choosing. Translated into more conventional terminology, a process that leads to efficient outcomes is "just" in the sense that it emerges from making the user pay for resources, provides a choice environment with perfect information and no externalities, and expects choices to be made in a rational utilitarian way. Under these circumstances, the process will lead to outcomes and factor rewards that are the best we can possibly do.

The second fundamental theorem of welfare economics, however, separates efficiency and equity. This is because the price and wealth effects of any given allocation of resources may go in different directions; there is, as a result, no single first-best equilibrium for both of them. Several equilibriums can each be efficient in a single period allocation, but they will be based on different distributional outcomes (the price versus wealth effect). There are many possible ways that societies can rank these equilibriums in terms of what they want from the economy, depending on the society's aggregate social welfare function. An aggregate social welfare function is what we collectively prefer to prefer, tempered by the kinds of trade-offs it embodies at a given state of technology and resources; this is effectively my definition of justice. The process of choice that is at the heart of mainstream economics' notion of justice therefore cannot guarantee that by following the choice procedure of the first welfare theorem, society will get the development process that implements its social welfare function.

Claims about optimal and just resource allocations converging with one another rely on other unrealistic assumptions as well. As noted in chapter 5, the most important such assumptions are that consumer preferences are convex (diminishing marginal rates of substitution), and production sets are convex (no economies of scale or any significant, irreversible bundling of options). These assumptions do not fit much of the reality of choice in the economy in general, and even less in the material environment of cities.

The relations between justice and efficiency become even more complex once we consider growth and development over time. How can we be sure that all immediately efficient actions are also those that generate the most long-term development? If the wealth effects mentioned above change the power of agents to affect future factor prices, then there is no way to guarantee how present actions connect to a future that maximizes some present preference. Moreover, if we decide that maximizing output in the long run is not the unique goal of development, then distributions along the way may matter for their own sake (fairness or individual fates) as well as for how each period affects subsequent periods in terms of output levels and distributional patterns (Pearce, Atkinson, and Mourato 2006). In other words, the process matters for its own sake, not merely for its utilitarian effects on the "ultimate" state of things (Rawls 2001).

As argued in chapter 3, the geography of the economy enters on the sides of both process and outcomes. Geography is a distribution—of people, output, and incomes—and some geographical distributions may contribute to maximizing output (efficiency). Yet maximizing output, if it requires changing the existing geographical distribution of people, output, and incomes, may have implications for justice as a social process (what people in places should or must do) as well as for outcomes (it may create richer and poorer places). Thus, the geographical unevenness of the economy adds an important dimension to the justice-efficiency relationship.

Two questions emerge from this starting point. The first is, How does geography contribute to efficiency and justice, and how much do the two overlap? The second is, Where they don't overlap entirely, should more developed places help less developed ones offset the consequences of the difference?

SOME EXAMPLES

A few examples will provide a sense of the issues of justice and efficiency in relationship to cities and regions.

Regional Inequalities in the Twenty-First Century   As I discussed in detail in chapter 3, much economic efficiency depends on agglomeration, and as I showed in chapters 4 and 6, certain local and regional economies are favored by their agglomerations, which raise their prices and wages, and usually in real terms. This generates a tendency for interplace real income disparities at various scales. Though there are some mechanisms that promote offsetting convergence, they are generally not powerful enough to erase interplace income disparities (Barro and Sala-i-Martin 1995). Aggregate output and wealth levels of economies are hence higher when there are territorial inequalities (Martin 2005).

The twenty-first century will be one in which city-regions will gain even more advantage on nonmetropolitan regions, and in more parts of the globe, than ever before. Furthermore, there will be considerable churn among city-regions in terms of their per capita incomes, with a distinctive hierarchy existing at any given time along with with a tendency for there to be winner and loser city-regions. What is a just distribution of income and activity in relation to this efficient development process (Baldwin, Martin, and Ottaviano 2001)?

Gentrification   In many cities, wealthier and highly skilled people move into centrally located neighborhoods, raising property values and making it impossible for some members of the previously dominant socioeconomic group to continue to live there. Gentrification is a spatial process by which the highly skilled locate themselves in relationship to their agglomerating jobs, which are also often located in the core of metropolitan cities, and they transform the neighborhoods in doing so. Such double clustering—residential and workplace—seems to enhance interactions by which such skilled people signal and learn, and enhance their advantages even more (Glaeser 2008). This process initially accelerates intraneighborhood (interpersonal) inequality, and if there is enough center-city gentrification, it may increase interneighborhood inequality as well. Some members of the formerly dominant group of the neighborhood will benefit from gentrification through the rapid rise in their property values, if they sell their property and move, or rent it to members of the new group. But this same process will then make it impossible for other members of the same group to live in the neighborhood, undermining their collective dominance of the neighborhood. Yet the same group, now displaced, may benefit from the wage spillover effects at the regional scale of a high-wage economy that depends on the gentrifiers who move into their former neighborhoods.

Is it fair for gentrification to occur merely because it meets the current needs of the highly skilled? Is it only just if it can occur without substantial displacement of other groups? Is it just only if the positive effects on the economy outweigh any negative effects on the most negatively impacted groups and individuals, or only if those negatively affected are actually compensated?

Ways of Life Economic integration among territories generates more output because it allows specialization to flourish; these are gains to trade. Integration may also increase the variety of products available, generating additional welfare increases within and between places. But the corollary of integration is that competition from imports and dedication to producing tradable exports can rearrange the local economy and in some cases destroy the preexisting local way of life (Benhabib 2006; Rauch and Trindade 2005; Cowen 2004). This is apparent when, for example, a hitherto-isolated region comes in contact with the world economy; but it has more subtle manifestations, as when an old manufacturing region in a developed country finds its comparative advantage redefined by competition from an emerging economy.

There are symbolically important cases of this. Indigenous ways of life in the Amazon basin are subtly transformed in the face of cattle ranching, soybean farming, and oil drilling. When farming villages in southern France, mining towns in Wales, or even working-class neighborhoods in Syracuse or Boston lose their flavor, either to abandonment or replacement by chain stores and new residents, has justice been done? For every Peruvian Indian who likes their new job on the oil rig, what about the others who want to preserve their way of life and not work in the oil fields? Is justice done if most individuals benefit yet the collective way of life disappears? Is it done if the worst-off individuals in the group whose way of life disappears also benefit, or just if there is merely an average "group gain," with some members losing out and objecting to the change? Or is it fundamentally unjust to change a way of life as an unintended effect of individual, efficient decisions to produce and trade (Lear 2006)? On the other hand, if a way of life is protected, it can have unintended impacts on people and places that are far away. An old manufacturing region that protects its way of life, say, may prevent a developing region from getting the opportunity to produce certain types of goods for it, and hence gain a foothold on development.

Should There Be Senates? Many countries have two-chamber legislatures, with the upper chamber getting a fixed level of representation, independent of population, and the lower getting representation that is proportional to the population. This typically results in higher-than-average transfers to the less populated areas. Is this a justifiable transfer, ensuring that the ways of life and local preferences of the smaller or less rich are preserved in the face of more populated, richer regions? Or is it a hold up of the latter by the former, with negative welfare consequences for the residents of the more populated areas?

Macworld or Multicultural Fiesta?   The production of culturally specific goods and services by different places has distributional consequences (income or pleasure) for people in producing and consuming regions. I alluded to this in chapter 10 by referring to the genius of cities as a source of particular ways of producing. I can deepen that discussion here.

In a multiregional world or national economy, the genius of cities is a form of "diversity between" places. Does it come at the price of "diversity within" places? If the world is diverse under autarky, and trade leads to the breakdown of collective structures and more imitation of the dominant goods/services pattern—which happens when costless trade and communication exist—then trade might reduce diversity. A reduction in diversity could also come about if there are economies of scale in production and duopoly behavior induces producers to cater to the middle of the market, rather than marginal or minority tastes. When widespread, this can lead to cultural destruction. Furthermore, consumers of imported cultural goods tend to gain, while consumers of exported goods will lose. If the latter are greater than the former, there is potential overall welfare loss (Rauch and Trindade 2005; Janeba 2004; Cowen 2004). For homogeneous goods, integration probably increases welfare, whereas for strongly heterogeneous or specialized goods based on community values, and especially those with consumption externalities, the effects of integration could be more mixed (McElreath, Boyd, and Richerson 2003; Rauch and Trindade 2005).

All these are examples of people versus place distributional trade-offs of productivity/output, wealth, preferences, and voice. What benefits individuals may not benefit their places or territories on average; what benefits individuals in the aggregate may not benefit all territories and may even exacerbate interplace inequalities. The outcomes to be considered must include both intended and unintended ones. Moreover, the processes that enable people to have individual voice (as producer, consumer, or individual) may not allow the average or even median preferences of the people in the place where they live to be satisfied.

Scale and Community: Who Is "Us" and Who Is "Them"?

Justice among places can only be considered in light of some clarity about the relevant range of places that want to be fair or just with one another. Insofar as places have explicitly decided that they form a union—a society in the sense that I defined it in chapter 8—then it follows that there is at least an entry point for discussing justice. It becomes justice within the relevant territory. The most relevant scale for us in this world are nation-states, which remain by far the scale at which people have agreed to submit to the same norms and have durable responsibilities to one another (Rodrik 2011). Within nations—at other scales such as cities, regions, and neighborhoods—there can be more or less intensive levels of us and them (Nagel 2005; Pogge 2002).

Where such agreement or union doesn't exist, things are thornier. With members of fully foreign nations, or ethnically or linguistically distinct regions, we have not explicitly agreed that we are members of the same society. What distributional arrangements or justice do we want with these versions of them (Rawls 1999)? Even if we are part of a political society (such as a stable nation-state), the question of "who is us" and "who is them" still shows up all the time, not only between groups in the population, but also at smaller territorial scales within the union. An extreme version of the "distant strangers" problem is groups that are distant in time in our own place—future generations of farmers or putative housing consumers—or in both space and time—those same groups but in other places.

The European Union provides a revealing example of the issues in dealing with communities. The European Commission's official position on European integration is that it should reconcile exchange with diversity—a "Europe of regions" (European Union 2004). This notion specifically refers to the promotion of durable collective differences between the European economies by preserving their specificities while creating a dense set of mutual responsibilities in the areas of trade, fiscal management, and a wide variety of regulatory policy areas. The tensions between these two sets of things are apparent, and the European Union is somewhere between a fully achieved us and a land of strangers.

Justice in NEG and the New Urban Economics

As was discussed in chapter 3, the geographical concentration of production generates pecuniary gains for firms (the proximity to suppliers and labor markets along with the ability to reduce overhead by being able to resort to external suppliers and labor pools) and possible dynamic efficiencies that raise the long-term rate of potential growth. If aggregate social welfare is equivalent to aggregate social income, then geographical concentration contributes to maximizing welfare. But if geographical concentration is associated, in the short and medium run at least, with higher interterritorial income inequality between urban and nonurban areas, between more densely developed countries and less developed ones, or even among cities of different sizes and industry compositions, then we cannot assume it maximizes aggregate welfare (Bairoch 1997; Combes, Mayer, and Thisse 2006).

A standard extension of this logic is to consider cases of regional policy, such as the European Union's (2004) framework for redistributing development funds from higher-income regions to lower-income ones with the stated goal of encouraging interterritorial equity. NEG theorists critique this type of formula because it reduces aggregate social welfare (output) insofar as the resources are diverted to lower-productivity uses. As I noted in chapter 12, the European Union has an urban structure with fewer big cities than the United States. If this is reinforced by a policy biased against agglomeration, so it goes, there will be a perverse overall effect of choosing equity at the price of making the European Union poorer (Martin 2005). In this case, if we want to maximize overall economic output, geographically uneven development is justified, even if it raises income inequalities within places (by raising returns to skills, which in turn raise economic performance of those places) and between places (for the same reason) (Charlot et al. 2006). It is important to know what underlies this reasoning: a standard social welfare function in which individuals each have a weight inversely proportional to their marginal utility of wealth.

Using the general spatial equilibrium framework, Glaeser (2008) takes a slightly different tack from NEG. He argues that place-based policies designed to help the poor actually worsen their fate by providing them incentives to remain where they are and remain together. This is a utilitarian critique that, if taken to its logical conclusion, implies that no territorial externalities or locational effects on people should be compensated, and no territorial income inequalities should be compensated either, because they reduce aggregate output. Thus, using the standard welfare function, the unemployed and unskilled worker in Manchester should move to London if they want to get a job, whereas the London banker doesn't have to move (because they have different marginal wealth utilities). The unskilled person in the poorer region should not be compensated if they can move though choose not to do so. But cities such as London have less need for the unskilled from the peripheral regions than they do for the skilled. And the unskilled in Manchester suffer an externality effect when the skilled leave to move to London, because the relative productivity of their local economy declines and the departure of the skilled hastens the departure of skill-based industries, and this in turn reduces the interactions between skilled and unskilled persons in the region as well as reducing the wage spillover effect from skilled tradable industries to less skilled local services. Hence, even in the standard NEG approach and using a standard social welfare function, it is not always clear that all agglomeration effects maximize overall social welfare.

Moreover, NEG logic would lead to different conclusions about the desirable spatial distributions of development if one employs other social welfare functions (known as the Kaldor-Hicks-Scitovsky functions because they assume a higher preference for equality than in the standard function). If, for example, the society has an aversion to interpersonal inequalities, then its notion of justice requires that the losers in the peripheral cities and regions be compensated for some of the losses they suffer from economic integration. Such losses could combine interpersonal inequality increases within the region and with respect to the winning people in other regions (see Just 2004; Scitovsky 1941; Kaldor 1939; Roemer 1996). Notice that such a justice standard is not one that intends to produce territorial equality but rather to compensate the individual inequality caused by location (which might, under some circumstances, include helping people to move).

A further argument from the general spatial equilibrium approach is that instead of helping the rich places where some poor people are concentrated, we should help individuals to move to cheaper places, especially because they suffer most from the high cost of living in rich places. But writing a check to a poor person does not ensure that they will subsequently use it to locate in a place where they will have access to collective goods such as schools and safety on which they depend more than average. The places with good schools and safe streets frequently block these people from getting in (through zoning, at a regional level, that bundles amenities and the local way of life, as discussed in chapter 5). And if these people do go to an entirely different region, nothing guarantees that they will have the collective goods they need once they arrive. Such poor people, lacking social networks in these other places, may remain vulnerable and have difficulty in achieving social mobility.

An inequality-averse social welfare function could also justify policies to help the richer places (Roemer 1996; Bénabou and Tirole 2005; Charlot et al. 2006). This is because while average incomes in peripheral areas are lower than in centers, there are major concentrations of needy people in rich cities and neighborhoods within them. When regional development assistance is provided to areas with low average incomes, the people who most suffer might be the disadvantaged ones in highly developed urban areas. Spending on a rural post office or town center has a regressive distributional effect if densely settled poor neighborhoods in big cities could benefit more from an expanded post office, public facility, or job training than the average beneficiary of such aid in a peripheral region.

To summarize, the insights of geographical economics can be used to begin to think about efficiency and justice, but there is a long way to go. For the moment, we lack sufficiently detailed empirical knowledge about the geography of income creation; the welfare preferences of the people concerned in the relevant territories, including the degree of utilitarianism and preferences about inequalities; the direct income distribution effects of the geography of income creation, interpersonal and interterritorial; the indirect income distribution effects such as externalities; and the extent to which mobility is an option and/or a preference. Most of the literature that ventures on this terrain has only partial knowledge of the empirics, and usually makes strong yet somewhat-arbitrary assumptions about preferences in adopting a welfare function. Most important, as we have seen above, when we adopt an inequality-averse social welfare function, the optimal geographical pattern is no longer evident. NEG needs to do a lot more work on examining alternative patterns in light of these issues.

Is There a Just Solution to Failure in Urban Land Markets?

The location of firms, households, and other activities within a city also reflects the way different preferences confront competitors for urban space, in light of different abilities to pay, and hence gives rise to a range of levels of satisfaction, as we saw in chapter 5. The differences from the interregional distributional issues considered above is that within a city-region, there are much lower mobility and interaction costs, and hence competition for space is keener.

At the intraurban scale, land prices heavily shape locations, but they also affect income distribution. The starting point is that land has a relatively inelastic supply. At any given location (say, the corner of Fifth Avenue and Fifty-Ninth Street in New York City), there is not all that much that can be done to stretch the supply (going up in the air is an option, with limits). Such a parcel has rare attributes relating to its access to other parcels as well as the long latency time and sunk costs of changing access. In the short run, therefore, the auctioning mechanism is more price than quantity (McCann 2001).

The Marxist analysis of urban land markets, stemming from David Harvey's (1976) seminal argument in *Social Justice and the City*, builds on this notion. Marxists contend that price reflects exchange value, which does not correspond to the land's use value. The market allocation mechanism cannot explicitly account for the intensity of preferences and differential ability to pay (budget constraints) for access to location or amenities. In addition, land property is a form of capital. As such, its ownership is unevenly distributed in the first place, reflecting the class structure of the society. Since the budget constraints of different classes are unequal, with the owner class having the ability systematically to outbid other potential users of land, this class will over time concentrate the ownership of this critical and scarce form of capital. The ownership class in turn wants to maximize their land property's exchange value, so private land markets establish land rents that systematically fail to satisfy many use values. Land markets discriminate in favor of the rich and the propertied in two ways: they satisfy more of their preferred uses, and the propertied get to accrue more capital in the process. Marxists see no efficiency effects coming from the role of land rent as a price signal (ibid.).

Standard market failure economics shares part of this reasoning to different ends. Land rent is a problem when it does not price in positive or negative externalities correctly. If positive externalities are not fully priced, then there will be too much concentration in the "good" places, since the price of access will be lower than the value; if negative externalities are not fully captured in reducing prices, there will be excessive aversion to less desirable places as a way to hedge against the eventual pricing in of their unpriced effects. So the primary task of land markets, which is to sort uses efficiently, is hampered. At the worst, land markets could lead to vicious circles of low-value "spatial traps" and an excessive buildup of values in other places (Ravallion and Jalan 1997). Mainstream economics thus can easily accommodate the idea that land values are socially produced (via location and infrastructure), and as such, that there is a possible case against the private ownership of land, although few economists are actually willing to advocate such a view.

It is more difficult for both the Marxist and mainstream market failure perspectives to define what an alternative land allocation system would look like. Mainstream approaches address themselves almost entirely to reducing inefficiencies: positive and negative externalities should be priced in (possibly by taxing certain location-specific rents and redistributing them; possibly by actively combating negative externalities). Even with the spatial concentration of activities, truly efficient land markets should have a more even distribution of land values and locational benefits than is the case with imperfect land markets. Yet these approaches pay no attention to the relationship between social welfare notions of the ability to pay and ability to enjoy, and the efficient organization of space and access to urban amenities. Nor do they tackle the interpersonal income distribution consequences of an efficient overall allocation of land.

If Marxism can be said to have an alternative social welfare function, it would replace exchange value with use value as the allocation mechanism (Roemer 1996). This would supposedly reduce the contribution of land rent to social inequality. Use value can only become the criterion for allocation through public, or at least collective, control over land use. But Marxists do not identify the alternative mechanism for deciding the highest use value of land, nor how to deal with conflicting preferences about which users get what. In a system for allocating land according to use values, the collective authority would still have to decide not only which of the uses preferred by people are higher priority but also whether the preferences of all people and in all categories are given equal weight. Alternatively, if some master "rational use" scheme is used to determine use value, then it needs criteria to rank uses (efficiency? equality?). In other words, even if the underlying income distribution were made radically more egalitarian, and landownership as a source of market and social power were reduced, there is no clear way to administer use values without running into the nexus of efficiency-equity-preferences. The Marxist critique offers little that serves as a guideline for achieving an urban form that enhances justice.

Public Choice and Cities

Public choice theory has had a powerful impact on urban economics through the Tiebout hypothesis of local government, as noted in chapter 5 (Tiebout 1957; Buchanan and Tullock 1962). The urban region is a fragmented political space in which the supply of land uses and amenities is varied, and households and firms sort themselves into the spaces where their preferences can be best satisfied. People and place distributions are therefore not in conflict; indeed, fragmentation and the variety of supply ensures that the maximum variety of preferences can be satisfied. Competition among local governments makes the supply change in a dynamic way, and if suppliers (localities) are sufficiently fragmented, then there are few principal-agent problems, as each principal (consumer) can find the agent (place) they want.

The analysis does not specify at exactly what scale (or granularity) places have to be fragmented in order to ensure that the supply accurately reflects demand. For the Tiebout mechanism to be scaled up to affect the interregional pattern of development, it would require extremely high levels of low-cost mobility of people and firms. Moreover, distant local and regional governments would have to be well informed about and responsive to the preferences of distant firms and people. Some of this clearly does go on, especially in the United States, in the form of smoke-stack chasing, attracting retired populations, and generally attracting inward investment (Donahue 1997). In chapter 2, however, I argued that amenity chasing is not a robust explanation of the interregional sorting of people and households.

Tiebout can also be thought of as a median-voter theorem of local government. In this case, as I showed in chapter 5, the problem is that when one buys into a place, usually one is buying a desired attribute that may be bundled with other aspects one doesn't want. Since we cannot break space down into little bits, so that each choice has a unique and separate space associated with it, then, we are back to the world of Condorcet problems (A is preferred to B, B to C, and C to A, so that highly desirable outcomes are not considered) and weak public choice mechanisms.

The problems are not confined to the choice or supply side; they also concern how places "decide" what to offer in a public choice process at the interregional scale. It is unclear whether places are acting by choice or constraint to offer something, since territorial competition has direct effects on local and regional tax collection, but in turn is costly to them (Donahue 1997). Public choice models justify competition, even through subsidies, via the all-encompassing assumption that competing expresses the preferences of the people in the region, and that competition between places will ultimately limit their distorting effects on specialization and location. But the average person's preferences and those of trained economists are likely to collide in making these detailed choices.

Another example concerns the unequal terms of trade for different comparative advantages. Suppose that a region does not have the possibility of specializing in activities that will generate high income. It can specialize in those for which it has a comparative advantage and thereby maximize its potential income under this constraint. We saw in chapters 2–4 that divergent development between city-regions is driven by the spatial dynamics that sort innovative, high-wage activity into some regions and not others. The lower-wage and lower-skill regions contribute to general (interregional and international) welfare by making tradable products cheaper for the people in these richer regions. But if this pattern generates high income inequality between places, then should not the lower-income places that "do the right thing" (contribute to aggregate interregional output maximization) be entitled to interplace assistance, given that these are externalities of the development pattern?

Furthermore, even if we assume that people sort themselves perfectly in order to jointly optimize all preferences, additional heroic assumptions are necessary to get to justice. All preferences for consumption, amenities, work, and income would have to be transitive and convex, and people would have to be able to use mobility to find the location that optimizes among all their preferences (as assumed in Glaeser 2008). It also requires the spatial indifference assumption about the locational behavior of firms—that they be like putty in order to be able to substitute factors. Examined closely, then, public choice does not give us a realistic way to get to just distributions of well-being across people and places.

The Liberal Approach to Justice

Liberal analytic philosophers, exemplified by John Rawls and Ronald Dworkin, start with individual preferences and choices, like most economists. But they argue that rational individuals prefer standards of justice that are different from the standard aggregate welfare function used in economics (Rawls 1971; Dworkin 2002). They claim that rational individuals are concerned with their position in society and not just their individual income, and they are concerned with future risks.

Rawls develops a heuristic device for this contention, known as the "original position," a state of nature where everyone is equal. He asks what people do when faced with huge uncertainty about whether they will be winners or losers, but where there is relatively high certainty that there will be considerable inequality. People will only prefer unknowable future inequalities if they can be sure that such inequalities will improve the situation of the least well off. Nobody wants to take the risk of ending up on the bottom and being in an absolutely worse situation.

This leads to the analytic device known as the *maximin* rule of choice. People will choose increasing inequality if two conditions are satisfied: on the one hand, if it raises efficiency and generates an "inequality surplus," and on the other hand, if the inequality surplus is divided out in amounts that can simultaneously provide incentives to the highest paid to generate the inequality surplus through extra efficiency (skill, effort, etc.) and raise the welfare of the least well off so that they are not worse off in absolute terms than in a world without the inequality surplus. Maximin, in other words, means maximizing the minimum payoff to everybody in the distribution.

To apply this to spatial development requires exploring how maximin affects both people and place distributions. Some targets are easy. One thinks of black ghettos in US cities, where those who are not mobile are worse off as a result of desegregation because they are abandoned by their group's more successful members, who move away (Wilson 1987). And at various points in the global development process (going back to the nineteenth century), many regions of the world whose industries were destroyed by European import competition ended up worse off, and so did many of their individuals (Darwin 2008). So under the maximin choice rule, more of the inequality surplus should have been diverted to them.

We can carry out a thought experiment about combinations of NEG efficiency tests and Rawls's maximin distributions. This is summarized in table 13.1.

In case 1A, there is an increase in the total output and a decrease in interregional disparities, where the wealth of the rich increases, but the wealth of the poor regions increases enough to cause the disparities to fall. In case 1B, by contrast, if the wealth of the rich regions declines, then the wealth of the poor must increase enough to allow the total efficiency to rise—a condition that has rarely been seen in the industrial era since 1820. Case 2A is a typical NEG story of agglomeration, where there is an increase in the total efficiency but an increase in disparities. If the wealth of poor regions increases, then the wealth of rich regions must increase

TABLE 13.1

The Maximin Approach to Interregional Inequality

Case	Productivity/ Efficiency	Interregional Inequalities	Poor Region Avg Wealth	Rich Region Avg Wealth	Maximin
1A	increase	decline	increase	increase	yes
1B	increase	decline	increase	decrease	yes
2A	increase	increase	increase	increase	yes
2B	increase	increase	decrease	increase	no
3A	decrease	decrease	increase	decrease	yes
3B	decrease	decrease	decrease	decrease	no
4A	decrease	increase	decrease	increase	no
4B	decrease	increase	decrease	decrease	no

more to generate the increase in inequalities, but this result satisfies the maximin test. If the wealth of the poor falls, by contrast, then the wealth of the rich region must rise by a larger magnitude in order to generate the increase in total output—something that is indeed possible yet does not satisfy maximin.

Turning to the cases where the overall output or productivity decreases, in case 3A there is also a decline in territorial inequalities. If the wealth of the poor regions increases, then the wealth of the rich ones must decline in greater magnitude in order to generate the decline in inequalities; this is the "shrinking pie" that is feared by some, leading them to advocate tolerance for increased inequality. It satisfies the maximin test, but not in a happy way. In case 3B, if the wealth of poor regions declines, then the wealth of the rich must decline even more to generate the decrease in inequalities—a sort of return to the pre-1820 world. In case 4A, there is a decrease in output and an increase in disparities—something like the worst of all worlds. If the wealth of rich regions rises, the wealth of the poor ones would have to decline in greater proportion in order to generate the decrease in output; clearly this does not satisfy maximin and there is no inequality surplus generated. In case 4B, if the wealth of the rich regions falls, then the wealth of the poor must fall even more in order to reduce inequalities; again, there is no inequality surplus and no maximin.

Thus, some increases in territorial inequalities could survive the Rawls test, especially within countries or highly integrated as well as developed trading areas. It is possible that both the worst-off individuals and the average development levels of the worst-off territories are better off with the inequality than without it. Notice that some such cases thus survive both the NEG and Rawls tests (1A, 1B, and 2A). Moreover, there are cases (3A) that survive the Rawls but not the NEG test.

Things become more complicated when people and place distributions conflict using the maximin test. What if the worst-off people in one place are worse off, but not in the other place? What if, using per capita income levels, the worst-off places are better off on average, yet some people in some places are worse off? These aren't necessarily fatal blows. In fact, they open up fascinating questions for empirical research on the effects of spatial development that go beyond those asked by the standard paradigm. The maximin rule also could be used to support many different policy recommendations. For example, the worst off people in one place could be encouraged to move to another place if it would move their incomes into the maximin bandwidth of being better off. This is more restrictive than the standard social welfare function, which suggests mobility if it makes people better off than their worst fate, even if not necessarily better off in absolute terms (Charlot et al. 2006).

Alternatively, some of the inequality surplus linked to the combination of spatial and interpersonal inequality could be transferred, but divided among people and place transfers so that both satisfy the maximin test. The people and place distributions would be brought under a single umbrella for simultaneous consideration. Sometimes neither of these compensatory measures is feasible. This can be because mobility does not generate enough benefit, or because there is insufficient inequality surplus to distribute to people and places to satisfy the maximin rule. In these cases, Rawls's social welfare function would exclude forms of spatial inequality that are allowed by NEG reasoning, going against what NEG says about efficient geographical patterns of output and income.

Dworkin (2002) outlines a different liberal approach to justice. For him, inequalities that are due to different levels of effort are not of concern to public policy. Differences in ability can be tolerated as long as they contribute to the overall social welfare. Suppressing entirely the rewards to certain differential abilities could leave the society without what can only be produced by the exercise of certain talents as well as the individual fulfillment that comes from exercising one's talent. But when equal abilities are combined with unequal resources, unjustified inequalities will come about.

Dworkin's categories of ability, resources, and effort don't scale up to the level of whole economies in a clear way. Yet a rough translation would be as follows: in economics, resources is something like factor endowments; ability is total factor productivity, including skills; and effort is whether a region achieves the institutional conditions to maximize its performance given the first two. Dworkin argues forcefully that if someone is doing the best they can (the effort criterion), with the resource endowments they have been given, then that is what we should expect of them, and any inequality suffered that is not due to being lazy (insufficient effort) should be compensated. In the world economy, there could be cases of exogenous shocks such as adverse terms-of-trade movements that penalize places even though they have nothing to do with their effort and everything to do with bad luck. Dworkin's framework, applied to these cases, suggests that they should not have to take the whole hit. He suggests that we should develop policies to deal with this injustice, such as forward insurance schemes against the vagaries of the economic process. Similarly, Sen (2009) opens up an intriguing notion that cities and regions could be provided incentives to do the best they can, knowing that they would be protected if it doesn't work out.

Social Choice and Geographical Inequalities

The preceding discussion shows that there is no single approach that enables us to define economic, social, or territorial justice. Should we just give up? The social choice perspective, at least a certain version of it, encourages us to keep on trying.

The notion of social choice—the idea that we can identify and act on collectively shared preferences—has a rocky history. From Lionel Robbins (1938) and Kenneth Arrow (1951), formal models in economics and philosophy have said that social choice is impossible (Roberts 1980). Modern institutional economics has been similarly skeptical, asserting that when organizations or institutions attempt to do things collectively, they end up frustrating preferences and generating a tendency to sclerosis, as all the organized interests dig in to keep what they have (Olson 1965). Only when market failures are huge can these downsides be smaller than the gains from creating organizations that implement collective choices. Adding geographical dimensions to efficiency-equity issues makes them so complex that it is easy to be pessimistic about the possibilities for identifying preferences and even more pessimistic for acting on them.

This complexity is the starting point for Sen's (2009) reformulation of the social choice framework. Sen embraces messiness by arguing that we should try to achieve comparatively better outcomes, not single-best, "transcendental" optima. In order to do "better, not best," Sen says that social choice is a process, but a process radically different from the economist's procedures of choice, and different as well from liberals like Rawls and Dworkin. Better choices can be pluralistic and partial, with complex trade-offs, yet it is better to make them than to be paralyzed by the quest for optimal or perfect outcomes.

The Status of Cities and Regions in a Social Choice Process

Sen says little about cities or regions as such, although he refers to many social groups that are rooted in place that can become the dramatis personae of social choice processes, and many of the problems for social choice stem from uneven economic development and how territories relate to one another in open-economy situations.

There is abundant evidence that people want to make choices about issues that are territorially patterned and bounded, or involve relations between territories (Rawls 1999). But other, nonterritorial groupings—class, education status, ethnicity (to the extent it's not territorially bounded), lifestyle, gender, sexual preference, and so on—also matter greatly to people. The latter do not necessarily conflict with territorially rooted preferences, but they can fragment them.

Attitudes and preferences of the population are sorted by geography, as I noted in chapter 12. We can learn what a black, young, well-educated female in one place versus another thinks about some question. Still, we know little about possible preferences *for* place development or preferences that come from location (as opposed to preferences that come from the sorting of certain kinds of people into that place). The kinds of things we need to know more about include the following questions: What are people's attachments to place as such? Do individuals consider place in an individualistic and utilitarian way (what it can do for me), collective ways (what I like about it), or a collective but utilitarian way (what it does for us)? What do they want from other places?

How do we accommodate the immanent yet unobservable utilities of place? These are aspects of being in a place that help and hurt us in ways we don't see clearly, and especially not over the relevant time horizons. Place characteristics aggregate individuals and create principal-agent dilemmas. But belonging—as I argued in chapter 7—also may help us clarify who we are and in some ways offers choice sets that aren't available on a strictly individual basis. Place as community both blocks and empowers individuals, yet how does it do so precisely, in which ways, in which places, and at what geographical scales? And does a social choice process have a role in making these unobservables more transparent so that they can become objects of choice processes? Were we to know more about these things, it would be possible to ask how aggregate welfare maximization relates to different subjective preferences for place.

In most countries, a wide variety of social categories—income, class, race, gender, and lifestyle—are considered communities, with input into collective choices. These nonterritorial communities then get politically expressed at the level of territories—neighborhoods, cities, regions, and countries. But this consideration of the preferences *of* neighborhoods, cities, and regions is not the same as preferences *for* neighborhoods, cities, and regions—that is, preferences for a certain kind of development. For a social choice process to work in matters of economic development, it will have to give place a status as subject and object. This would enable us to generate a social welfare function that incorporates people and their places, and this could then be the starting point for social choice processes for and across places.

Social Choice, Urban and Regional Policy

Some kind of interterritorial assistance and redistribution probably has to happen in a world where development's efficiencies are so tightly linked to the creation of interterritorial inequalities. The challenge to urban and regional policy is to minimize the potential inefficiencies, dead-weight costs, and unintended effects of such assistance.

Some of the inequality surplus in the world should be systematically invested in assistance, and this assistance should be guided by a deeper understanding of preferences for place development. What does development mean? It involves some combination of individual (people) and average (place) welfare. Sen (2009) suggests that there are universal goals: freedom and liberty; the ability to live our lives and be happy; and the development of our capabilities. But the precise definitions of these and how they relate to each other quantitatively and qualitatively cannot be predetermined, nor need they be identical for all places. Once again, we need to know what the preferences of people in specific places are for these two distributions. These preferences can differ, and so there can be a plurality of legitimate possible outcomes. The redistribution of the inequality surplus must therefore allow a certain degree of autonomy of places in determining their desired people-place distributions; this is the pluralistic aspect of social choice.

How could inequality surpluses be used to advance these goals? Interplace justice can be thought of in this regard as a semicontractual relationship. Development choices should have to be justified within the general categories agreed on between territories to make them eligible to potentially receive the inequality surpluses generated by other places. And there obviously have to be counterparty rights—that is, living up to the obligations that come with taking inequality surpluses. The contractual lever consists of requiring places receiving aid to agree to broad substantive goals and defend them through the process of reason, or forego their share of the inequality surplus. The ability to define one's own goals, preferences, and values in doing this is a powerful incentive within these constraints. This is exactly the kind of deal that will likely result from the European Union's euro crisis, which is active at the time of this writing.

Implementing social choice in administrative bureaucracies is a huge challenge, because bureaucracies have little ability to handle messiness. One needs to think only of the European structural funds or US federal assistance programs to cities in order to see this; both are largely reduced to checklist-type formulas, usually justified by simplistic cost-benefit analyses (often themselves using incorrect assumptions). To implement a pragmatic but reason- and evidence-based social choice framework for territorial development assistance would require nothing less than the reinvention of public administration (Farole, Rodríguez-Pose, and Storper 2011; Barca Report 2009).

Social choice in public policy would require abandoning the checklist minimalism of the administrative state and learning how to function in a more experimental manner (Haussman and Rodrik 2003). Minimalism, according to Charles Sabel and William Simon (2010), is excessively preoccupied with static efficiency norms, and insufficiently attentive to risks and opportunities. "Experimentalist intervention is a more promising approach in the public policy areas characterized by uncertainty about both the definition of the relevant problem and its solution." But in order to engage in this type of messiness, actors must understand that "self-discovery is part of the coordination problem and process" (ibid., 1).

Preferences for Cities and Uncertainty

City-region development, like all economic development, is radically uncertain and nontransparent to its principal actors over any relevant time framework. Most people have little idea when they make present-day choices of how those choices will interact with a multitude of other forces and thus influence outcomes down the line. This uncertainty applies to both the individuals within a place and people in one place making choices that affect the lives of people in other places. As noted in chapter 10, part of the uncertainty is related to the actor's situation: short-term horizons, framing, herd effects, and limited investment in thinking and gathering information. But much of it is that even if all those "errors" were corrected, development is too noisy and complex to model with any level of certainty.

This is one reason why Rawls's notion of starting from a tabula rasa of the original position may be interesting in a moral sense. It suggests that people do not want to be made worse off by unknown future events. Rawls's solution to this dilemma of forward uncertainty is that there should be a master game where we work out the bottom line of maximin for the future. It is hard to imagine how his idea could be implemented or institutionalized: Should we set up a "great commission?" Sen argues that we should muddle through by developing better information and providing it to the principals, so that they can participate in the choice process. Sen's proposal could sound naive if it were formulated as a once-and-for-all utopian state of the world. But it is a framework for using reason as a procedure, gathering much more refined empirical evidence about what people want, and informing them about trade-offs involved in pursuing development pathways that satisfy different bundles of preferences.

The fields of development studies along with urban and regional studies cannot provide this information at the present time because they are not set up to do so. Uncertainty and the messiness of development will not go away, yet we do a poor job of presenting the range of future possibilities. As a result, people cannot understand their current choices in relationship to the way they might generate different bundles of future effects, and which current preferences might possibly be satisfied by these bundles. We will never predict the future, and there will often be positive future developments that we cannot possibly imagine today, as well as negative ones. Still, we need a conceptual and pragmatic revolution in how we develop information about the relationship between current choices and future city-regional development. The starting point for doing this is for scholars and policymakers to start to ask about and find out what neighborhoods, cities, regions, and nations consider to be just ways of relating to one another.

Conclusion
Dear Policymaker

SOME KEYS FOR YOU

TO: The Commission on Urban and Regional Development
RE: Report of the Research Committee
FR: Michael Storper, chair of the Research Committee

As chair of the Research Committee, I am grateful for the unusual opportunity to explore the state of what we know about the causes and dynamics of urban and regional development. The commission did this out of a desire to look at deep, long-term causes. Our report is highly academic, and so we want to provide you with a "bottom line" here.

Cities are workshops, not playgrounds: economic development is fundamentally about the development of the productive forces of a region. The development of the region's productive forces will largely determine its skill mix, population changes, and income level.

Economic geography shows us how sectors develop, how they are affected by trade costs, and how they shape the economies of cities and regions. Economic activities do two things: they develop in places, and they sort between cities and countries. The interaction of development and sorting give the economy its geographical dynamic, and shape the economic fates of city-regions.

Activities exit from places when their agglomeration economies weaken. They cluster in places when they require the sharing of productive inputs, labor pools, or interaction for innovation. In light of this, the supply of amenities has more of a role in determining where people and activities locate within the metropolitan region than in determining the region's overall growth rate or performance relative to other regions in the urban system.

Nonetheless, a huge amount of urban policy worldwide is based on versions of the amenity theory of urban development and its cousin, the "playground" model. These approaches are misguided. The high-end versions of such policies are designed to attract the skilled, rich, or creative by providing them the environments that they supposedly crave. The low-end versions are designed basically to keep housing cheap. These policies are only relevant for attracting the limited populations that do not have to work: the wealthy and retired. They may also affect urban tourism, but that is arguably a productive sector of the economy that sells amenities to people who are visiting. There is nothing wrong with supplying amenities for their own sake. But these policies tend to monopolize political attention and crowd out discussions of the most basic challenge for city-regions, which is how to generate income.

Winning in the development process depends on successful specialization and respecialization. In an open world economy, local economic development depends fundamentally on doing what it takes to maintain or improve the region's position in the shifting economy-wide division of labor (clustering versus exiting and sorting). Each city-region's economy has a local development process shaped by this wider dynamic. The key element of any developmental process for a city-region is to specialize as favorably as possible. City-regions are members of different development clubs: high, middle, and low ranks on the overall ladder of specialization, skills, and incomes. Each of these has its own set of challenges for successful specialization.

At the top end are wealthy but congested, high-cost and high-income cities. These city-regions must create, capture, or keep activities that belong to the innovative high end of the goods- and services-producing economy. Such activities tend to be highly clustered. The city-regions that get them have local genius. Yet this genius has to be kept dynamic and sometimes needs to be reinvented. Such regions rely on having large pools of people with high levels of and highly specialized skills. The capture of new activities is somewhat accidental, and unfortunately we do not know how to influence it by policy. But city-regions can maximize the probability of creating and capturing new high-end parts of the economy by having lots of star scientists and other content creators, and connecting them well to local business communities. They can pay attention to the conditions that sustain anchor firms in emerging areas of the economy and especially to linking them to the production networks of the region. They can foster high-skill immigration that is specialized to the areas in which the region's economy is specialized. And they can hope that robust leaders and other kinds of brokers emerge, and try to sustain them with a strong regional society while not allowing narrow communities to block them.

Finally, high-cost and high-income cities should not play to their weak points. It is futile to privilege the creation of low-wage and low-skill jobs in high-cost regions, even if this appears to be humane. Such regions can never succeed by trying to be cheaper than lower-income regions. The low-wage and low-skill workforce of high-cost regions strongly benefits from the successful development of the high-wage and high-skill core through wage spillovers. And urban and regional gentrification is probably the best sign of success in the core sectors of a high-wage economy. Instead of opposing it, some of the inequality surplus of a successful regional economy can be diverted to spreading the economic and urban benefits of a dynamically successful regional economy. The "high road" is the only road for these regions.

Middle-income regions have a different set of challenges that affect their development club. Their challenge is to get past the middle-income trap, where once they exhaust the advantages they have from cheap land and labor in the early stages of development, they must respecialize, because some of their activities will leave, and in any case their incomes will stagnate. This requires internal development to widen the capacities of the local economy as well as allow it to move up product and productivity ladders; to do so, they must raise education and skill levels, and start to nourish the robust actors that could alter their specializations. Middle-income city-regions can derive benefits from externally provided "bootstrapping" investments—such as major private or public research centers, or a rapid increase in the quality of the local university system, major local health providers (research hospitals), and national laboratories. Nevertheless, they will no longer move up the income and skills ladder by attracting more investments in routine production sectors.

For lower-income city-regions, there are two key development challenges. The first is "getting into the game." This is equivalent to a country that wants to enter the global economy: it must discover its initial comparative advantage, and must simultaneously discover the transport/communication links that make its local factors more exploitable in the economy-wide division of labor. Within countries, some infrastructure development is transformational in this sense: if it fundamentally changes the price of a factor in a way that changes the role of cities in the division of labor and reallocates production into a new geographical pattern. This doesn't happen often, but when it does, it can cause a whole new class of cities to enter the game, as happened in the development of the US Sun Belt in the second half of the twentieth century. Local development, once again, is intimately related to the overall geography of the economy and urban system, especially for those cities at the lower end of the income ladder (Farole, Rodriguez-Pose, and Storper 2011).

Institutions combine with economic geography to shape urban productivity. A city-region's economy is a set of activities, set within the physical system of the city-region. By definition, dense urban economies are systems of intensive interactions—among firms, between firms and customers, and between workers, households, and firms, with all of this embedded in interactions with government, education, and a wide variety of other organizations. Physical proximity is key to their ability to interact successfully, and this depends in part on the physical system of the city and its infrastructure. But the physical interactions and human networks among key actors, and rules and norms that govern them—the key informal institutions of the city-region—jointly shape the productivity of urban interactions.

Institutions also shape local economic evolution and responses to external challenges. Institutions are also the essential factor in the ongoing adjustment process, and determine whether the region "moves up, falls down, or stays even" in the open-economy game of continually changing specializations and roles. The regional institutions that most matter are largely hidden from the naked eye because they are the region's groups of networked actors as well as the bridges and coalitions among them. If these are diverse, well linked, and deeply involved, they will have more connections, and more deal makers and actors who shift skills into new areas and develop existing ones; if they are narrow, poorly interlinked, and not involved, the probability of meeting the challenges of the open economy and its shifting divisions of labor are greatly reduced.

We know relatively little about how to create such networks, but bridging the region's strong communities together into a strong regional society should be high on the priority list of regional leaders. Where such communities are weak or their interactions feeble, a key long-term priority should be to create ways of convening them, creating the awareness of the complex but hard-to-observe dynamics of the regional economy. Leadership that convenes is subtle, yet it is possibly the most valuable type of institution building to be done.

Globalization and local interaction are two complementary sides of development. The globalization of technology, transport, and communication enhances local interactions at the same time that it replaces certain local functions with long-distance imports. But the winner regions have more growth of local interaction than the regions in other development clubs. Those cities with local productive forces that use distantly provided inputs and information to enhance the complexity as well as quality of their own outputs will have a big boost to local interaction.

Particularly strong forms of local interaction amount to a form of local genius. Local genius is a highly desirable form of regional development, difficult to imitate but also difficult to nurture. Face-to-face contact is an especially strong form of local interaction, and it performs vital functions in coordinating deal making and relationships in the modern economy. Demand is growing for face-to-face interaction, especially in certain kinds of cities with multiple genius sectors. When many forms of local genius collide in a city, the resulting buzz affects their codevelopment, and explains the resilience of the biggest and highest-income city-regions.

Regional dynamics are deeply inscribed in the national development process. It is not possible for all city-regions to be at the top of the income hierarchy or stay there permanently. It is not possible for an omniscient national government to know how or plan for the variety of regional development processes in the different development clubs. There can be wasteful forms of intercity competition, overlap, and redundancy in investments, however, and wasteful or inappropriate infrastructure investments to link them together. Infrastructure investments that are appropriate to one development club are not necessarily the right ones for another, so building metro systems is right for Los Angeles or New York today, but probably not yet right for Phoenix. Development will, for political reasons, probably tend to be spread out too much relative to an optimally efficient geographical pattern. But national policies for infrastructure, education, R & D, and such could probably function better in most countries if they had more explicit ways of recognizing the different development clubs along with their specific needs.

Justice, efficiency, and cities. The stakes in city-region development are enormous—for how we live and our welfare. Yet there is virtually no real public conversation about urban efficiency, and even less about its relationship to justice. Local or regional dialogues should not be that difficult to organize, but they would require a much more developed language for framing choices for the public.

A national conversation about the urban system and cities in general is in principle a possibility. This is possible because unlike in the international development debate, there is no international community that is the equivalent of the nation-state (Rodrik 2011). And yet, no country has organized this discussion for its public in a way that the major relationships of efficiency and distributional outcomes could be considered in an open, transparent manner.

These social choice conversations should be organized for the public, or at least articulated by scholars and policy agencies. They require a major overhaul of how the "urban" is dealt with in political life.

Economic geography, institutions, innovation, and justice: these are the keys to understanding city-region development. For each of them, we have abundant existing tools of analysis, and many of them have been explored in this book. I have also identified the areas where we have inadequate knowledge and thus that can be areas of future progress. There is significant knowledge of how policy has affected some of these areas as well. These keys to the city can be used open up doors to better scholarship and practice.

Notes

Chapter 2. Workshops of the World Economy: People, Jobs, and Places

1. This chapter draws heavily from Kemeny and Storper 2012. I thank Tom Kemeny for his collaboration, but he is not responsible for the use made of our joint work here.

2. Thus, Glaeser and Gottlieb (2009) write: "Since the pioneering work of Mills (1967), Rosen (1979) and Roback (1982), cross-city work has almost always assumed that the free migration of workers creates a spatial equilibrium where utility levels are equalized." They also note that "the high mobility of labor leads urban economists to assume a spatial equilibrium, where elevated New York incomes do not imply that New Yorkers are better off. Instead, welfare levels are equalized across space and high incomes are offset by negative urban attributes such as high prices or low amenities. . . . By assuming that workers choose their locations, urban economists gain at least the possibility of explaining the large concentrations of people in urban areas."

3. Though Los Angeles is certainly sunny, it is not typically included in the Sun Belt, because California has followed a distinctive development trajectory, as compared with the southern states that usually receive this moniker. I discuss the peculiarities of California in more detail below.

4. Some of the correlations are insignificant, and so we might reasonably question the extent to which we can conclude that high-income cities are also best endowed with a wide range of amenities.

5. We also tried including mean January temperature in place of the broader climate measure. Results incorporating this variable were not meaningfully different from those reported below.

6. We must choose an imperfect method of determining Sun Belt membership, since "Sun Belt" is a rhetorical device rather than a hard-and-fast dividing line. We define a city as being part of the Sun Belt if it is located in a state that belonged to the Confederacy during the American Civil War. Confederate states constitute typical definitions of the US South, and for much of the twentieth century their development stood in stark contrast to other parts of the country.

7. Moreover, the p-value on the regression indicates that the overall specification is insignificant. In other words, the model with quadrants as covariates does no better at predicting urban population growth between 1980 and 2000 than a model with no predictors whatsoever.

8. Transport economists have long debated whether transport can shift the pattern of production (Leunig 2007; Anas, Arnott, and Small 1998), and most agree that the shift in factor prices made possible by transport innovations must be significant for it to act as an independent cause of change.

9. Per capita income in the five-county Los Angeles metro area was 94 percent that of the ten-county San Francisco metro area in 1970, but it had declined to 66 percent by 2005.

10. Quality-of-life indexes, used to instrument for amenities, include those of Mercer, the *Readers' Digest*, and the *Economist*. All rank the San Francisco Bay Area far higher in terms of quality of life than the Los Angeles area.

11. In this model as well as a large accompanying literature, the assumption is that regulation determines the rate of expansion of the housing base and hence the labor force (Glaeser and Gyourko 2005). But an alternative model (Van Nieuwerburgh and Weill 2009) assigns housing price differences to productivity differences, reflected in wage dispersion, between metropolitan areas.

Chapter 3. The Motor of Urban Economies: Specialization

1. Frédéric Robert-Nicoud (2005), however, has been able to identify the spatial equilibriums analytically.

2. Paul Krugman noted this fact in his Nobel lecture. Edward Glaeser and Janet Kohlhase (2003) also make this point, but not for the purpose of distinguishing the agglomerative tendencies of different sectors. Rather, they argue that urbanization is now propelled by the clustering behavior of skilled workers. I will return to this point below.

3. Puga (2010) reviews the different attempts to measure the input-sharing contribution to agglomeration. The result is only significant when highly dispersed sectors are eliminated. In my view, this simply means that input sharing is not strong enough to induce colocation, which should be one of the effects of input sharing (cf. Melitz and Ottaviano 2008).

4. Unless we introduce the degree of stability/instability to the employment contract, it is difficult to explain why firms would not choose to spread themselves out and avoid competition in the local labor market.

5. This move to cheaper land can occur at either the intrametropolitan scale (by moving to the urban fringe) or an interregional scale (e.g., to the Sun Belt). Some authors have begun to consider the relationship between the two, but it is still not well understood (Thisse 2010; Rossi-Hansberg, Sarte, and Owens 2009). Glenn Ellison, Edward Glaeser, and William Kerr (2010) find that sharing is the strongest among the three, but that their weights are not highly different.

Chapter 4. Disruptive Innovation: Geography and Economics

1. A standard response to this latter claim is that what I am calling innovative rents is just productivity differences, and hence there is nothing nonstandard in evidence. But productivity measures for this purpose use the willingness to pay as a source of the value of output, and do so over heterogeneous goods; they are simple tautologies. The only productivity comparisons that are watertight are those that compare homogeneous goods or units of value in relation to homogeneous inputs along with their unit prices. Nobody can do this for city-regions. In asking whether New York's finance industry has high prices because of rents or productivity, and comparing it to making cars, is like comparing apples to oranges.

2. Using a Google search on January 25, 2008, the term "MAR externalities" brought up 221,000 listings; on June 13, 2012, that number increased to 509,000 results.

3. One major debate between more neoclassical models of economic development and more heterodox ones is how long the rents can be enjoyed by the region or country before they are bid away due to rising costs, technological change, or some other force, and how such short- to medium-term rents relate to longer-term economic development processes. Once again, strict neoclassical work emphasizes the return to equilibrium, whereas work based on an evolutionary or "history matters" frame of reference stresses a circular, cumulative perpetuation of advantage.

4. What of the scenario of the localized learning, sharing, and reuse of technologies, creating localized increasing returns? This is a well-documented phenomenon. But the circle of beneficiaries of such processes would be limited if the use of such technologies remained localized, if for no other reason than that producers would be strongly tempted to extract monopoly rents for the knowledge involved. That they do so is a claim of much of the regional economics literature, as it is one potential explanation for why certain regions can support high labor and land prices. At some point in the development process, however, the benefits of such technologies seem to leak out to the wider economy, and this is likely to involve codification of the knowledge, delocalization, and the bidding away of monopoly rents through the entry of new competing producers. *Both* of these processes deepen and widen the basis for Romer growth effects. There is, as usual, debate over this—between those who believe the long-term source of innovation involves a Schumpeterian process, and those who believe it comes from a simple production function in innovation. For a review that favors the latter perspective, see Jones 2004. For the former, see Aghion and Howitt 1997.

5. In the literature on local sources of technological change, reference is also made to "Jacobs externalities" (Jacobs 1969). The common interpretation of Marshall is that he called our attention to intrasectoral technological spillovers, and thus to the benefits of specialization, whereas Jane Jacobs emphasized diversity and the learning that comes from encountering the unknown, and hence the benefits of a nonspecialized local economy. Yet one finds no reference to Jacobs-Romer externalities, curiously. In any event, my point would hold for such a construction: if there are Jacobs-type sources of technological change, in order to contribute to economy-wide increasing returns they would have to undergo economic and geographical diffusion, or delocalization—otherwise they, too, would be captured as localized technology rents.

6. Along these lines, Fujita and Thisse (2002) along with Baldwin and Martin (2004) emphasize the geographical concentration of skilled workers, who then innovate, and whose innovations are sources of the long-term growth dynamic of the economy; this primary innovation-driven concentration is supplemented by the home market effect. Both sets of authors remark that Krugman and his colleague Anthony Venables (1995) cannot develop an effective explanation of persistent income divergence without a model of the renewal of advantages in high-income places—something like Myrdal's "backwash" effects. Recently, dynamic models of the geography of high productivity have appeared (Melitz 2003; Melitz and Ottaviano 2008; Baldwin, Martin, and Ottaviano 2001), based on selection effects linked to export propensity, but for these to be fully effective, we would need dynamic models that are linked to the geography of innovation, which is the major source of the rents that propel development.

7. For example, the end of the postwar growth period in the United States also seems to have slowed down processes of convergence, while the advent of the high-tech and then financial booms appears to have accelerated divergence. This seems to correspond to, respectively, a phase in which the economy was dominated by deagglomeration to one in which agglomeration increased in importance, corresponding as well to different levels of technological maturity in the underlying propulsive activities.

Chapter 5. Cities and Individuals: How We Shape Cities, But Not the Way We Want To

1. This chapter draws from Manville and Storper 2006. I thank Mike Manville for his collaboration, but he should not be held responsible for any changes I have introduced into this version of our work.

2. The powerful support lent to Paris by the French central government makes its revival less spectacular than that of central cities in the United States or Britain.

3. The density of the urbanized area outside Phoenix's central city is about thirty-two hundred people per square mile. The urbanized area outside Boston's central city is about two thousand people per square mile.

4. See Leamer and Storper 2001; Storper and Venables 2004. And yet, a lot of the productivity growth from information technology came from discount retail—a creature of the suburban "old economy." Advances in telecommunications (Walmart owns its own satellite) and logistics have allowed for just-in-time delivery, better inventory control, and inefficiency gains from big-box stores. So the New Economy has both centripetal and centrifugal aspects; it centralizes and decentralizes.

5. As Richard Easterlin (1987) pointed out in *Birth and Fortune*, the generation that came of age during the midcentury urban decline was inordinately small. Decline also coincided with a period of highly restricted immigration. More recent native-born cohorts have been much bigger, and immigration levels are the highest they have been in decades.

6. In one way, Florida's use of gays as a proxy for tolerance is problematic. Although gays certainly face discrimination, they are much more likely than many other minorities (Latino immigrants, for example) to have a similar appearance and socioeconomic status as the majority. Discrimination against gays can thus be more difficult than against other minorities because it requires more information.

7. Indeed, the level of immigrant segregation in US cities correlates highly with the availability of public transportation, since immigrants frequently organize their lives around public transport while native-born residents organize their lives around the car (Cutler, Glaeser, and Vigdor 2005).

8. Many of these observations came from or were inspired by an online conversation on the decline of urban architecture begun by Tyler Cowen on the *Marginal Revolution* blog. See http://www.marginalrevolution.com/marginalrevolution/2004/08/has_urban_archi.html (accessed October 20, 2012).

9. For a discussion of technical obsolescence, see Downs 1997.

10. For instance, cities that pursued urban renewal programs frequently removed those populations that would object to such policies, and created popula-

tions that benefited from them. Doubtless this gave renewal a temporary veneer of stability.

11. I owe this example to Paul Cheshire.

12. The logic behind this is that a person with conflicting preferences would be irrational and open to having their wealth drained through a series of perpetual disadvantageous exchanges.

13. Schelling (1978) was probably the first economist to explore this subject in depth.

14. Thanks to Ian Gordon for clarifying my reasoning on this latter point.

15. Many of Tiebout's critics respond only to his seminal article, and not the subsequent improvements made to it by Wallace Oates (1969) and Bruce Hamilton (1975).

16. Thanks to Gilles Duranton for pointing this out.

Chapter 6. Winner and Loser Regions: The "Where" of Development

1. Once again, a lot of urban economics would ascribe the greater volatility of regional population change in the San Francisco Bay Area and Los Angeles to their greater openness to one another than countries; but if this were the case, they should also show real income or utility equalization.

2. There are a few exceptions such as the city of Toronto or Miami-Dade County, but even there the consolidation of powers is far short of actually eliminating local governments and the patchwork of decision-making scales in those regions.

3. Heterogeneity simply could be due to the fact that the more people there are, the higher the probability that their preferences will be dispersed, or because a higher population raises the probability that it will involve ethnic, religious, or linguistic fragmentation, which often corresponds to different preferences. Income inequality could also be a source of divergent preferences.

Chapter 7. Communities and the Economy

1. There is a general debate about this question of whether such forms can be optimal or just second best (Bowles and Gintis 2002, 2004).

2. Sociology stresses the role of socialization and group experience is demonstrably important in socialization, but says little about how socialization relates to the wide diversity of choices made by individuals in the same social groups (Bénabou and Tirole 2005; Alesina and Angeletos 2005; Alesina and Fuchs-Schundeln 2005).

3. There is some literature on the degree of endogeneity of preferences and role of situations. See Alesina and Fuchs-Schundlen 2005; Alesina and LaFerrara 2005; Alesina and Angeletos 2005; Bénabou and Tirole 2005; Bowles 1998).

4. This can include involuntary communities such as those imposed by exclusion or discrimination; once "forced" into the club, if we want what it can provide us (even as an undesired second best), we must accept its interactions (Young and Durlauf 2001).

Chapter 8. Robust Action: Society, Community, and Economic Development

1. This was the view of Pierre Guillaume Frédéric le Play and others from certain European historical schools.

2. The empirical indicator of these studies has always been the intensity of associational life, although there is considerable controversy over which empirical measures should be used and how to interpret them (Norris 2002).

3. Arnaldo Bagnasco called my attention to this point in a conversation (see also Bagnasco 2003).

4. The analytic basis for this contention can be found below.

5. Public choice theory does not share this interest in coalitions and states, holding instead that the aggregation of interests can and should be generated spontaneously as well as temporarily. In this view, the questions of both who bonds and how they bridge with other groups emerge from rational action under a condition of full information transparency along with low to nil transactions costs. Such "Coasian" bargains assume away precisely the conditions that, as I argued in chapter 7, create necessary and efficiency-enhancing roles for groups.

6. This also echoes Seymour Martin Lipset's (1963) notion of crosscutting, diversified alliances as generating a kind of moderating, generalized bridging.

7. There is of course a fourth area, macroeconomics, but that is beyond the scope of the present book.

8. We are reminded here of the fundamental distinction, introduced by Frank Knight ([1921] 2005), between risk and uncertainty. When confidence is weak or absent, the problem is that risks can no longer be estimated and thus minimized, and actors must face true uncertainty, with strongly negative effects on many of the foundations of long-term growth.

9. These have an indirect link to Sen's (1999) notion that extreme inequality expresses the lack but also impedes the construction of the social bonds that are crucial to development, because it discourages the provision of certain necessary social goods and deprives the poorest of the preconditions (basic resources) that would enable them to contribute to their own as well as society's development.

10. In the formal sense, scale lowers the transaction costs and raises the payoffs to addressing preferences shared on a large scale.

11. In French, the principle of universality is known as the *principe de généralité*.

12. This section is based on Rodríguez-Pose and Storper 2005, and Andrés Rodríguez-Pose initially developed the ideas for it.

13. This is the opposite of the problem taken on by Donald Davis and David Weinstein (2002). They show the persistence of places after shocks as an example of path dependencies; I suggest that there are shocks that can create new places, but then places lock in these shocks to make them durably important.

Chapter 9. Technology, Globalization, and Local Interaction

1. This case study and model were developed jointly with Gilles Duranton, and originally was discussed in a coauthored work (Duranton and Storper 2008).

2. Gertler (2004) actually goes further and argues that transaction costs are not driven solely by τ, a pure transport cost parameter. Instead, cultural and language differences made the coordination of machine producers with their North American customers much more difficult than it was with their local customers (which is consistent with the robustness of the common language dummy in gravity equations). Gertler (2004) also insists on institutional differences. German machines were designed for workers who maintain them lavishly and make a heavy personal investment to understand the details of their workings. North American workers are typically reluctant to make such long-term investment because of their much higher job turnover.

3. It could be added that trade between adjacent countries remains a large part of world trade (Leamer and Storper 2001). All this is also consistent with more indirect evidence such as studies of agglomeration in Europe, which routinely fail to uncover much systematic changes in the location patterns of industries despite European integration (Midelfahrt-Knarvik and Overman 2002; Storper, Chen, and De Paolis 2002).

4. To develop a general equilibrium model with detailed microeconomic foundations, theoretical consistency requires us to specify why countries trade and offer detailed microeconomic foundations for transaction costs. In order to keep the model tractable, fairly specific assumptions are necessary. My modeling strategy is to accept these requirements although they reduce the scope of the model. I begin in this section with a simple sketch of how my basic approach works in a simple, partial equilibrium setup. This shows that my core argument is fairly general and relies on a more limited set of assumptions.

5. Another interesting result of Berthelon and Freund (2004) is that the increase in the sensitivity to distance is not apparently related to the type of good being traded. A similar result occurs in the model here. This is because trade flows must be balanced. Consequently, trade in final goods (imported by country 1) will show the same effects as the trade in machines (imported by country 2).

6. Thanks to Andrea Ascani for valuable research assistance on this section.

7. There have been some technical critiques of this initial finding (Thompson and Fox-Kean 2005), and some doubters (Boschma 2005). But the finding continues to be reproduced as robust in empirical research, using both patent data and other indicators (Branstetter 2001; Döring and Schnellback 2006; Sonn and Storper 2008).

8. Though Granovetter's (1973) concept of "embeddedness" is concerned with the same issue.

9. Likewise, there are many stories of an initial rush to place customer service back offices and call centers in faraway emerging economies, and that some of these had to be repatriated because it was impossible to coordinate for adequate quality over such great geographical and cultural distances. In these services, there are discretionary interactions that cannot be engineered into routines. As information technology develops further, it may make such routines more comprehensive, but the human capital investments to make them work will remain high, and hence the total coordination costs will continue to create limits on such outsourcing.

Chapter 10. Local Context: The Genius of Cities

1. In the case of rich versus poor countries, differences in productivity should define comparative advantages.

2. Using purchasing power parity exchange rates to the euro.

3. Therefore, the Paris daily free newspaper *Métro* noted on December 4, 2007, that the prize for "Fooding" in 2007 went to Pierre Jancou, with his restaurant Racines, which has only thirty-six seats, with ten of them outside. His secret: "I search for artisans for vegetables, meat and cheeses, and here we just showcase the products, without chi-chi."

4. In the highly prestigious restaurants in France, of course, there's a formal division of labor in the kitchen, rigidly codified by education and practice.

5. Thanks to Monica Viarengo of the restaurant Farina in San Francisco for explaining the Italian "method" to me.

6. Known in economics, of course, as the first welfare theorem.

7. Many economists would reply that this is not a problem, since we can depend on prices to reveal—even if only after the fact—the value of what we do not know and hence correct the problem. But we do not know the precise prices for each type of potentially relevant information, and we cannot separate them from all the prices for everything else.

8. See http://www.rulesofthumb.com.

9. The notion of context has affinity with my earlier notion of a "world," which is a collective environment defined by the conventional ways actors coordinate with one another to reduce uncertainty. Those conventions, in effect, collectively stabilize many of the anchors and frameworks for individual action in a given type of environment (Storper and Salais 1993). Behavioral economics, however, provides the microfoundations that are missing in the literature on conventions.

Chapter 11. Face-to-Face Contact

1. This chapter is based on Storper and Venables 2004. I thank Tony Venables for his permission to use this material here.

2. The concept of socialization belongs upstream of economists' notions of human capital, screening, and selection, because it is concerned with the generation of initial capacities for action and discrimination, not merely their rational deployment. For models of the economics of group identity, see Akerlof and Kranton 2000.

3. At this stage of the game, there is no incentive for players to not reveal their true signal or the effort expended in obtaining the signal. A richer model might link the share of the project's surplus to effort, in which case there are incentives to misrepresent.

4. The game has a similar structure to "chicken" in which two Californian kids drive toward each other. The last to swerve is the winner.

5. Notice that this meeting is about information sharing, not about collective decision taking. In the latter context, Osborne and his colleagues (2000) argue that meeting costs can reduce the quality of decision taking by reducing attendance.

6. This section draws on work done with Riel Miller (Miller and Storper 2008).

Chapter 12. Exit or Voice? Politics, Societies, and City-Systems

1. This case study is based on Crescenzi, Rodríguez-Pose, and Storper (2007), in a highly abridged and somewhat-modified format. I want to thank my coauthors for allowing me to include this material here.

2. "A patent is a member of the triadic patent families if and only if it has been applied for and filed at the European Patent Office (EPO), at the Japanese Patent Office (JPO) and if it has been granted by the US Patent and Trademark Office (USPTO)" (Eurostat 2006a; Eurostat 2006b, 6). Patent families are supposed to improve international comparability by suppressing the home advantage.

3. Or €8,049.5 in the EU25 and €8,422.6 in the eurozone versus €20,487 in the United States, measured in purchasing power parity, based on full-time equivalents.

4. Although the effects of the 1982 patenting system reform are debated (see Jaffe and Lerner 2004).

5. Zimmermann (2005, 448) points out that the European Union shows "a split labour market that is characterized by high levels of unemployment for low-skilled people and a simultaneous shortage of skilled workers. This lack of flexible high-skilled workers and the aging process has created the image of an immobile labour force and the eurosclerosis phenomenon (thus preventing) the best allocation of resources and hence economic efficiency."

References

Abrams, P. 1983. *Historical Sociology*. Ithaca, NY: Cornell University Press.

Acemoglu, D., and S. H. Johnson. 2012. *Why Nations Fail: The Origins of Power, Prosperity, and Poverty*. New York: Crown.

Acemoglu, D., S. H. Johnson, and J. A. Robinson. 2004. "Institutions as the Fundamental Cause of Long-Run Growth." Working paper 10481, National Bureau of Economic Research, Cambridge, MA. http://www.nber.org/wp10481 (accessed October 18, 2012).

Ács, Z. 2002. *Innovation and the Growth of Cities*. Cheltenham, UK: Edward Elgar.

Ács, Z., P. Braunerhjelm, D. Audretsch, and B. Carlsson. 2009. "The Knowledge Spillover Theory of Entrepreneurship." *Small Business Economics* 32 (1): 15–30.

Adams, J. D. 2005. "Comparative Localization of Academic and Industrial Spillovers." In *Clusters, Networks, and Innovation*, ed. S. Breschi and F. Malerba, 379–408. Oxford: Oxford University Press.

Aghion, P. 1998. "Inequality and Economic Growth." In *Growth, Inequality, and Globalization*, ed. P. Aghion and J. Williamson, 5–102. Cambridge: Cambridge University Press.

Aghion, P., A. Alesina, and F. Trebbi. 2002. "Endogenous Political Institutions." Working paper 9006, National Bureau of Economic Research, Cambridge, MA. http://www.nber.org/papers/w9006 (accessed October 18, 2012).

Aghion, P., and P. Howitt. 1997. *Endogenous Growth Theory*. Cambridge, MA: MIT Press.

Akerlof, G. A., and R. E. Kranton. 2000. "Economics and Identity." *Quarterly Journal of Economics* 115:715–53.

Akerlof, G. A., and R. Shiller. 2009. *Animal Spirits: How Human Psychology Drives the Economy and Why It Matters for Global Capitalism*. Princeton, NJ: Princeton University Press.

Albouy, D. 2008. "Are Big Cities Bad Places to Live? Estimating Quality of Life across Metropolitan Areas." Working paper 14472, National Bureau of Economic Research, Cambridge, MA.

Alchian, A., and W. R. Allen. 1964. *University Economics*. Belmont, CA: Wadsworth.

Alesina, A., and G.-M. Angeletos. 2005. "Fairness and Redistribution." *American Economic Review* 95 (3): 960–80.

Alesina, A., R. Baqir, and W. Easterly. 1999. "Public Goods and Ethnic Divisions." *Quarterly Journal of Economics* 114:1243–84.

Alesina, A., and E. Fuchs–Schundeln. 2005. "Goodbye Lenin (or Not?): The Effect of Communism on People's Preferences." Working Paper 11700, National Bureau of Economic Research, Cambridge, MA. http://www.nber.org/papers/w11700 (accessed October 18, 2012).

Alesina, A., and E. La Ferrara. 2005. "Ethnic Diversity and Economic Performance." *Journal of Economic Literature* 43 (3): 762–800.

Alesina, A., S. Ozler, N. Roubini, and P. Swagel. 1996. "Political Instability and Economic Growth." *Journal of Economic Growth* 1:189–212.

Alesina, A., and D. Rodrik, D. 1994. "Distributive Politics and Economic Growth." *Quarterly Journal of Economics* 109:465–90.

Alesina, A., and F. Spolaore. 2006. *The Size of Nations*. Cambridge, MA: MIT Press.

Algan, Y., and P. Cahuc. 2007. *La sociéte de défiance: Comment le modèle social français s'autodétruit* [The society of distrust: How the French social model is destroying itself]. Paris: Editions de l'Ecole Normale Supérieure.

Allen, R. C. 2009. *The British Industrial Revolution in Global Perspective*. Cambridge: Cambridge University Press.

Almeida, P., and B. Kogut. 1999. "Localization of Knowledge and the Mobility of Engineers in Regional Networks." *Management Science* 45:905–17.

———. 2005. "Geographies of Knowledge Formation in Firms." *Industry and Innovation* 12:465–86.

Amin, A., and P. Cohendet. 1999. "Learning and Adaptation in Decentralized Business Networks." *Environment and Planning D* 17:87–104.

———. 2005. *Architectures of Knowledge: Firms, Capabilities, and Communities*. Oxford: Oxford University Press.

Amsden, A. H. 1992. *Asia's Next Giant: South Korea and Late Industrialization*. Oxford: Oxford University Press.

———. 2001. *The Rise of the "Rest": Challenges to the West from Late-Industrializing Economies*. Oxford: Oxford University Press.

Anas, A., R. Arnott, and K. Small. 1998. "Urban Spatial Structure." *Journal of Economic Literature* 36:1426–64.

Anderson, J. E., and E. van Wincoop. 2003. "Gravity with Gravitas: A Solution to the Border Puzzle." *American Economic Review* 93 (1): 170–92.

Anderson, J. E., and E. van Wincoop. 2004. "Trade Costs." *Journal of Economic Literature* 42 (3): 691–751.

Andersson, R., J. M. Quigley, and M. Wilhelmsson. 2005. "Agglomeration and the Spatial Distribution of Creativity." Berkeley, CA: Berkeley Electronic Press.

Anselin, L., A. Varga, and Z. Ács. 1997. "Local Geographic Spillovers between University Research and High Technology Innovations." *Journal of Urban Economics* 42:422–48.

———. 2000. "Geographic and Sectoral Characteristics of Academic Knowledge Externalities." *Papers in Regional Science* 79:435–43.

Antràs, P. 2003. "Firms, Contracts, and Trade Structure." *Quarterly Journal of Economics* 118 (4): 1374–418.

Appiah, K. A. 2010. *The Honor Code: How Moral Revolutions Happen*. New York: W. W. Norton.

Archibugi, D., and S. Iammarino. 2002. "The Globalization of Technological Innovation: Definition and Evidence." *Review of International Political Economy* 9 (1): 98–122.

Ariely, D. 2008. *Predictably Irrational: The Hidden Forces That Shape Our Decisions*. New York: Harper.

Arrow, K. J. 1951. *Social Choice and Individual Values*. New York: John Wiley.

———. 1962. "The Economic Implications of Learning-by-Doing." *Review of Economic Studies* 29:155–73.

Arthur, W. B. 1989. "Competing Technologies, Increasing Returns, and Lock-In by Historical Events." *Economic Journal* 99:116–31.

———, ed. 1994. *Increasing Returns and Path Dependence in the Economy*. Ann Arbor: University of Michigan Press.

Audretsch, D. B. 2003. "Innovation and Spatial Externalities." *International Regional Science Review* 26 (2): 167–74.

Audretsch, D. B., and M. P. Feldman. 1996. "R & D Spillovers and the Geography of Innovation and Production." *American Economic Review* 86:630–40.

Austin, J. L. 1962. *How to Do Things with Words*. Oxford: Clarendon Press.

Aydogan, N. 2002. "Social Capital and Growth in Silicon Valley." Working paper, University of California at Irvine, Department of Economics.

Bagnasco, A. 2003. *Societa fuori squadra: Come cambia l'organizzazione sociale*. Milan: Il Mulino.

Bairoch, P. 1997. *Victoires et déboires: Histoire économique et sociale du monde du XVIeme siècle à nos jours* [Victories and setbacks : Economic and social history of the world from the sixteenth century to the present day]. Paris: Gallimard.

Balconi M. 2002. "Tacitness, Codification of Technological Knowledge, and the Organisation of Industry. *Research Policy* 31:357–79.

Balconi, M., S. Breschi, and F. Lissoni. 200. "Networks of Inventors and the Role of Academia: An Exploration of Italian Patent Data." *Research Policy* 33:127–45.

Baldwin, R. E. 2006. *Globalization: The Great Unbundling(s)*. Helsinki: Economic Council of Finland.

Baldwin, R. E., and R. Forslid. 1997. "The Core-Periphery Model and Endogenous Growth: Stabilizing and Destabilizing Integration." *Economica* 67 (3): 307–24.

———. 2006. "Trade Liberalization with Heterogeneous Firms." Working paper 12192, National Bureau of Economic Research, Cambridge, MA. http://www.nber.org/papers/w12192 (accessed October 18, 2012).

Baldwin, R. E., R. Forslid, P. Martin, G.I.P. Ottaviano, and F. Robert-Nicoud. 2003. *Economic Geography and Public Policy*. Princeton, NJ: Princeton University Press.

Baldwin, R. E., and P. Martin. 2004. "Agglomeration and Regional Growth." In *Handbook of Regional and Urban Economics*, ed. J. V. Henderson and J.-F. Thisse, 2671–711. Amsterdam: Elsevier.

Baldwin, R. E., P. Martin, and G.I.P. Ottaviano. 2001. "Global Income Divergence, Trade, and Industrialization: The Geography of Growth Take-Offs." *Journal of Economic Growth* 6 (1): 5–37.

Barca Report. 2009. "The Union and Cohesion Policy: Thoughts for Tomorrow." European Comission, Brussels. http://ec.europa.eu/regional_policy/policy/future/barca_en.htm (accessed October 19, 2012).

Barro, R., and X. Sala-i-Martin. 1995. *Economic Growth*. New York: McGraw-Hill.

Bartels, L. M. 2008. *Unequal Democracy: The Political Economy of the New Gilded Age*. Princeton, NJ: Princeton University Press.

Bateson, G. 1973. *Steps toward an Ecology of Mind.* London: Paladin Press.

Bathelt, H. 2007. "Buzz-and-Pipeline Dynamics: Towards a Knowledge-Based Multiplier Model of Clusters." *Geography Compass* 1:1282–98.

Bathelt, H., A. Malmberg, and P. Maskell. 2004. "Clusters and Knowledge: Local Buzz, Global Pipelines and the Process of Knowledge Creation." *Progress in Human Geography* 28:31–56.

Bathelt, H., and N. Schuldt. 2008 "Between Luminaries and Meat Grinders: International Trade Fairs as Temporary Clusters." *Regional Studies* 42:853–68.

Batty M. 2003. "The Geography of Scientific Citation." *Environment and Planning: A* 35 (5): 761–65.

Baumgartner, J R. 1988. "Physicians' Services and the Division of Labor across Local Markets." *Journal of Political Economy* 96 (October): 948–82.

Becattini, G., and F. Sforzi, eds. 2002. *Lezioni sullo sviluppo locale* [Lessons of local development]. Turin: Rosenberg and Sellier.

Behrens, K., A. Lamorghese, G.I.P. Ottaviano, and T. Tabuchi. 2004. "Testing the Home Market Effect in a Multi-Country World." Working paper 2005055, Center for Operations Research and Econometrics, Université Catholique de Louvain, Louvain, Belgium.

Bell, D. 1976. *The Cultural Contradictions of Capitalism.* New York: Basic Books.

Bellah, R. N., R. Madsen, W. Sullivan, A. Swidler, and R. Tipton. 1985. *Habits of the Heart: Individualism and Commitment in American Life.* New York: Harper and Row.

Belussi, F. 1987. "Benetton: Information Technology in Production and Distribution: A Case Study of the Innovative Potential of Traditional Sectors." Working paper, Science Policy Research Unit, Sussex, UK.

Bénabou, R., and J. Tirole. 2005. "Belief in a Just World and Redistributive Policies." Working paper, Department of Economics, Princeton University, Princeton, NJ.

Benedikt, M. 1997. *Center.* Vol. 10, *Value.* Austin: University of Texas Press.

Benhabib, S. 2006. *Democracy and Difference.* Princeton, NJ: Princeton University Press.

Berthelon, M., and C. L. Freund. 2004. "On the Conservation of Distance in International Trade." Policy research working paper 3293, World Bank, Washington, DC.

Bishop, B. 2008. *The Big Sort: Why the Clustering of Like-Minded America Is Tearing Us Apart.* New York: Houghton-Mifflin.

Black, D., G. Gates, S. Sanders, and L. Taylor. 2002. "Why Do Gay Men Live in San Francisco?" *Journal of Urban Economics* 51 (1): 54–76.

Black, D., and V. Henderson. 1999. "A Theory of Urban Growth." *Journal of Political Economy* 107:252–84.

Boldrin, M., and D. K. Levine. 2006. "Globalization, Intellectual Property, and Economic Prosperity." *Spanish Economic Review* 8:23–34.

Borrás, S. 2004. "System of Innovation Theory and the European Union." *Science and Public Policy* 31 (6): 425–33.

Borts, G., and J. Stein. 1964. *Economic Growth in a Free Market.* New York: Columbia University Press.

Boschma, R. A. 2005. "Proximity and Innovation: A Critical Assessment." *Regional Studies* 39:61–74.

Boschma, R. A., and R. C. Kloosterman, eds. 2005. *Learning from Clusters: A Critical Assessment from an Economic-Geographical Perspective*. Frankfurt: Springer.

Boschma, R. A., and J. Lambooy. 1999. "Evolutionary Economics and Economic Geography." *Journal of Evolutionary Economics* 9:411–29.

Boschma, R. A., and R. Martin. 2007. "Constructing an Evolutionary Economic Geography." *Journal of Economic Geography* 7 (5): 537–48.

Bottazzi, L., and G. Peri. 2003. "Innovation and Spillovers in Regions: Evidence from European Patent Data." *European Economic Review* 47:687–710.

Bowles, S. 1998. "Endogenous Preferences: The Cultural Consequences of Markets and Other Economic Institutions." *Journal of Economic Literature* 36:75–111.

Bowles, S., and H. Gintis. 2002. "Social Capital and Community Governance." *Economic Journal* 112:419–36.

———. 2004. "Persistent Parochialism: Trust and Exclusion in Ethnic Networks." *Journal of Economic Behavior and Organization* 55:1–23.

Boyer, R. 1985. *Places-Rated Almanac: Your Guide to Finding the Best Places to Live in America*. Chicago: Rand McNally.

Branstetter, L. G. 2001. "Are Knowledge Spillovers International or Intranational in Scope? Microeconometric Evidence from US and Japan." *Journal of International Economics* 53:53–79.

Braunerhjelm, P., and M. Feldman. 2006. *Cluster Genesis: Technology-Based Industrial Development*. Oxford: Oxford University Press.

Bremer, J., and J. Kasarda. 2002. "The Origins of Terror." *Milken Institute Review* 4 (4): 34–48.

Breschi, S., and M. Lissoni. 2005. "'Cross-Firm' Inventors and Social Networks: Localised Knowledge Spillovers Revisited." *Annales d'Economie et de Statistique* 79–80:189–209.

Breschi, S., and F. Malerba, eds. 2005. *Clusters, Networks, and Innovation*. Oxford: Oxford University Press.

Brookings Institution. 2010. *The State of Metropolitan America*. Washington, DC: Brookings Institution.

Brown, J. S., and P. Duguid. 1991. "Organizational Learning and Communities of Practices." *Organization Science* 2:40–57.

———. 2000. *The Social Life of Information*. Boston: Harvard Business School Press.

Buchanan, J., and G. Tullock. 1962. *The Calculus of Consent*. Ann Arbor: University of Michigan Press.

Bunnell, T., and N. Coe. 2001. "Spaces and Scales of Innovation." *Progress in Human Geography* 25:569–89.

Cairncross, F. 2001. *The Death of Distance: 2.0 How the Communications Revolution Will Change Our Lives*. London: Texere.

Camuffo, A., P. Romano, and A. Vinelli. 2001. "Back to the Future: Benetton Transforms Its Global Network." *MIT Sloan Management Review* 46:43–52.

Carlino, G., S. Chatterjee, and R. Hunt. 2001. "Knowledge Spillovers and the New Economy of Cities. Working paper 01-14, Federal Reserve Bank of Philadelphia.

Carlino, G., and L. Mills. 1996. "Convergence and the US States: A Time-Series Analysis." *Journal of Regional Science* 36 (4): 587–616.

Carlino, G., and A. Saiz. 2008. "City Beautiful." Working paper 08-22, Federal Reserve Bank of Philadelphia.

Carruthers, J. 2002. "Growth at the Fringe: The Influence of Political Fragmentation in United States Metropolitan Areas." *Papers in Regional Science* 82:475–99.

Casson, M. 1995. *Entrepreneurship and Business Culture*. Aldershot, UK: Edward Elgar.

Castellacci, F., and D. Archibugi. 2008. "The Technology Clubs: The Distribution of Knowledge across Nations." *Research Policy* 37:1659–73.

Chapple, K., and T. W. Lester. 2010. "The Resilient Regional Labor Market? The US Case." *Cambridge Journal of Regions, Economy, and Society* 3 (1): 85–104.

Charlot, S., and G. Duranton. 2006. "Cities and Workplace Communication: Some Quantitative French Evidence." *Urban Studies* 43:1365–94.

Charlot, S., C. Gaigné, F. Robert-Nicoud, and J.-F. Thisse. 2006. "Agglomeration and Welfare: The Core-Periphery Model in Light of Bentham, Kaldor, and Rawls." *Journal of Public Economics* 90:325–47.

Cheshire, P., and S. Sheppard. 1995. "On the Price of Land and the Value of Amenities." *Economica* 62:247–67.

Ciccone, A. 2000. "Agglomeration Effects in Europe." *European Economic Review* 46:213–27.

Ciccone, A., and R. E. Hall. 1996. "Productivity and the Density of Economic Activity." *American Economic Review* 86 (1): 54–70.

Clark, T., R. Lloyd, K. K., Wong, and P. Jain. 2002. "Amenities Drive Urban Growth." *Journal of Urban Affairs* 24 (5): 493–515.

Cohen, S., and G. Fields. 1999. "Social Capital and Capital Gains in Silicon Valley." *California Management Review* 41 (2): 108–30.

Coleman, J. 1990. *Foundations of Social Theory*. Cambridge, MA: Harvard University Press.

Combes, P.-P., and G. Duranton. 2006. "Labour Pooling, Labour Poaching, and Spatial Clustering." *Regional Science and Urban Economics* 36 (1): 1–28.

Combes, P.-.P, G. Duranton, L. Gobillon, D. Puga, and S. Roux. 2009. "The Productivity Advantages of Larger Cities: Distinguishing Agglomeration from Firm Selection." Discussion papers 7191, Centre for Economic Policy Research, London.

Combes, P.-P., and M. Lafourcade. 2005. "Transport Costs: Measures, Determinants, and Regional Policy Implications for France." *Journal of Economic Geography* 5:319–49.

Combes, P.-P., T. Mayer, and J.-F. Thisse. 2006. *Economic Geography*. Princeton, NJ: Princeton University Press.

Cooke, P. 2006. "Global Bioregional Networks: A New Economic Geography of Bioscientific Knowledge." *European Planning Studies* 14:1265–85.

Costa, D., and M. Kahn. 2000. "Power Couples: Changes in the Locational Choice of the College Educated, 1940–2000." *Quarterly Journal of Economics* 112 (3): 827–72.

Cowan, R. 2005. "Network Models of Innovation and Knowledge Diffusion." In *Clusters, Networks, and Innovation*, ed. S. Breschi and F. Malerba, 29–53. Oxford: Oxford University Press.

Cowen, T. 2004. *Creative Destruction: How Globalization Is Changing the World's Cultures*. Princeton, NJ: Princeton University Press.

Cox, K. R. 1993. "The Local and the Global in the New Urban Politics: A Critical View." *Environment and Planning D: Society and Space* 11 (4): 433–48.

Crescenzi, R. 2005. "Innovation and Regional Growth in the Enlarged Europe: The Role of Local Innovative Capabilities, Peripherality, and Education." *Growth and Change* 36:471–507.

Crescenzi, R., A. Rodríguez-Pose, and M. Storper. 2007. "On the Geographical Determinants of Innovation in Europe and the United States." *Journal of Economic Geography* 7 (6): 673–709.

———. 2012. "The Territorial Dynamics of Innovation in India and China." *Journal of Economic Geography* 12 (5): 929–42.

Crozier, M. 1964. *The Bureaucratic Phenomenon*. Chicago: University of Chicago Press.

Csikszentmihalyi, M. 1997. *Creativity: Flow and the Psychology of Discovery and Invention*. New York: Harper Perennial.

Cutler, D., E. L. Glaeser, and J. Vigdor. 2008. "Is the Melting Pot Still Hot?" *Review of Economics and Statistics* 90 (3): 478–97.

Dahl, R. (1961) 2005. *Who Governs? Democracy and Power in an American City*. Reprint, New Haven, CT: Yale University Press.

Dahl, M. S., and C. Pedersen. 2004. "Knowledge Flows through Informal Contacts in Industrial Clusters: Myth or Reality?" *Research Policy* 33:1673–86.

Darwin, J. 2008. *After Tamerlane: A Global History of Empire since 1405*. New York: Bloomsbury Press.

Davis, D. R., and D. E. Weinstein. 2002. "Bones, Bombs, and Break Points: The Geography of Economic Activity." *American Economic Review* 92 (5): 1269–89.

Debreu, G. 1974. "Excess Demand Functions." *Journal of Mathematical Economics* 1:15–21.

Delmas, M. A. 2002. "Innovating against European Rigidities: Institutional Environment and Dynamic Capabilities." *Journal of High Technology Management Research* 13:19–43.

Desmet, K., and M. Fafchamps. 2005. "Changes in the Spatial Concentration of Employment across U.S. Counties: A Sectoral Analysis, 1972–2000." *Journal of Economic Geography* 5 (3): 261–84.

Desmet, K., and E. Rossi-Hansberg. 2010. "On Spatial Dynamics." *Journal of Regional Science* 50 (1): 43–64.

DeVol, R., A. Bedroussian, and K. Klowden. 2011. *Best Performing Cities, 2011*. Santa Monica, CA: Milken Institute. http://www.milkeninstitute.org/publica tions/publications.taf?function=detail&ID=38801293&cat=resrep (accessed October 18, 2012).

Disdier, A.-C., and K. Head. 2005. "The Puzzling Persistence of the Distance Effect on Bilateral Trade." Mimeo, University of British Columbia.

Dobbs, R., S. Smit, J. Remes, J. Manyika, C. Roxburgh, and A. Restrepo. 2011. *Urban World: Mapping the Economic Power of Cities*. San Francisco: McKinsey Global Institute.

Donahue, J. 1997. "Tiebout? Or Not Tiebout? The Market Metaphor and America's Devolution Debate." *Journal of Economic Perspectives* 11 (Fall): 73–81.

Döring, T., and J. Schnellenbach. 2006. "What Do We Know about Geographical Knowledge Spillovers and Regional Growth? A Survey of the Literature." *Regional Studies* 40:375–95.

Dosi, G. 1998. "Sources, Procedures, and Microeconomic Effects of Innovation." *Journal of Economic Literature* 26 (3): 1120–71.

Dosi G., P. Llerena, and M. Sylos Labini. 2006. "The Relationships between Science, Technologies, and Their Industrial Exploitation: An illustration through the Myths and Realities of the So-Called 'European Paradox.'" *Research Policy* 35 (10): 1450–64.

Douglass, M., and J. Friedmann, eds. 1997. *Cities for Citizens*. Chichester: John Wiley and Sons.

Downs, A. 1997. "The Challenge of Our Declining Big Cities." *Housing Policy Debate* 8 (2): 359–408.

Drennan, M. P., and J. Lobo. 2007. "Specialization Matters: The Knowledge Economy and United States Cities." Unpublished manuscript, University of California at Los Angeles, School of Public Affairs.

Drennan, M. P., J. Lobo, and D. Strumsky. 2004. "Unit Root Tests of Sigma Income Convergence across US Metropolitan Areas." *Journal of Economic Geography* 4:583–95.

Drennan, M. P., E. Tobier, and J. Lewis. 1996. "The Interruption of Income Convergence and Income Growth in Large Cities in the 1980s." *Urban Studies* 33 (1): 63–82.

Duranton, G. 2007. "Urban Evolutions: The Fast, the Slow, and the Still." *American Economic Review* 97 (1): 197–221.

Duranton, G., and D. Puga. 2000. "Diversity and Specialisation in Cities: Why, Where, and When Does It Matter?" *Urban Studies* 37 (3): 533–55.

———. 2001. "Nursery Cities: Urban Diversity, Process Innovation, and the Life Cycle of Products." *American Economic Review* 91 (5): 1454–77.

———. 2004. "Micro-Foundations of Urban Agglomeration Economies." In *Handbook of Regional and Urban Economics*, ed. J. V. Henderson and J.-F. Thisse, 4:2064–117. Amsterdam: Elsevier.

———. 2005. "From Sectoral to Functional Urban Specialisation." *Journal of Urban Economics* 57:343–70.

Duranton, G., and M. Storper. 2008. "Rising Trade Costs? Agglomeration and Trade with Endogenous Transaction Costs." *Canadian Journal of Economics* 41 (1): 292–319.

Durkheim, E. (1893) 1984. *The Division of Labor in Society*. Translated by W. D. Halls. Reprint, New York: Free Press.

Durlauf, S. N.2004. "Neighborhood Effects." In *Handbook of Regional and Urban Economics*, ed. J. V. Henderson and J.-F. Thisse, 4:2173–242. Amsterdam: Elsevier.

Dworkin, R. 2002. *Sovereign Virtue: The Theory and Practice of Equality*. Cambridge, MA: Harvard University Press.

Earle, C. 1992. *Geographical Inquiry and American Historical Problems*. Stanford, CA: Stanford University Press.

Easterlin, R. 1987. *Birth and Fortune: the Impact of Numbers on Personal Welfare*. New York: Basic Books.

Easterly, W. 2001. *The Elusive Quest for Growth*. Cambridge, MA: MIT Press.

Edler J., H. Fier, and C. Grimpe. 2011. "International Scientist Mobility and the Locus of Knowledge and Technology Transfer." *Research Policy* 40:791–805.

Eisingerich, A. B., S. J. Bell, and P. Tracey P. 2010. "How Can Clusters Sustain Performance? The Role of Network Strength, Network Openness, and Environmental Uncertainty." *Research Policy* 39:239–53.

Ellison, G., E. L. Glaeser, and W. R. Kerr. 2010. "What Causes Industry Agglomeration? Evidence from Coagglomeration Patterns." *American Economic Review* 100 (3): 1195–213.

Engel, J. A. 2007. *Local Consequences of the Global Cold War*. Washington, DC: Woodrow Wilson Center.

Ergas, H. 1987. "Does Technology Policy Matter?" In *Technology and Global Industry*, ed. B. Guile and H. Brooks, 191–245. Washington, DC: National Academy Press.

Essletzbichler, J., and D. Rigby. 2004. "Competition, Variety, and the Geography of Technology Evolution." *Tijdschrift voor Economische en Sociale Geografie* 96:48–62.

European Commission. 2005. "EU's Higher Education Achievements and Challenges: Frequently Asked Questions (FAQ)." Memo 05/133, EU Publications Office, Brussels.

European Union. 2004. "Exploiting Europe's Territorial Diversity for Sustainable Economic Growth." Paper presented at the ministerial conference, Rotterdam, November 29.

Eurostat. 2006a. "Patent Applications to the EPO at National Level." Statistics in Focus, vol. 3, Eurostat Publications Office, Brussels.

Eurostat. 2006b. "Patent Applications to the EPO in 2002 at Regional Level." Statistics in Focus, vol. 4, Eurostat Publications Office, Brussels.

Evans, P. 1995. *Embedded Autonomy: States and Industrial Transformation*. Princeton, NJ: Princeton University Press.

Fallick, B., C. A. Fleischman, and J. B. Rebitzer. 2006. "Job-Hopping in Silicon Valley: Some Evidence concerning the Microfoundations of a High-Technology Cluster." *Review of Economics and Statistics* 88:472–81.

Farole, T. C., A. Rodríguez-Pose, and M. Storper. 2010. "Human Geography and the Institutions That Underlie Economic Growth: A Multi-Disciplinary Literature Review." *Progress in Human Geography* 35 (1): 58–80.

———. 2011. "Cohesion Policy in the European Union: Growth, Geography, Institutions." *Journal of Common Market Studies* 49 (5): 1089–111.

Faulconbridge J. R. 2006. "Stretching Tacit Knowledge beyond a Local Fix? Global Spaces of Learning in Advertising Professional Service Firms." *Journal of Economic Geography* 6:517–40.

Fehr, E., and S. Gachter. 2000. "Fairness and Retaliation: The Economics of Reciprocity." *Journal of Economic Perspectives* 14 (3): 159–81.

Feldman, M. P. 1994. *The Geography of Innovation*. Boston: Kluwer.

———. 2003. "The Locational Dynamics of the US Biotechnology Industry: Knowledge Externalities and the Anchor Hypothesis." *Industry and Innovation* 10:311–28.

Feldman, M. P. 2005. "The Entrepreneurial Event Revisited: Firm Formation in a Regional Context." In *Clusters, Networks, and Innovation*, ed. S. Breschi and F. Malerba, 136–68. Oxford: Oxford University Press.

Feldman, M. P., and D. B. Audretsch. 1999. "Innovation in Cities: Science-Based Diversity, Specialisation, and Localised Competition." *European Economic Review* 43 (2): 409–29.

Feldman, M. P., and T. D. Zoller. 2011. "Dealmakers in Place: Social Capital Connections in Regional Entrepreneurial Economies." Unpublished paper, University of North Carolina, Chapel Hill.

Filatotchev I., X. Liu, J. Lu, and M. Wright. 2011. "Knowledge Spillovers through Human Mobility across National Borders: Evidence from Zhongguancun Science Park in China." *Research Policy* 40:453–62.

Fine, C. 2006. *A Mind of Its Own: How Your Brain Distorts and Deceives*. Cambridge, UK: Icon Books.

———. 2001. *The Homevoter Hypothesis*. Cambridge, MA: Harvard University Press.

Fischer, C. S. 2010. *Made in America: A Social History of American Culture and Character*. Chicago: University of Chicago Press.

Florida, R. 2002. *The Rise of the Creative Class*. New York: Basic Books.

———. 2005. *Cities and the Creative Class*. London: Routledge.

Fogel, R. W. 2000. *The Fourth Great Awakening and the Future of Egalitarianism*. Chicago: University of Chicago Press.

Fosfuri, A., M. Motta, and T. Rønde. 2001. "Foreign Direct Investment and Spillovers through Workers' Mobility." *Journal of International Economics* 53:205–22.

Frank, R. 2001. *Luxury Fever*. New York: Free Press.

Franklin, R. 2003. "Migration of the Young, Single, and College Educated." In *2000 Special Reports*, CENSR-12. Washington, DC: US Bureau of the Census.

Frenken, K., F. G. van Oort, and T. Verburg. 2007. "Related Variety, Unrelated Variety, and Regional Economic Growth." *Regional Studies* 41:685–97.

Frey, W. H. 1993. "The New Urban Revival in the United States." *Urban Studies* 30 (4–5): 741–74.

Fritsch, M. 2002. "Measuring the Quality of Regional Innovation Systems: A Knowledge Production Function Approach." *International Regional Science Review* 25 (1): 86–101.

Fuchs, G., and P. Shapira, eds. 2005. *Rethinking Regional Innovation and Change: Path Dependency or Regional Breakthrough*. Frankfurt: Springer.

Fujita, M., and P. Krugman. 1995. "When Is the Economy Monocentric? Von Thunen and Chamberlin Unified." *Regional Science and Urban Economics* 25 (4): 505–28.

Fujita, M., P. Krugman, and T. Mori. 1999. "On the Evolution of Hierarchical Urban Systems." *European Economic Review* 43:209–51.

Fujita, M., and J.-F. Thisse. 2002. *Economics of Agglomeration*. Cambridge: Cambridge University Press.

———. 2009. "Paul Krugman's New Economic Geography: Past, Present, and Future." Working paper, CORE–Université Catholique, Louvain, Belgium.

Fujita, M., P. Krugman, and A. J. Venables. 1999. *The Spatial Economy: Cities, Regions, and International Trade*. Cambridge, MA: MIT Press.

Fukuyama, F. 1996. *Trust: The Social Virtues and the Creation of Prosperity*. New York: Free Press.

Furtado, C. 1959. *Formacão económica do Brasil* [Development of the Brazilian economy]. Rio de Janeiro: Fundo da Cultura.

Gabaix, X., and Y. Ioannides. 2004. "The Evolution of City-Size Distributions." In *Handbook of Urban and Regional Economics*, ed. J. V. Henderson and J.-F. Thisse, 4:2341–78. Amsterdam: Elsevier.

Gambetta, D., ed. 1988. *Trust: Making and Breaking Cooperative Relations*. Oxford: Oxford University Press.

Garfinkel, H. 1987. *Studies in Ethnomethodology*. Oxford: Blackwell.

Garreau, J. 1992. *Edge City*. New York: W. W. Norton.

George, D. 2001. *Preference Pollution*. Ann Arbor: University of Michigan Press.

Gertler M. S. 2003. Tacit Knowledge and the Economic Geography of Context, or the Undefinable Tacitness of Being (There). *Journal of Economic Geography* 3:75–99.

———. 2004. *Manufacturing Culture: The Institutional Geography of Industrial Practice*. Oxford: Oxford University Press.

Ghemawat, P., and J. L. Nueno. 2003. ZARA: Fast Fashion. Harvard Business School Cases, case number 704397. http://cb.hbsp.harvard.edu/cb/web/product _detail.seam?E=45234&R=703497-PDF-ENG&conversationId=1931149 (accessed October 18, 2012).

Giddens, A. 1984. *The Constitution of Society*. Cambridge, UK: Polity Press.

———. 1990. *The Consequences of Modernity*. Stanford, CA: Stanford University Press.

Gilovich, T., D. Griffin, and D. Kahneman, eds. 2002. *Heuristics and Biases: The Psychology of Intuitive Judgment*. Cambridge: Cambridge University Press.

Glaeser, E. L. 1998. "Are Cities Dying?" *Journal of Economic Perspectives* 12:139–60.

———. 2003. "Reinventing Boston, 1640–2003." Working paper 10166, National Bureau of Economic Research, Cambridge, MA. http://www.nber.org/ papers/w10166 (accessed October 19, 2012).

———. 2007. "The Economic Approach to Cities." Paper, Department of Economics, Harvard University, Cambridge, MA.

———. 2008. *Cities, Agglomeration, and Spatial Equilibrium*. Oxford: Oxford University Press.

———. 2010. *Triumph of the City*. New York: Macmillan.

Glaeser, E. L., and J. Gottlieb. 2009. "The Wealth of Cities: Agglomeration Economies and Spatial Equilibrium in the United States." Paper, Department of Economics, Harvard University, Cambridge, MA. http://www.economics.harvard .edu/faculty/glaeser/papers_glaeser (accessed October 19, 2012).

Glaeser, E. L., and J. Gyourko. 2005. "Urban Decline and Durable Housing." *Journal of Political Economy* 113:345–76.

Glaeser, E. L., H. D. Kallal, J. A. Scheinkman, and A. Schleifer. 1992. "Growth in Cities." *Journal of Political Economy* 100 (6): 1126–52.

Glaeser, E. L., and J. E. Kohlhase. 2003. "Cities, Regions, and the Decline of Transport Costs." *Papers in Regional Science* 83 (1): 197–228.

Glaeser, E. L., J. Kolko, and A. Saiz. 2001. "Consumer City." *Journal of Economic Geography* 1 (1): 27–50.

Glaeser, E. L., R. La Porta, F. Lopez-de-Silanes, and A. Schleifer. 2004. "Do Institutions Cause Growth?" *Journal of Economic Growth* 9 (3): 271–303.

Glaeser, E. L., and D. C. Maré. 2001. "Cities and Skills." *Journal of Labor Economics* 19:316–42.

Glaeser, E. L., and K. Tobio. 2008. "The Rise of the Sunbelt." *Southern Economic Journal* 74 (3): 610–43.

Goffman, E. 1959. *The Presentation of Self in Everyday Life*. New York: Doubleday.

———. 1982. *Interaction Rituals: Essays on Face-to-Face Behavior*. New York: Pantheon Books.

Gordon, I. R., and P. McCann. 2005. "Innovation, Agglomeration, and Regional Development." *Journal of Economic Geography* 5:523–43.

Görg, H., and F. Strobl. 2005. "Spillovers from Foreign Firms through Workers Mobility: An Empirical Investigation." *Scandinavian Journal of Economics* 107:693–709.

Granovetter, M. 1973. "The Strength of Weak Ties." *American Journal of Sociology* 78:1360–80.

———. 1985. "Economic Action and Social Structure: The Problem of Embeddedness." *American Journal of Sociology* 91:481–510.

———. 1995. *Getting a Job: A Study of Job Contacts and Careers*. Chicago: University of Chicago Press.

———. 2001. "A Theoretical Agenda for Economic Sociology." In *The New Economic Sociology: Developments in an Emerging Field*, ed. M. Guillen, R. Collins, P. England, and M. Meyer, 35–59. New York: Russell Sage Foundation.

———. 2005. "The Impact of Social Structure on Economic Outcomes." *Journal of Economic Literature* 19 (1): 33–50.

Graves, P. 1976. "A Reexamination of Migration, Economic Opportunity, and the Quality of Life." *Journal of Regional Science* 16:107–12.

———. 1980. "Migration and Climate." *Journal of Regional Science* 20 (2):227–38.

———. 1983. "Migration with a Composite Amenity: The Role of Rents." *Journal of Regional Science* 23 (4): 541–47.

Greenwood, M. 1997. "Research on Internal Migration in the United States: A Survey." *Journal of Economic Literature* 13 (2): 397–433.

Gregersen, B., and B. Johnson. 1997. "Learning Economies, Innovation Systems, and European Integration." *Regional Studies* 31:479–90.

Greif, A. 1993. "Contract Enforceability and Economic Institutions in Early Trade: Evidence on the Maghribi Traders." *American Economic Review* 83:525–48.

Grémion, P. 1976. *Le pouvoir périphérique: Bureaucrates et notables dans le système politique français* [Power at the edges: Bureaucrats and notables in the French political system]. Paris: Editions du Seuil.

Greunz, L. 2003. "Geographically and Technologically Mediated Knowledge Spillovers between European Regions." *Annals of Regional Science* 37:657–80.

Griliches, Z. 1979. "Issues in Assessing the Contribution of R & D to Productivity Growth." *Bell Journal of Economics* 10:92–116.

———. 1986. "Productivity, R & D, and Basic Research at the Firm Level in the 1970s." *American Economic Review* 76:141–54.

Grossman, G. M., and E. Helpman. 1991. "Quality Ladders and the Theory of Growth." *Review of Economic Studies* 58 (1): 43–61.

———. 2001. *Special Interest Politics*. Cambridge, MA: MIT Press.

Grossman, G. M., and E. Lai. 2004. "International Protection of Intellectual Property." *American Economic Review* 94:1635–53.

Guiso, L., P. Sapienza, and L. Zingales. 2010. "Civic Capital as the Missing Link." Working paper 15845, National Bureau of Economic Research, Cambridge, MA. http://www.nber.org/papers/w15845 (accessed October 19, 2012).

Gul, F., and W. Pesendorfer. 2001. "Temptation and Self-Control." *Econometrica* 69 (6): 1403–35.

Habbakuk, H. 1962. *American and British Technology in the Nineteenth Century*. Cambridge: Cambridge University Press.

Håkanson, L. 2005. "Epistemic Communities and Cluster Dynamics: On the Role of Knowledge in Industrial Districts." *Industry and Innovation* 12:433–63.

Hall, P. 1998. *Cities in Civilization*. New York: Pantheon.

Hall, P., and D. Soskice, eds. 2001. *Varieties of Capitalism*. Oxford: Oxford University Press.

Hamilton, B. 1975. "Property Taxes and the Tiebout Hypothesis: Some Empirical Evidence." In *Fiscal Zoning and Land Use Controls*, ed. E. S. Mills and W. E. Oates, 13–20. Lexington, MA: Heath-Lexington.

Hammond, G. W., and E. C. Thompson. 2008. "Determinants of Income Growth in Metropolitan and Nonmetropolitan Labor Markets." *American Journal of Agricultural Economics* 90 (3): 783–93.

Hanson, G. H. 2005. "Market Potential, Increasing Returns, and Geographic Concentration." *Journal of International Economics* 67 (1): 1–24.

Hart, D. M. 2001. "Antitrust and Technological Innovation in the US: Ideas, Institutions, Decisions, and Impacts, 1890–2000." *Research Policy* 30:923–36.

Hart, O., and J. Moore. 2005. "On the Design of Hierarchies: Coordination versus Specialization." *Journal of Political Economy* 113:675–702.

Harvey, D. 1976. *Social Justice and the City*. Baltimore: Johns Hopkins University Press.

Haselton, M. G., D. Nettle, and P. W. Andrews. 2005. "The Evolution of Cognitive Bias." In *The Handbook of Evolutionary Psychology*, ed. D. M. Buss, 724–46. Hoboken, NJ: Wiley and Sons.

Haussman, R., and D. Rodrik. 2003. "Economic Development as Self-Discovery." *Journal of Development Economics* 72 (2): 603–33.

Head, K., and T. Mayer. 2004. "The Empirics of Agglomeration and Trade." In *Handbook of Regional and Urban Economics*, ed. J. V. Henderson and J.-F. Thisse, 4:2609–69. Amsterdam: Elsevier.

Helpman, E. 2004. *The Mystery of Economic Growth*. Cambridge, MA: Belknap Press.

———. 2011. *Understanding Global Trade*. Cambridge, MA: Belknap Press.

Henderson, J. V. 1974. "The Sizes and Types of Cities." *American Economic Review* 64 (4): 640–56.

Henderson, J. V. 2010. "Cities and Development." *Journal of Regional Science* 50 (1): 515–40.

Hilber, C., and C. Mayer. 2004. "Why Do Households without Children Support Local Public Schools?" Working paper 10804, National Bureau of Economic Research, Cambridge, MA. http://www.nber.org/papers/w10804 (accessed October 19, 2012).

Hillberry, R., and D. Hummels. 2008. "Trade Responses to Geographic Frictions: A Decomposition Using Micro-Data." *European Economic Review* 52 (3): 527–50.

Hirschman, A. O. 1958. *The Strategy of Economic Development*. New Haven, CT: Yale University Press.

———. 1970. *Exit, Voice, and Loyalty: Responses to Decline in Firms, Organizations, and States*. Cambridge, MA: Harvard University Press.

Hodgson, G. 1993. *Economics and Evolution*. Ann Arbor: University of Michigan Press.

Hoekman J., K. Frenken, and F. Van Oort. 2008. "Collaboration Networks as Carriers of Knowledge Spillovers: Evidence from EU-27 Regions." DIME working paper 2008.3, Dynamics of Knowledge Accumulation, Competitiveness, Regional Cohesion, and Economic Policies series, Brussels.

Hounshell, D. 1984. *From the American System to Mass Production, 1800–1932*. Baltimore: Johns Hopkins University Press.

Hummels, D. 2007. "Transportation Costs and International Trade in the Second Era of Globalization." *Journal of Economic Perspectives* 21 (3): 131–54.

Hummels, D., and A. Skiba. 2004. "Shipping the Good Apples Out? An Empirical Confirmation of the Alchian-Allen Conjecture." *Journal of Political Economy* 112 (6): 1384–402.

Husserl, E. 1968. *The Ideas of Phenomenology*. The Hague: Nijhoff.

Jacobs, J. 1969. *The Economy of Cities*. New York: Random House.

Jaffe, A. B. 1986. "Technological Opportunity and Spillovers of R & D: Evidence from Firms' Patents, Profits, and Market Share." *American Economic Review* 76:984–1001.

———. 1989. "Real Effects of Academic Research." *American Economic Review* 79:957–70.

Jaffe, A. B., and J. Lerner. 2004. *Innovation and Its Discontents: How Our Broken Patent System Is Endangering Innovation and Progress, and What to Do about It*. Princeton, NJ: Princeton University Press.

Jaffe, A. B., and M. Trajtenberg. 2002. *Patents, Citations, and Innovations*. Cambridge, MA: MIT Press.

Jaffe, A. B., M. Trajtenberg, and R. Henderson. 1993. "Geographic Localization of Knowledge Spillovers as Evidenced by Patent Citations." *Quarterly Journal of Economics* 108:577–98.

Jaher, F. C. 1984. *The Urban Establishment: Upper Strata in Boston, New York, Charleston, Chicago, and Los Angeles*. Urbana: University of Illinois Press.

Janeba, E. 2004. "International Trade and Cultural Identity." Working paper, National Bureau of Economic Research, Cambridge, MA. http://www.nber.org/papers/w10426 (accessed October 19, 2012).

Jayet, H. 1983. "Chômer plus souvent en région urbaine, plus longtemps en région rurale" [Labor turnover is greater in urban areas, but unemployment periods longer in rural areas]. *Economie et Statistique* 153:47–57.

Johnson B., E. Lorenz, and B-Å. Lundvall. 2002. "Why All This Fuss about Codified and Tacit Knowledge?" *Industrial and Corporate Change* 11:245–62.

Jones, C. I. 2004. "Growth and Ideas." Working paper 10767, National Bureau of Economic Research, Cambridge, MA. http://www.nber.org/papers/w10767 (accessed October 19, 2012).

Jones, B. D., and F. Baumgartner. 2005. *The Politics of Attention: How Government Prioritizes Problems.* Chicago: University of Chicago Press.

Just, R. 2004. *The Welfare Economics of Public Policy.* Cheltenham, UK: Edward Elgar.

Kahneman, D., E. Diener, and N. Schwartz. 1998. *Understanding Well-Being: Scientific Perspectives on Enjoyment and Suffering.* New York: Russell Sage Foundation.

Kahneman, D., and A. Tversky. 1979. "Prospect Theory: An Analysis of Decision under Risk." *Econometrica* 47:263–91.

Kaldor, N. 1939. "Welfare Properties of Economics and Interpersonal Comparisons of Utility." *Economic Journal* 49:549–51.

Kasarda, J., S. J. Appold, S. Sweeney, and S. Sieff. 1997. "Central-City and Suburban Migration Patterns: Is a Turnaround on the Horizon?" *Housing Policy Debate* 8 (2): 307–58.

Kemeny, T. 2009. "International Technology Gaps in the Age of Globalization." PhD diss., University of California at Los Angeles.

———. 2011. "Are Technology Gaps Growing or Shrinking in the Age of Globalization?" *Journal of Economic Geography* 11 (1): 1–35.

Kemeny, T., and M. Storper. 2012. "The Sources of Urban Development: Wages, Housing, and Amenity Gaps across American Cities." *Journal of Regional Science* 52 (1): 85–108.

Kenney, M., ed. 2000. *Understanding Silicon Valley.* Stanford, CA: Stanford University Press.

Kenyon, D. 1997. "Theories of Interjurisdictional Competition." *New England Economic Review* (March–April): 14–28.

Kenyon, D., and J. Kincaid, eds. 1991. *Competition among States and Local Governments: Efficiency and Equity in American Federalism.* Washington, DC: Urban Institute Press.

Kim, S. 2002. "The Reconstruction of the American Urban Landscape in the Twentieth Century." Working paper 8857, National Bureau of Economic Research, Cambridge, MA. http://www.nber.org/papers/w8857 (accessed October 19, 2012).

Kim, S., and M. Law. 2012. "History, Institutions, and Cites: A View from the Americas." *Journal of Regional Science* 52 (1): 10–39.

Kirzner, I. 1973. *Competition and Entrepreneurship.* Chicago: University of Chicago Press.

Klepper, S. 2005. "Employee Start-ups in High-Tech Industries." In *Clusters, Networks, and Innovation*, ed. S. Breschi and F. Malerba, 199–233. Oxford: Oxford University Press.

Knight, F. (1921) 2005. *Risk, Uncertainty, and Profit*. Reprint, New York: Cosimo.

Kotkin, J. 2005. "We Don't Need a 'Cool' Mayor." *Los Angeles Times*, May 19, B10.

Krugman, P. 1991a. "Increasing Returns and Economic Geography." *Journal of Political Economy* 99:483–99.

———. 1991b. *Geography and Trade*. Cambridge, MA: MIT Press.

———. 2011. "The New Economic Geography: Now Middle Aged." *Regional Studies* 45 (1): 1–7.

Krugman, P., and A. Venables. 1995. "Globalisation and the Inequality of Nations." *Quarterly Journal of Economics* 110 (4): 857–80.

Kuisel, R. 1981. *Le capitalisme et l'Etat en France: Modernisation et dirigisme au XXème siècle* [State capitalism in France: Modernization and dirigisme in the twentieth century]. Paris: Gallimard.

Kuran, T. 1997. *Private Truths, Public Lies: The Social Consequences of Preference Falsification*. Cambridge, MA: Harvard University Press.

Lakoff, G., and M. Johnson. 1980. *Metaphors We Live By*. Chicago: University of Chicago Press.

Lamont, M. 1992. *Money, Morals, and Manners: The Culture of the French and American Upper Middle Class*. Chicago: University of Chicago Press.

Lanier, J. 2010. *You Are Not a Gadget*. New York: Alfred A. Knopf.

Laslett, J. M., and S. M. Lipset, eds. 1984. *Failure of a Dream? Essays in the History of American Socialism*. Berkeley: University of California Press.

Laursen, K., F. Masciarelli, and A. Prencipe. 2011. "Regions Matter: How Localized Social Capital Affects Innovation and External Knowledge Acquisition." *Organization Science* 1–17.

Leamer, E. E. 1983. "Let's Take the Con Out of Econometrics." *American Economic Review* 73 (1): 31–43.

———. 2010. "Tantalus on the Road to Asymptopia." *Journal of Economic Perspectives* 24 (3): 31–46.

———. 2012. *The Craft of Economics*. Cambridge, MA: MIT Press.

Leamer, E. E., and M. Storper. 2001. "The Economic Geography of the Internet Age." *Journal of International Business Studies* 32 (4): 641–66.

Lear, J. 2006. *Radical Hope: Ethics in the Face of Cultural Devastation*. Cambridge, MA: Harvard University Press.

Le Galès, P. 2004. *Le Retour des villes européennes? Sociétés urbaines, mondialisation, gouvernement et gouvernance*. Paris: Presses de Sciences Po.

Leonardi, R. 1995. "Regional Development in Italy, Social Capital, and the Mezzogiorno." *Oxford Review of Economic Policy* 11 (2): 165–79.

Lerner J. 2009. "The Empirical Impact of Intellectual Property Rights on Innovation: Puzzles and Clues." *American Economic Review* 99:343–48.

Leunig, T. 2007. "Time Is Money: A Re-assessment of the Passenger Social Savings from Victorian British Railways." *Journal of Economic History* 66: 635–73.

Levy, J. 1999. *Tocqueville's Revenge: State, Society, and Community in Contemporary France*. Cambridge, MA: Harvard University Press.

Levy, F., and R. Murnane. 2005. *The New Division of Labor: How Computers Are Creating the Next Job Market*. Princeton, NJ: Princeton University Press.

Lin, N. 2000. *Social Capital: A Theory of Social Structure and Action.* New York: Cambridge University Press.

Lindert, P. H. 2004. *Growing Public: Social Spending and Economic Growth since the Eighteenth Century.* Cambridge: Cambridge University Press.

Lipset, S. M. 1963. *Political Man.* Garden City, NY: Doubleday Anchor.

Logan, J., and H. Molotch. 1987. *Urban Fortunes.* Berkeley: University of California Press.

Long, N. 1971. "The City as Reservation." *Public Interest* 25 (Fall): 22–38.

Lorentzen, A. 2008. "Knowledge Networks in Local and Global Space." *Entrepreneurship and Regional Development* 20:533–45.

Lucas, R. E., Jr. 1988. "On the Mechanics of Economic Development." *Journal of Monetary Economics* 22:3–42.

Lundvall, B.-Å., and B. Johnson. 1994. "The Learning Economy." *Journal of Industry Studies* 1:23–42.

Maddison, A. 1982. *Phases of Capitalist Development.* New York: Oxford University Press.

Maggioni, M. A., M. Nosvelli, and E. Uberti. 2006. "Space vs. Networks in the Geography of Innovation: A European Analysis." Working paper 2006.153, Fondazione Eni Enrico Mattei, Milan.

Malecki, E. J. 2010. "Everywhere? The Geography of Knowledge." *Journal of Regional Science* 50 (1): 493–514.

Malmberg, A., and P. Maskell. 2006. "Localized Learning Revisited." *Growth and Change* 37:1–18.

Mantel, R. 1974. "On the Characterization of Aggregate Excess Demand." *Journal of Economic Theory* 7:348–53.

Manville, M., and D. Shoup. 2005. "People, Parking, and Cities." *Journal of Urban Planning and Development* 131 (4): 233–45.

Manville, M., and M. Storper. 2006. "Behaviour, Preferences, and Cities: Urban Theory and Urban Resurgence." *Urban Studies* 43 (8): 1–28.

Markusen, J., and N. Trofimenko. 2007. "Teaching Locals New Tricks: Foreign Experts as a Channel of Knowledge Transfer." Working paper 12872, National Bureau of Economic Research, Cambridge, MA. http://www.nber.org/papers/wp12872 (accessed October 19, 2012).

Marshall, A. 1919. *Industry and Trade.* London: Macmillan.

Martin, P. 2005. "The Geography of Inequalities in Europe." *Swedish Economic Policy Review* 12:83–108.

Martin, P., and G.I.P. Ottaviano. 1999. "Growing Locations: Industry Location in a Model of Endogenous Growth." *European Economic Review* 43 (2): 281–302.

Martin, R., and P. Sunley. 2006. "Path Dependence and Regional Economic Evolution." *Journal of Economic Geography* 6:395–437.

Maskell, P., H. Bathelt, and A. Malmberg. 2006. "Building Global Knowledge Pipelines: The Role of Temporary Clusters." *European Planning Studies* 14: 997–1013

Mayer, W. G. 1993. *The Changing American Mind: How and Why American Public Opinion Changed between 1960 and 1988.* Ann Arbor: University of Michigan Press.

McCann, P. 2001. *Urban and Regional Economics*. Oxford: Oxford University Press.

McElreath, R., R. Boyd, and P. Richerson. 2003. "Shared Norms and the Evolution of Ethnic Markers." *Current Anthropology* 44 (1): 122–29.

McLaughlin, G. E. 1949. *Why Industry Moves South: A Study of Factors Influencing the Recent Location of Manufacturing Plants in the South*. Washington, DC: National Planning Association, Committee of the South.

Mehrabian, A. 1981. *Silent Messages: Implicit Communications of Emotions and Attitudes*. Belmont, CA: Wadsworth.

Melitz, M. J. 2003. "The Impact of Trade on Intra-Industry Reallocations and Aggregate Industry Productivity." *Econometrica* 71 (6): 1695–725.

Melitz, M. J., and G.I.P. Ottaviano. 2008. "Market Size, Trade, and Productivity." *Review of Economic Studies* 75 (1): 295–316.

Meisenzahl, R. R., and J. Mokyr. 2012. "The Rate and Direction of Invention in the British Industrial Revolution: Incentives and Institutions." In *The Rate and Direction of Inventive Activity Revisited*, ed. S. Stern and J. Lerner, 443–79. Chicago: University of Chicago Press for the National Bureau of Economic Research.

Midelfart-Knarvik, H., and H. G. Overman. 2002. "Delocation and European Integration: Is Structural Spending Justified." *Economic Policy* 17:322–69.

Midelfart-Knarvik, H., H. G. Overman, S. Redding, and A. J. Venables. 2002. "The Location of European Industry." *European Economy* 2:216–73.

Miller, R., and M. Storper. 2008. "Near and Far: Imagining the Future of Telepresence." Working paper, Sciences Po, Paris.

Mokyr, J. 1991. *The Lever of Riches: Technological Creativity and Economic Progress*. New York: Oxford University Press.

Molotch, H. 1976. "The City as a Growth Machine." *American Sociological Review* 82 (2): 309–32.

———. 2002. *Where Stuff Comes From*. London: Routledge.

Morck, R., and B. Yeung. 2011. "Economics, History, and Causation." Working paper 16678, National Bureau of Economic Research, Cambridge, MA. http://www.nber.org/papers/w16678 (accessed October 19, 2012).

Moreno, R., R. Paci, and S. Usai. 2005a. "Geographical and Sectoral Clusters of Innovation in Europe." *Annals of Regional Science* 39 (4): 715–39.

———. 2005b. "Spatial Spillovers and Innovation Activity in European Regions." *Environment and Planning A* 37:1793–812.

Moretti, E. 2012. *The New Geography of Jobs*. Boston: Houghton Mifflin Harcourt.

Mowery, D. C. 1998. "The Changing Structure of the U.S. National Innovation System: Implications for International Conflict and Cooperation in R & D Policy." *Research Policy* 27 (6): 639–54.

Mowery, D. C., and A. A. Ziedonis. 2001. "The Geographic Reach of Market and Nonmarket Channels of Technology Transfer: Comparing Citations and Licenses of University Patents." Working paper 8568, National Bureau of Economic Research, Cambridge, MA. http://www.nber.org/papers/wp8568 (accessed October 19, 2012).

Muth, R. F. 1971. "Migration: Chicken or Egg?" *Southern Economic Journal* 37:295–306.

Myers, D., and E. Gearin. 2001. "Current Preferences and Future Demand for Denser Residential Environments." *Housing Policy Debate* 12 (4): 633–60.

Myrdal, G. 1957. *Economic Theory and the Underdeveloped Regions*. London: Duckworth.

Nagel, T. 2005. "The Problem of Global Justice." *Philosophy and Public Affairs* 33:115–50.

National Science Foundation. 2006. *Science and Engineering Indicators 2006*. Washington, DC: National Science Foundation.

Nohria, N., and R. Eccles. 1992. *Networks and Organizations: Structure, Form, and Action*. Boston: Harvard Business School Press.

Nonaka, I., and H. Takeuchi. 1995. *The Knowledge-Creating Company*. Oxford: Oxford University Press.

Norris, P. 2002. *Democratic Phoenix: Reinventing Political Activism*. Cambridge: Cambridge University Press.

North, D. 2005. *Understanding the Process of Economic Change*. Princeton, NJ: Princeton University Press.

Norton, R. D., and J. Rees. 1979. "The Product Cycle and the Spatial Decentralization of American Manufacturing." *Regional Studies* 13 (2): 141–51.

Oates, W. 1969. "Local Spending on Property Values." *Journal of Political Economy* 6 (November–December): 957–71.

OECD (Organization for Economic Cooperation and Development). 2001. "Using Patent Counts for Cross-Country Comparisons of Technology Output," *STI Review* 27:129–46.

———. 2005. *OECD Employment Outlook*. Paris: OECD.

———. 2006. *Compendium of Patent Statistics*. Paris: OECD.

Office of Management and Budget, US President. 2003. *OMB Metropolitan Areas and Components, 1993, with FIPS Codes*. Washington, DC: Office of Management and Budget.

Olson, G. M., and J. S. Olson. 2000. "Distance Matters." *Human-Computer Interaction* 15 (2): 139–78.

Olson, M. 1965. *The Logic of Collective Action: Public Goods and the Theory of Groups*. Cambridge, MA: Harvard University Press.

O'Malley, E. 1998. "Industrial Policy in Ireland and the Problem of Late Development." In *Latecomers in the Global Economy*, ed. M. Storper, S. Thomadakis, and L. Tsipouri, 203–23. London: Routledge.

Osborne, M., J. R. Rosenthal, and M. A. Turner. 2000. "Meetings with Costly Participation." *American Economic Review* 90:927–43.

Ottaviano, G., and G. Peri. 2006. "The Economic Value of Cultural Diversity: Evidence from US Cities." *Journal of Economic Geography* 6 (1): 9–44.

Owen-Smith, J., and W. W. Powell. 2004. "Knowledge Networks as Channels and Conduits: The Effects of Spillovers in the Boston Biotechnology Community." *Organization Science* 15:5–21.

———. 2008a. "Accounting for Emergence and Novelty in Boston and Bay Area Biotechnology." In *Cluster Genesis: The Emergence of Technology Clus-*

ters and Their Implications for Government Policy, ed. P. Braunerhjelm and M. Feldman, 61–86. Oxford: Oxford University Press.

———. 2008b. "Networks and Institutions." In *The SAGE Handbook of Organizational institutionalism*, ed. R. Greenwood, O. Christine, R. Suddaby, and K. Sahlin-Andersson, 594–621. London: SAGE Publications.

Oxley, J. E., and R. C. Sampson. 2004. "The Scope and Governance of International R & D Alliances." *Strategic Management Journal* 25:723–49.

Padgett, J. F., and C. K. Ansell. 1993. "Robust Action and the Rise of the Medici, 1400–1434." *American Journal of Sociology* 98:1259–319.

Padgett, J. F., and P. McLean. 2006. "Organizational Invention and Elite Transformation: The Birth of the Partnership System in Renaissance Florence." *American Journal of Sociology* 111 (5): 1463–568.

Padgett, J. F., and W. W. Powell. 2012. *The Emergence of Organizations and Markets*. Princeton, NJ: Princeton University Press.

Partridge, M. 2010. "The Dueling Models: NEG versus Amenity Migration in Explaining US Engines of Growth." *Papers in Regional Science* 89 (3): 513–36.

Pascal, A. 1987. "The Vanishing City." *Urban Studies* 24 (6): 597–603.

Pastor, M., W. Lester, and J. Scoggins. 2009. "Why Regions? Why Now? Who Cares?" *Journal of Urban Affairs* 31 (3): 269–96.

Pearce, D., G. Atkinson, and S. Mourato. 2006. "Cost-Benefit Analysis and the Environment: Recent Developments." Report, Organization for Economic Cooperation and Development, Paris.

Peri, G. 2005. "Skills and Talent of Immigrants: A Comparison between the European Union and the United States." Working paper, Institute of European Studies, University of California at Berkeley.

Perloff, H. 1963. *How a Region Grows*. New York: Committee for Economic Development.

Perroux, F. 1950. "Economic Space: Theory and Applications." *Quarterly Journal of Economics* 64 (1): 89–104.

Persson, T., and G. Tabellini. 2002. *Political Economics: Explaining Economic Policy*. Cambridge, MA: MIT Press.

———. 2006. "Democracy and Development: The Devil Is in the Details." Working paper 11993, National Bureau of Economic Research, Cambridge, MA. http://www.nber.org/papers/wp11993 (accessed October 19, 2012).

Peterson, P. 1981. *City Limits*. Chicago: University of Chicago Press.

Pike, A., A. Rodríguez-Pose, and J. Tomaney. 2006. *Local and Regional Development*. London: Routledge.

Piore, M. J., and C. F. Sabel. 1984. *The Second Industrial Divide*. New York: Basic Books.

Pizzorno, A. 1980. *I soggetti del pluralismo: Classi, partiti, sindicati*. Bologna: Il Mulino.

Pogge, T. 2002. *World Poverty and Human Rights: Cosmopolitan Responsibilities and Reforms*. Cambridge, UK: Polity Press.

Polanyi, K. 1944. *The Great Transformation*. Boston: Beacon Press.

Polanyi, M. 1966. *The Tacit Dimension*. London: Routledge.

Pomeranz, K. 2000. *The Great Divergence*. Princeton, NJ: Princeton University Press.

Porter, K., K. B. Whittington, and W. W. Powell. 2005. "The Institutional Embeddedness of High-Tech Regions: Relational Foundations of the Boston Biotechnology Community." In *Clusters, Networks, and Innovation*, ed. S. Breschi and F. Malerba, 261–96. Oxford: Oxford University Press.

Postrel, V. 2003 *The Substance of Style*. New York: HarperCollins.

Powell, W. W. 1990. "Neither Market nor Hierarchy: Network Forms of Social Life." *Research in Organizational Behavior* 12:295–336.

Powell, W. W., K. Packalen, and K. B. Whittington. 2012. "Organizational and Institutional Genesis: The Emergence of High-Tech Clusters in the Life Sciences." In *The Emergence of Organizations and Markets*, ed. J. Padgett and W. W. Powell, 434–65. Princeton, NJ: Princeton University Press.

Powell, W. W., and J. Owen-Smith. 2012. "An Open Elite: Arbiters, Catalysts, or Gatekeepers in the Dynamics of Industry Evolution?" In *The Emergence of Organizations and Markets*, ed. J. Padgett and W. W. Powell, 466–95. Princeton, NJ: Princeton University Press.

Powell, W. W., D. R. White, K. W. Koput, and J. Owen-Smith. 2005. "Network Dynamics and Field Evolution: The Growth of Inter-Organizational Collaboration in the Life Sciences." *American Journal of Sociology* 110 (4): 1132–205.

Pratt, A. C. 2002. "Firm Boundaries? The Organization of New Media Production in SF, 1996–98." Unpublished manuscript, Department of Geography, London School of Economics.

Prebisch, R. 1950. *The Economic Development of Latin America and Its Principal Problems*. New York: United Nations, 1950.

Pred, A. R. 1973. *Urban Growth and the Circulation of Information: The US Urban System, 1790–1840*. Cambridge, MA: Harvard University Press.

———. 1977. *City Systems in Advanced Economies*. London: Hutchinson.

Pred, A. R., and T. Hagerstrand. 1967. *Innovation Diffusion as a Spatial Process*. Chicago: University of Chicago Press.

Przeworski, A. M., J. A. Alvarez, F. Cheibub, and L. Limongi. 2000. *Democracy and Development: Political Institutions and Well-Being in the World, 1950–1990*. Cambridge: Cambridge University Press.

Puga, D. 2010. "The Magnitude and Causes of Agglomeration Economies." *Journal of Regional Science* 50 (1): 203–20.

Puga, D., and G. Duranton. 2001. "From Sectoral to Functional Specialisation." Discussion paper 2971, Center for Economic Policy Research, London School of Economics. http://ssrn.com/abstract=285959 (accessed October 19, 2012).

Puhani, P. A. 2001. "Labour Mobility: An Adjustment Mechanism in Euroland? Empirical Evidence for Western Germany, France, and Italy." *German Economic Review* 2 (2): 127–40.

Putnam, R. 2000. *Bowling Alone: The Collapse and Revival of American Community*. New York: Simon and Schuster.

Putnam, R., R. Leonardi, and R. Y. Nanetti. 1993. *Making Democracy Work*. Princeton, NJ: Princeton University Press.

Rappaport, J. 2007. "Moving to Nice Weather." *Regional Science and Urban Economics* 37 (3): 375–98.

Rauch, J. E., and V. Trindade. 2005. "Neckties in the Tropics: A Model of International Trade and Cultural Diversity." Working paper, National Bureau of

Economic Research, Cambridge, MA. http://www.nber.org/papers/w11890 (accessed October 19, 2012).

Ravallion, M., and J. Jalan. 1997. "Spatial Poverty Traps?" Policy research paper 1862, World Bank, Washington, DC.

Rawls, J. 1971. *A Theory of Justice*. Cambridge, MA: Harvard University Press.

———. 1999. *The Law of Peoples*. Cambridge, MA: Harvard University Press.

———. 2001. *Justice as Fairness: A Restatement*. Cambridge, MA: Harvard University Press.

Reades, J. E. 2010. "The Place of Telecommunications Spatial Decision-Making by Firms in the Age of Global Communications." PhD diss., University College London.

Redding, S. J. 2010. "The Empirics of New Economic Geography." *Journal of Regional Science* 50 (1): 297–311.

Reynolds, P. D., S. M. Camp, W. D. Bygrave, E. Autio, and M. Hay. 2001. *Global Entrepreneurship Monitor: 2001 Executive Report*. Kansas City, MO: Kauffman Center for Entrepreneurial Leadership at the Ewing Marion Kauffman Foundation.

Rigby, D. L., and J. Essletzbichler. 1997. "Evolution, Process Variety, and Regional Trajectories of Technological Change in US Manufacturing." *Economic Geography* 73:269–84.

Roback, J. 1982. "Wages, Rents, and the Quality of Life." *Journal of Political Economy* 90 (6): 1257–78.

Robbins, L. 1938. "Interpersonal Comparisons of Utility: A Comment." *Economic Journal* 48 (192): 635–41.

Robert-Nicoud, F. 2005. "The Structure of Simple 'New Economic Geography' Models (or, on Identical Twins)." *Journal of Economic Geography* 5 (2): 201–34.

Rodríguez-Pose, A., and R. Crescenzi. 2008. "Research & Development, Spillovers, Innovation Systems, and the Genesis of Regional Growth in Europe." *Regional Studies* 42 (1): 51–67.

Rodríguez-Pose, A., and M. Storper. 2005. "Better Rules or Stronger Communities? On the Social Foundations of the Institutional Change and Its Economic Effects." *Economic Geography* 82 (1): 1–25.

Rodrik, D. 1999. *The New Global Economy and Developing Countries: Making Openness Work*. Essay number 24, Overseas Development Council Policy, Washington, DC.

———. 2003. "Growth Strategies." Working paper 10050, National Bureau of Economic Research, Cambridge, MA. http://www.nber.org/papers/w10050 (accessed October 19, 2012).

———. 2011. *The Globalization Paradox: Democracy and the Future of the World Economy*. New York: W. W. Norton.

Rodrik, D., A. Subramanian, and F. Trebbi. 2004. "Institutions Rule: The Primacy of Institutions over Geography and Integration in Economic Development." *Journal of Economic Growth* 9 (2): 131–65.

Roemer, J. E. 1996. *Theories of Distributive Justice*. Cambridge, MA: Harvard University Press.

Romer, P. M. 1986. "Increasing Returns and Long-Run Growth." *Journal of Political Economy* 94 (5): 1002–37.

———. 1994. "The Origins of Endogenous Growth." *Journal of Economic Perspectives* 8 (1): 3–22.

Rose-Ackerman, S. 1983. "Beyond Tiebout: Modelling the Political Economy of Local. Government." In *Local Provision of Public Services: The Tiebout Model after Twenty-Five Years*, ed. George Zodrow, 55–83. Waltham, MA: Academic Press.

Rosen, S. 1983. "Specialization and Human Capital." *Journal of Labor Economics* 1 (1): 43–49.

Rosenberg, N. 1982. *Inside the Black Box: Technology and Economics*. Cambridge: Cambridge University Press.

Rosenthal, S. R., and W. C. Strange. 2001. "The Determinants of Agglomeration." *Journal of Urban Economics* 50:191–229.

Rosenvallon, P. 2004. *Le modèle politique français* [The French political structure]. Paris : Editions du Seuil.

Ross, L., and R. Nisbet. 1991. *The Person and the Situation*. Philadelphia: Temple University Press.

Rossi-Hansberg, E., P. D. Sarte, and R. Owens III. 2009. "Firm Fragmentation and Urban Patterns." *International Economic Review* 50 (1): 143–86.

Rossi-Hansberg, E., and M. Wright. 2007. "Urban Structure and Growth." *Review of Economic Studies* 74:597–624.

Russell Sage Foundation. 2011. *Chartbook of Social Inequality*. New York: Russell Sage Foundation. http://www.russellsage.org/research/chartbooks (accessed October 20, 2012).

Sabel, C. F., and W. H. Simon. 2010. "Minimalism and Experimentalism in the Administrative State." Working paper, Columbia University Law School, New York.

Sabel, C. F., and J. Zeitlin. 1985. *World of Possibilities*. New York: Cambridge University Press.

Safford, S. 2009. *Why the Garden Club Couldn't Save Youngstown: The Transformation of the Rust Belt*. Cambridge, MA: Harvard University Press.

Sahlins, M. 1995. *How Natives Think*. Chicago: University of Chicago Press.

Saks, R. E. 2007. "Job Creation and Housing Construction: Constraints on Metropolitan Area Growth." *Journal of Urban Economics* 64:178–95.

Sala-i-Martin, X. 2006. "The World Distribution of Income: Falling Poverty and Convergence [space][ellipsis symbol][space] period." *Quarterly Journal of Economics* 121:351–97.

Saliola, F., and A. Zanfei. 2009. "Multinational Firms, Global Value Chains, and the Organization of Knowledge Transfer." *Research Policy* 38:369–81.

Sandel, M. 1996. *Democracy's Discontent: America in Search of a Public Philosophy*. Cambridge, MA: Belknap Press.

Saxenian, A. L. 1994. *Regional Advantage: Culture and Competition in Silicon Valley and Route 128*. Cambridge, MA: Harvard University Press.

———. 2000. "The Origins and Dynamics of Production Networks in Silicon Valley." In *Entrepreneurship: The Social Science View*, ed. R. Swedberg, 384–403. Oxford: Oxford University Press.

———. 2006. *The New Argonauts*. Cambridge, MA: Harvard University Press.

Saxenian, A., and J.-H. Hsu. 2005. "The Silicon Valley–Hsinchu Connection: Technical Communities and Industrial Upgrading." In *Clusters, Networks, and*

Innovation, ed. S. Breschi and F. Malerba, 235–60. Oxford: Oxford University Press,

Schelling, T. 1978. *Micromotives and Macrobehavior*. New York: W. W. Norton.

Schumpeter, J. A. 1991. *The Economics and Sociology of Capitalism*. Edited by R. Swedberg. Princeton, NJ: Princeton University Press.

Scitovsky, T. 1941. "A Note on Welfare Properties in Economics." *Economic Journal* 64:284–89.

———. 1976. *The Joyless Economy: An Inquiry into Human Satisfaction and Consumer Dissatisfaction*. New York: Oxford University Press.

Scott, A. J. 1993. *Technopolis: High Technology Industry and Regional Development in Southern California*. Berkeley: University of California Press.

———. 2005. *On Hollywood: The Place, the Industry*. Princeton, NJ: Princeton University Press.

———. 2009. "Jobs or Amenities? Destination Choices of Migrant Engineers in the USA." *Papers in Regional Science* 1–21.

Scott, A. J., and M. Storper. 1987. "High Technology Industry and Regional Development: A Theoretical Critique and Reconstruction." *International Social Science Journal* 112 (May): 215–32.

Scranton, P. 1983. *Proprietary Capitalism*. New York: Cambridge University Press.

———. 1991. *Endless Novelty: Specialty Production and American Industrialization, 1865–1925*. Princeton, NJ: Princeton University Press.

Searle, J. 1969. *Speech Acts: An Essay in the Philosophy of Language*. New York: Cambridge University Press.

Sedgley, N., and B. Elmslie. 2004. "The Geographic Concentration of Knowledge: Scale, Agglomeration, and Congestion in Innovation across U.S. States." *International Regional Science Review* 27 (2): 111–37.

Sen, A. 1999. *Development as Freedom*. New York: Alfred A. Knopf.

———. 2002. *Rationality and Freedom*. Cambridge, MA: Harvard University Press.

———. 2009. *The Idea of Justice*. Cambridge, MA: Harvard University Press.

Sewell, W., Jr. 1996. "Historical Events as Transformations of Structures: Inventing Revolution at the Bastille." *Theory and Society* 25:841–81.

Shea, C. 2004. "The Road to Riches?" *Boston Globe*, February 29, D1.

Shoup, D. 2005. *The High Cost of Free Parking*. Chicago: Planner's Press.

Simmie, J., and R. L. Martin. 2010. "The Economic Resilience of Regions: Towards an Evolutionary Approach." *Cambridge Journal of Regions, Economy, and Society* 3:27–43.

Smith, K. 2007. "Does Europe Perform Too Little Corporate R & D?" Paper presented at the DRUID (Danish Research Unit on Industrial Dynamics) Summer Conference, Copenhagen Business School, Copenhagen, Denmark, June.

Sonn, J. W., and M. Storper. 2008. "The Increasing Importance of Geographical Proximity in Technological Innovation: An Analysis of U.S. Patent Citations, 1975–1997." *Environment and Planning A* 40 (5): 1020–39.

Sonnenschein, H. 1972. "Market Excess Demand Functions." *Econometrica* 40:549–63.

————.1973. "Do Walras' Identity and Continuity Characterize the Class of Community Excess Demand Functions?" *Journal of Economic Theory* 6:345–354.

Sperling, B., and P. Sander. 2004. *Cities Ranked and Rated*. 2nd ed. New York: Frommer's.

Stein, J. A. 2004. "Is There a European Knowledge System?" *Science and Public Policy* 31 (6): 435–47.

Sternlieb, G. 1971. "The City as Sandbox." *Public Interest* 25:14–21.

Stigler, G. 1951. "The Division of Labor Is Limited by the Extent of the Market." *Journal of Political Economy* 59:185–97.

Stiglitz, J. 1982. "The Theory of Local Public Goods Twenty-Five Years after Tiebout." In *Local Provision of Public Services: The Tiebout Model after Twenty-Five Years*, ed. G. Zodrow, 17–53. Waltham, MA: Academic Press.

Storper, M. 1995. "The Resurgence of Regional Economies, Ten Years Later: The Region as a Nexus of Untraded Interdependencies." *European Urban and Regional Studies* 2 (3): 191–221.

Storper, M., Y. C. Chen, and F. De Paolis. 2002. "Trade and the Location of Industries in the OECD and European Union." *Journal of Economic Geography* 2 (2): 73–107.

Storper, M., L. Lavinas, and A. Mercado. 2006. "Society, Community, and Development: A Tale of Two Regions." In *Geographies of Innovation*, ed. K. Polenske, 310–39. Cambridge: Cambridge University Press.

Storper, M., and R. Salais. 1997. *Worlds of Production: The Action Frameworks of the Economy*. Cambridge, MA: Harvard University Press.

Storper, M., and A. J. Venables. 2004. "Buzz: Face-to-Face Contact and the Urban Economy." *Journal of Economic Geography* 4:351–70.

Storper, M., and R. Walker. 1989. *The Capitalist Imperative: Territory, Technology, and Industrial Growth*. Oxford: Basil Blackwell.

Surowiecki, J. 2004. *The Wisdom of Crowds*. New York: Doubleday.

Swanstrom, T. 1983. *The Crisis of Growth Politics*. Lawrence: University of Kansas Press.

Swope, C. 2003. "Chasing the Rainbow: Is a Gay Population an Engine of Urban Revival?" *Governing* 17 (1): 18–24.

Tabarrok, A., and T. Cowen. 1998. "Who Benefits from Progress?" *Kyklos* 51 (3): 379–97.

Teaford, J. 1990. *The Rough Road to Renaissance*. Baltimore: Johns Hopkins University Press.

Texas Politics. 2011. "Texas Politics, Texas Culture." *Texas Politics*. http://texas-politics.laits.utexas.edu/10_printable.html (accessed October 19, 2012).

Thaler, R. 1985. "Mental Accounting and Consumer Choice." *Marketing Science* 14 (3): 199–214.

————. 1994. *The Winner's Curse*. Princeton, NJ: Princeton University Press.

Thisse, J.-F. 2010. "Toward a Unified Theory of Economic Geography and Urban Economics." *Journal of Regional Science* 50 (1): 281–96.

Thompson, P., and M. Fox-Kean. 2005. "Patents Citations and the Geography of Knowledge Spillovers: A Reassessment." *American Economic Review* 95:450–60.

Thompson, W. (1968) 1996. "The City as a Distorted Price System." In *Readings in State and Local Public Finance*, ed. M. Drennan and D. Netzer, 372–83. Reprint, London: Blackwell.

Tiebout, C. 1957. "A Pure Theory of Local Expenditures." *Journal of Political Economy* 64:416–24.

Tocqueville, A. de. (1830) 1986. *De la démocratie en Amérique* [Democracy in America]. 2 vols. Reprint, Paris: Gallimard.

Turner, F. 2006. *From Counterculture to Cyberculture: Stewart Brand, the Whole Earth Catalog, and the Rise of Digital Utopianism*. Chicago: University of Chicago Press.

Turner, F. J. 1921. *The Frontier in American History*. New York: Holt.

———. 1925. "The Significance of the Section in American History." *Wisconsin Magazine of History* 8 (3): 255–80.

———. 1932. *The Significance of Sections in American History*. New York: Holt.

Vandamme, F. 2000. "Labour Mobility within the European Union: Findings, Stakes, and Prospects." *International Labour Review* 139 (4): 437–55.

Van Niewerburgh, S., and P.-O. Weill. 2009. "Why Has House Price Dispersion Gone Up?" Paper, Department of Economics, University of California at Los Angeles. http://www.econ.ucla.edu/poweill/houseprice.pdf (accessed October 19, 2012).

Varga, A. 1998. *University Research and Regional Innovation*. Boston: Kluwer Academic Publishers.

———. 2000. "Local Academic Knowledge Spillovers and the Concentration of Economic Activity." *Journal of Regional Science* 40:289–309.

Wade, R. 1990. *Governing the Market: Economic Theory and the Role of Government in East Asian Industrialization*. Princeton, NJ: Princeton University Press.

Walker, R. A. 2008. *The Country in the City*. Seattle: University of Washington Press.

Weber, M. (1921) 1968. *Economy and Society*. Translated by G. Roth and C. Wittich. Reprint, New York: Bedminster Press.

Whitley, R. 2004. "The Social Construction of Organizations and Markets: The Comparative Analysis of Business Recipes." In *The New Economic Sociology*, ed. Frank Dobbin, 162–87. Princeton, NJ: Princeton University Press.

Wieser, R. 2005. "Research and Development Productivity and Spillovers: Empirical Evidence at the Firm Level." *Journal of Economic Surveys* 19 (4): 587–621.

Wilson, W. J. 1987. *The Truly Disadvantaged*. Chicago: University of Chicago Press.

Woeffray, O. 2012. "Regional Governance: A Case Study of the Metropolitan Transportation Commission." Master's thesis, Sciences Po, Paris.

World Bank. 2009. *World Development Report: Reshaping Economic Geography*. Washington, DC: World Bank.

World Intellectual Property Organization. 2007. *Patent Report of the World Intellectual Property Organization*. http://www.wipo.int/ipstats/en/statistics/patents/patent_report_2007.html (accessed October 19 2012).

Yamamoto, D. 2008. "Scales of Regional Income Inequalities in the USA, 1955–2003." *Journal of Economic Geography* 8:79–103.

Yellen, J. 1977. "Factor Mobility, Regional Development, and the Distribution of Income." *Journal of Political Economy* 85 (1): 79–96.

Young, A. 1928. "Increasing Returns and Economic Progress." *Economic Journal* 38:527–42.

Young, H. P., and S. Durlauf. 2001. *Social Dynamics.* Washington, DC: Brookings Institution.

Zimmermann, K. F. 1995. "Tackling the European Migration Problem." *Journal of Economic Perspectives* 9:45–62.

———. 2005. "European Labour Mobility: Challenges and Potentials." *Economist* 127 (4): 425–50.

Zucker, L. G., and M. R. Darby. 2006. "Movement of Star Scientists and Engineers and High-Tech Firm Entry." Working paper 12172, National Bureau of Economic Research, Cambridge, MA. http://www.nber.org/papers/wp12172 (accessed October 19, 2012).

Zucker, L. G., M. R. Darby, and J. Armstrong. 1998. "Geographically Localized Knowledge: Spillovers or Markets?" *Economic Inquiry* 36:65–86.

Index

CPSIA information can be obtained
at www.ICGtesting.com
Printed in the USA
JSHW020425030922
30113JS00002B/82